W9-BBK-043

The Cult of the Constitution

The

CULT

of the

CONSTITUTION

MARY ANNE FRANKS

STANFORD UNIVERSITY PRESS
Stanford, California

STANFORD UNIVERSITY PRESS
Stanford, California

Printed in the United States of America on acid-free, archival-quality paper

Library of Congress Cataloging-in-Publication Data

Names: Franks, Mary Anne, author.

Title: The cult of the constitution / Mary Anne Franks.

Description: Stanford, California : Stanford University Press, 2019. | Includes bibliographical references and index.

Identifiers: LCCN 2018050188 (print) | LCCN 2018055321 (ebook) | ISBN 9781503609105 (e-book) | ISBN 9781503603226 (cloth; alk. paper)

Subjects: LCSH: Civil rights—United States. | United States. Constitution. 1st Amendment. | United States. Constitution. 2nd Amendment. | Freedom of expression—United States. | Firearms—Law and legislation— United States. | Equality before the law—United States.

Classification: LCC KF4749 (ebook) | LCC KF4749 .F685 2019 (print) | DDC 342.7308/5—dc23

LC record available athttps://lccn.loc.gov/2018050188

Cover design by Kevin Barrett Kane
Text design by Kevin Barrett Kane
Typeset at Stanford University Press in 10/15 Sabon

CONTENTS

BAD FAITH

I still remember the day I was saved.

I was 8 years old. I was sitting, as I had sat nearly every Sunday morning of my childhood, in a hard oak pew with my mother and brothers, all of us dressed as respectably as our poverty would allow. As he did every Sunday at the close of services, our preacher stood in front of the altar, flanked by a Christian flag on one side and an American flag on the other, asking who among us was ready to come forward and accept Jesus into their heart. Some Sundays three or four sinners would stumble down the aisle toward salvation; sometimes no one left the pews. When those seeking salvation got to the front, they would huddle down with our pastor, and their voices would drop too low to be heard by those of us remaining in our seats. Very often they would weep. The end was always the same: Our pastor would lift his head and hands up and say the person's name out loud, and the congregation would join him in rejoicing that one more soul had escaped eternal damnation and joined the fellowship of the church.

By the day I decided to be saved, I had watched all this happen hundreds of times. I had heard how the streets of heaven were paved with gold and how no death and no suffering would ever be found there. I had heard the thunderous warnings about the burning fires of hell, where the sinners who had been too proud to repent would spend all of their days in torment and isolation. I had heard that all one had to do to obtain immortal life, avoid damnation, and be welcomed into the fold of the faithful was to accept Jesus as my Lord and Savior.

It sounded so easy. I had come very close to stepping out into the aisle several times before, but I had shrunk back at the thought of all the eyes in the pews and of the preacher's booming voice so close to my ear. I was seized with the fear that if I did step out in the aisle, the deacons would shake their heads forbiddingly and send me back, explaining that the offer of salvation was not meant for people like me.

In all of those hundreds of Sunday mornings, I had never seen anyone who looked like me get saved. We were the only Asian members of our tiny, all-white Southern Baptist church. We were also one of only a handful of Asian families in the entire town of Pine Bluff, Arkansas, a city whose population was almost evenly divided between white and black. We were a minority even within that minority, as my brothers and I were the biracial children of a Taiwanese mother and a white father. Our father had died when we were young, and my mother was raising the three of us by herself, and I was convinced that our poverty was the first thing people saw when they looked at us, like the mark on Cain's forehead.

Church was in many ways a refuge. No one was likely to call me a "chink," or shout gibberish at me as they pulled their eyelids back into slants, or mock my mismatched, secondhand clothes. Church meant gospel songs, grape juice and tiny tasteless wafers for communion, and a gift-wrapped present with my name on it at Christmastime. But I could never shake the feeling that even in church, we were at best pitied and tolerated rather than warmly embraced.

I wondered if salvation would change that.

That day, as our elderly church pianist hammered out the final hymn of the Sunday service, the fear of eternal damnation and the desire to belong to a community won out over my other anxieties. I made my way down the aisle, and, to my immense relief, I wasn't turned back. That Sunday, I was the one kneeling down before the altar with our preacher, I was the one tearfully accepting Jesus into my heart, and I was the one being presented to the congregation as the newest member of an eternal fellowship, forever and ever amen.

As I grew older, I found myself increasingly frustrated by the contrast between what I was taught about the Bible in church and my own study of the text. First were the problems I encountered in attempting to take the Bible literally, as Southern Baptists do. Genesis, for example, presented no end of difficulties. It made no sense to me why God, if he were all powerful, would need to rest after only six days of work. I was confounded by the reference to Cain's marriage, wondering where the only living son of the first two human beings had found a wife. And I kept tripping over the passage in which God says, "The man has now become like one of us, knowing good and evil" after Adam eats the forbidden fruit, wondering who God was speaking to and why he used the first-person plural.

Then there were the contradictions between the Old and the New Testament. We were often told in sermons and Sunday school that to be a Christian meant being compassionate, nonjudgmental, and forgiving, but so much of the Old Testament seemed to exalt in God's vengeance and cruelty. These passages stood in such a sharp contrast to the New Testament, which emphasized God's humility and humanity in the form of Jesus Christ. The Old Testament's steady stream of rapes, executions, and plagues jarred with New Testament stories of feeding the hungry and tending to the sick; "eye for an eye" seemed fundamentally out of step with the commandment to "turn the other cheek."

As I continued to read the Bible on my own over the years, I could not help but notice how many of the Old Testament stories most treasured by the people of my faith were stories of domination: men's domination of women, masters' domination of slaves, favored tribes' domination of other peoples, God's domination of all humanity. What seemed even more peculiar was how many of these stories told of powerful, favored men being brought to rage and ruin by those weaker than themselves: servants, members of disfavored tribes, and, most of all, women. There was Adam—the first man, namer of all things, father of humanity—deprived of eternal life by a woman's seductive curiosity. Joseph—interpreter of dreams and favorite son of Jacob—thrown into prison on the word of a loose woman falsely crying rape. Then there was Samson—strongest man in the world, blessed by God—reduced to a blind weakling by a faithless woman with a pair of scissors. And of course the story of Noah and the

Great Flood, in which God himself—omnipresent, omnipotent—is driven into such rage by his disobedient children that he wipes them from the face of the earth.

These stories troubled me all the more as I began to see their resonance in the political and cultural beliefs of the larger conservative community around me. This was a community that believed that men were the head of the household, that white people were more hardworking and virtuous than black people, and that deviant forces (including homosexuality, promiscuity, and abortion) were constantly threatening to destroy our society. Instead of carefully reading scripture to shape its worldview, my community seemed to be using its worldview to shape its reading of scripture.

My college studies in literature, philosophy, and religion deepened my skepticism about the faith I was raised in. Literary theory taught me how to read a text; philosophy taught me how to evaluate moral systems; and religious studies taught me that Christianity was only one faith among many.

The work of the eighteenth century philosopher Immanuel Kant had probably the most profound impact on my thinking during these years. The first time I encountered his famous "categorical imperative"—"Act only according to that maxim whereby you can at the same time will that it should become a universal law"—I was struck by its resemblance to the New Testament command to "do unto others as you would have them do unto you." But Kant's imperative is more than a moral command. It is a test, not only of the morality but the *intelligibility* of our actions. A rule that applies only to others and not to ourselves is no rule at all, but merely a self-serving preference upon which no coherent moral system can be built.

The principle that Kant articulates in the categorical imperative is sometimes called "reciprocity," and it is a concept that is affirmed by religious and philosophical traditions all over the world. What ultimately led me to abandon the religion of my childhood was my realization that it betrayed this fundamental principle, despite it being at the heart of Christianity itself.

By the time I finished my undergraduate studies and left for England to study on a Rhodes Scholarship, I no longer comfortably identified as either a Christian or a conservative.

After completing my doctorate in literature at Oxford, I turned to the study of law. I was drawn to constitutional law in particular, and even more specifically to the Reconstruction Amendments. These amendments expanded and transformed the Constitution in a way that paralleled the way the New Testament expanded and transformed the Bible. The Fourteenth Amendment makes clear that it is both impermissible and illogical to read the Constitution selectively either in terms of which rights it protects or of whose rights it protects; as such, the Fourteenth Amendment struck me as the constitutional expression of the Golden Rule. The equal protection clause seemed to be the keystone of the Constitution, the source of the entire text's moral legitimacy and structural intelligibility.

For more than a decade now, my work as a legal scholar and advocate has been dedicated to the principle of constitutional reciprocity. I have focused on the rights of free speech and self-defense, two rights that have been interpreted in ways that overprotect certain groups and underprotect others. I have worked to combat intimate privacy invasions that diminish the ability of women and minorities to express themselves freely and gun policies that jeopardize their equal rights to self-preservation.

Much of my work on free speech and privacy has focused on nonconsensual pornography (often called "revenge porn"), a form of abuse that disproportionately affects women and causes irreparable damage to victims' reputations, psychological health, job prospects, and personal relationships. I authored the first model criminal statute criminalizing nonconsensual pornography in 2013, which has since served as the template for both state and federal legislation on the issue. I served as the reporter for the Uniform Law Commission's (ULC) Uniform Civil Remedies for Unauthorized Disclosure of Intimate Images Act, which was approved in July 2018. I have provided expert testimony regarding the impact of intimate privacy violations on freedom of expression and have worked with legislators and tech industry leaders on policies to protect equal rights to free speech.

My work on protecting equal rights of self-defense has focused on the disparate impact of gun violence on women and minorities. I have worked with the Florida League of Women Voters to educate lawmakers about the effects of stand-your-ground laws and testified against legislation that would have allowed guns to be carried on campuses across the state.

In the wake of the February 2018 mass shooting at Marjory Stoneman Douglas High School in Parkland, Florida, my two areas of particular focus—gun violence and online abuse—collided in an unsettling way. It was horrifying to watch the young survivors of the shooting become the targets of vicious online harassment, threatened with violence and death simply for speaking out against gun violence and political corruption. Here were children exercising their First Amendment rights in the midst of unimaginable pain, only to be vilified as crisis actors bent on destroying the Second Amendment. It wasn't long before someone created an image of Emma Gonzalez, one of the most visible and eloquent Parkland student activists, appearing to show her ripping up the U.S. Constitution. My experiences working on free speech, gun rights, and online abuse issues drove home the disheartening lesson of this book: Fundamentalism is as alive and well in law as it is in religion. I have seen firsthand how often people use the Constitution the way religious fundamentalists use the Bible—selectively, self-servingly, and in bad faith.

Much as the evangelical community I was raised in focused on verses about homosexuality or women's inferiority while ignoring the Golden Rule, constitutional fundamentalists focus on individual rights of speech and bearing arms while disregarding the equal protection guarantees of the Fourteenth Amendment. This is not just a tactic of conservatives, whose affinity for Christian fundamentalism is no secret, but also of self-identified liberals. I was not particularly surprised when National Rifle Association supporters and Breitbart readers denounced my work on gun violence as an attack on the Constitution; I was more taken aback when American Civil Liberties Union representatives and self-identified liberals made similar claims about my efforts to protect intimate privacy rights.

As I have fielded e-mails, phone messages, and social media posts threatening me with job loss, rape, and death, I have been struck by another parallel between religious and constitutional fundamentalism: the tendency to engage in a tactic I call victim-claiming. Often used in conjunction with victim-blaming, which attempts to deprive victims of sympathy, victim-claiming attempts to generate sympathy for perpetrators. Victim-claiming is a reversal technique that puts the powerful in the the space of the vulnerable, the abuser in the space of the abused. It is the theme that disturbed me as a young reader of the Bible, which often portrays powerful men as suffering at the hands of their supposed inferiors. The point of such passages seemed to be the justification of the use of violence by the powerful against the vulnerable.

The fundamentalist reading of the Constitution, especially of the First and Second Amendments, produces the same effect. The most powerful and privileged people in America—white men—cast themselves as an underclass engaged in a protracted struggle against the women and minorities seeking to censor and disarm them.

I was moved to write this book because I believe that good faith can conquer bad. I believe that good faith in the Constitution, in particular, is both possible and necessary. I wrote this book to make the case against fundamentalism and for the principle of reciprocity expressed in Christianity's Golden Rule, Kant's categorical imperative, and the Fourteenth Amendment's equal protection clause. I wrote this book to advocate for the position that the only rights any of us should have are the rights that all of us should have. If only some of us are saved, all of us are lost.

As I was writing this book, I struggled with the fear that it too often states the obvious, that it lacks subtlety, that its moral claims are so blindingly apparent that there is no need to state them explicitly. On one particularly difficult day of writing I happened across the following passage:

[W]e have now sunk to a depth at which the restatement of the obvious is the first duty of intelligent men. It is not merely that at present the rule of naked force obtains almost everywhere. Probably that has always been the case. Where this age differs from those immediately preceding it is that a liberal intelligentsia is lacking. Bully-worship, under various disguises, has become a universal religion, and such truism as that a machine-gun is still a machine-gun even when a "good" man is squeezing the trigger . . . have turned into heresies which it is actually becoming dangerous to utter.

George Orwell wrote these lines in 1939. I have pushed aside my fears about the obviousness of this book and the simplicity of its claims because I fear something else much more: what our future will look like if the obvious is left unsaid.

The Cult of the Constitution

WHO WE ARE

"You will not replace us."

On the night of August 11, 2017, hundreds of white men[1] marched through Charlottesville, Virginia, waving torches and chanting, "You will not replace us," "Jews will not replace us," and "Blood and Soil," a translation of the Nazi slogan "Blut und Boden." In their path was a small group of University of Virginia students who had linked arms around a statue of Thomas Jefferson, the university's founder. Skirmishes broke out; witnesses reported that the marchers attacked the students with their torches and with chemical sprays.

The following morning, a much larger group of demonstrators gathered in the city's recently renamed Emancipation Park for the "Unite the Right" rally organized by a white supremacist named Jason Kessler. Some of the demonstrators carried Confederate flags and displayed swastikas. Others wore military-style tactical gear and carried assault rifles, taking advantage of Virginia's open-carry law. These demonstrators were met by hundreds of counter-protesters, and violent confrontations began almost immediately. Video footage shows one man firing a gun into a crowd of people and six men beating a young African American man in a parking garage.[2] Virginia Governor Terry McAuliffe declared a state of emergency, and the crowds were ordered to disperse.

In the afternoon, one of the far-right demonstrators drove his car full speed into a crowd of unarmed counter-protesters. The attack injured thirty-five people and killed a 32-year-old woman named Heather Heyer. Two state troopers, who were monitoring the demonstration from the air, died when their helicopter crashed. Responding to criticism that law enforcement had failed to maintain order, Governor McAuliffe claimed that the heavily armed demonstrators "had better equipment than our state police had."[3]

The demonstrators were ostensibly protesting the city's planned removal of a statue of Confederate General Robert E. Lee and the renaming of Lee Park as Emancipation Park. Before the march, city officials had attempted to move the rally to a larger location farther from downtown for public safety reasons. Kessler, represented by the American Civil Liberties Union (ACLU) of Virginia, successfully argued in a lawsuit that moving the demonstration would violate the First Amendment.

It was not the first time a left-leaning civil liberties organization had defended the prerogative of a white supremacist group to march in a town that did not want them there. Forty years before the events in Charlottesville, the ACLU famously fought for the right of the National Socialist Party of America (NSPA) to march through the Illinois suburb of Skokie, home to nearly a thousand Holocaust survivors. The neo-Nazi marchers planned to wear Nazi storm trooper uniforms and carry signs proclaiming "Free Speech for the White Man."[4] At the time, the ACLU was widely perceived as a liberal organization, and its support of the rightwing extremist group was met with surprise and condemnation in many quarters. Today, however, the ACLU's defense of the NSPA is often cited as an example—sometimes as the quintessential example—of courageous and principled commitment to free speech. The Skokie case helped define what is sometimes called the absolutist approach to the First Amendment, which maintains that even the most extreme and repugnant forms of expression must be protected. The ACLU's advocacy on behalf of white supremacist efforts to demonstrate in Charlottesville in 2017 earned the organization similar criticism and praise prior to the event.

But Charlottesville turned out quite differently than Skokie. The 1977 Skokie march never took place. The NSPA had originally planned to march in Marquette Park in Chicago, and it had been cleared to do so by the time the Skokie case was settled. The small group marched there instead without dramatic incident. By contrast, the Charlottesville march erupted in violence, and that violence was repeatedly and vividly broadcast through both mainstream and social media. The injuries and deaths resulting from the demonstration in Charlottesville cast the consequences of free speech absolutism in a very different light.

Two days after the demonstration, Governor McAuliffe highlighted the Virginia ACLU's role in ensuring that the rally took place downtown rather than in what the city considered to be a safer location a few miles away: "We were, unfortunately, sued by the ACLU. The judge ruled against us. That rally should not have been in the middle of downtown."[5] A board member of the Virginia ACLU resigned following the demonstration, stating that he would not "be a fig leaf for Nazis."[6] In a joint statement posted a few days after the demonstration, three California ACLU affiliates appeared to break ranks with the Virginia ACLU's decision to defend Kessler. According to the California statement,

> [T]he First Amendment does not protect people who incite or engage in violence. If white supremacists march into our towns armed to the teeth and with the intent to harm people, they are not engaging in activity protected by the United States Constitution. The First Amendment should never be used as a shield or sword to justify violence.[7]

The organization's national leadership was quick to counter the impression that a rift had developed within the ACLU. Within days, Anthony Romero, the ACLU's executive director, told the *Wall Street Journal* that the ACLU would not support armed demonstrators in the future: "If a protest group insists, 'No, we want to be able to carry loaded firearms,' well, we don't have to represent them."[8] While Romero and other ACLU representatives insisted that this was not a change in ACLU policy, the statement drew criticism from those who perceived the ACLU to be backing away from its absolutist commitment to First Amendment rights, as well as those who believed that the organization was denigrating Second Amendment rights.[9] A statement by the national ACLU one day after the

California affiliate's statement did little to clear up the confusion.[10] According to the statement, the national ACLU agreed with "every word in the statement from our colleagues in California. The First Amendment absolutely does not protect white supremacists seeking to incite or engage in violence." But "[a]t the same time," the statement continued, "we believe that even odious hate speech, with which we vehemently disagree, garners the protection of the First Amendment when expressed non-violently."[11]

The national ACLU's statement attempted to sidestep the issue grimly highlighted in Charlottesville: the contested boundary between speech and violence. The claim that the First Amendment protects speech but not violence assumes, as an initial matter, that speech and violence can always be meaningfully separated. This was not the first time that assumption had been challenged, but the weapons prominently displayed amid the swastikas and Confederate flags in Charlottesville brought the challenge into particularly sharp relief. Particularly when the First Amendment absolutism endorsed by organizations such as the ACLU collides with the Second Amendment absolutism endorsed by organizations such as the National Rifle Association, speech and violence become difficult to disentangle.[12] The Charlottesville demonstration accelerated already intense debates over First Amendment protections for hateful speech and the Second Amendment rights of citizens to openly display loaded weapons in volatile situations.

The "Unite the Right" rally also highlighted the role of the Internet in mobilizing and amplifying extremist groups committed to both online and offline violence. The small group of neo-Nazis planning the 1977 Skokie march relied on in-person communications and printed flyers. By contrast, the "Unite the Right" rally had been organized and advertised on various white supremacist and neo-Nazi websites, attracting a broad coalition of extremists from around the country. The march's attendees "shared advice on weaponry and tactics, including repeatedly broaching the idea of driving vehicles through opposition crowds" through online chat applications and websites.[13] On August 14, 2017, one such website, a popular white nationalist propaganda site named the Daily Stormer, published a piece celebrating Heather Heyer's murder, calling her a "fat, childless, 32-year-old slut"[14] and urging its readers to target her funeral.

In the days following the rally, the Daily Stormer's domain registration was canceled, first by the domain name service provider GoDaddy and later by Google's domain management service.[15] Twitter and Facebook both removed content associated with the Daily Stormer from their platforms, and the Internet security company Cloudflare terminated the Daily Stormer's account.[16] While some praised tech companies for taking a stand against the site, the Electronic Frontier Foundation (EFF), a prominent civil liberties and digital rights organization, criticized these responses. The EFF asserted "that no one—not the government and not private commercial enterprises—should decide who gets to speak and who doesn't."[17]

Charlottesville raised questions not only about *what* the Constitution is meant to protect, but also *who* the Constitution is meant to protect. The spectacle in Charlottesville was freighted with symbolism: white male protesters rallying around a statue of the leader of the Confederate Army as a diverse group of counter-protesters locked arms around the statue of the author of the Declaration of Independence. Robert E. Lee fought to preserve the institution of slavery; Thomas Jefferson proclaimed, "all men are created equal." Indeed, the fierce debate over the removal of Confederate monuments across the country is a testament to how deeply divided Americans continue to be over issues of race and national identity. These divisions often map neatly onto political affiliations, making it seem that the conflict can be further reduced to conservative versus liberal, Republican versus Democrat. It is tempting to characterize America's contemporary identity crisis as the choice between Lee and Jefferson, between bigotry and egalitarianism. But the harsh reality is that a choice between Lee and Jefferson is not much of a choice at all.

"I think there is blame on both sides" for what happened in Charlottesville, President Donald Trump told reporters on August 15, 2017.[18] This remark was criticized by figures across the political spectrum for promoting a false equivalence between the violent actions of white supremacists, most notably the murder of Heyer, and the conduct of the largely unarmed counter-protesters. But the remark also contained an inadvertent truth. In their repeated invocations of the First and Second Amendments, the neo-Nazi demonstrators in Charlottesville echoed the neo-Nazi demonstrators planning to march in Skokie forty years earlier:

The Constitution is first and foremost for white men. While conservatives officially distance themselves from this sentiment and liberals denounce it, the Constitution has indeed functioned to protect white male supremacy since the day it was written.

The term "white male supremacy" requires elaboration. It differs from the more commonly used expression "white supremacy" in two important ways. First and most obviously, it includes the word "male," intentionally highlighting the gendered as well as racialized nature of America's social and political hierarchy. The term "white male supremacy" is meant to make the patriarchal foundation of power visible, illuminating the intimate connections between racial and sexual inequality.[19]

Second, "white male supremacy," as the term is used in this book, refers not only to ideology of violent extremists who openly call for the exclusion or elimination of women and nonwhite men, but also to groups and individuals who express "softer" forms of racial and gender superiority, including members of the so-called alt-right as well as more mainstream conservatives. It also includes the ideology of many self-described liberals who espouse commitment to racial and gender equality in theory but reinforce existing hierarchies of power in practice. White male supremacy can be subtle and even seemingly benevolent as well as overt and violent. And because white male supremacy is an ideology, not an identity, its adherents are not limited to people who are white or male.

White male supremacy demands, in essence, that the interests of white men *take priority* over those of all others. In this sense, the concept of white male supremacy mirrors the concept of constitutional supremacy. As stated in Article VI, Clause 2, the Constitution is "the supreme Law of the Land." This "supremacy clause" acknowledges that other laws may be created and enforced, but none may conflict with and all are ultimately subordinate to the ultimate authority of the Constitution. In a similar fashion, those who adhere to the ideology of white male supremacy may tolerate the expansion of rights to women and nonwhite men, but only to the extent that these rights do not conflict with or undermine the rights of white men.[20] White male supremacy is thus profoundly antidemocratic.

Though the ideology of white male supremacy is pervasive, relatively few people are willing to openly endorse it. While there are some extremists who will proudly assert their belief in racial and gender superiority, it is more common for white male supremacy to be disguised and diffused within some seemingly neutral belief system. That system can be a religion, an economic theory, or, as is the focus of this book, a Constitution.

As Sanford Levinson observes in his book *Constitutional Faith*, "'worship of the Constitution' is a thread running through much American political rhetoric."[21] This "rhetoric of reverence" for the Constitution is, in the words of historian Michael Kammen, "more than offset by the reality of ignorance."[22] The majority of Americans have never read the Constitution in its entirety,[23] and even fewer have familiarized themselves with the vast body of Supreme Court doctrine interpreting its ambiguities and complexities. This lack of knowledge does little to dampen American enthusiasm for the Constitution or certainty about its meaning.

The combination of reverence and ignorance is at the heart of all fundamentalism. While cults are often characterized by excessive devotion to a charismatic leader, the object of cultlike devotion can also be an idea or a text. Many radical religious groups are fanatically devoted to sacred scriptures such as the Bible or the Koran. Common characteristics of religious fundamentalism include the idealization of authority figures, selective and self-serving interpretations of sacred texts, an unfounded sense of persecution, and a belief in natural hierarchies.

Constitutional fundamentalists exhibit these same tendencies. They idealize the founding fathers, read passages from the Constitution in isolation and out of context, believe themselves and their values to be constantly under attack, and rationalize extreme inequality as the product of natural competition. The cult of the Constitution allows Americans to downplay and disavow the role of white male supremacy in America's past and present.

The disavowal of white male supremacy was everywhere on display in the days following the violence in Charlottesville. A common refrain from prominent figures on both the right and left was that what happened in Charlottesville was fundamentally un-American. Tim Kaine, Virginia senator and former Democratic vice presidential nominee, stated that the "violence and bigotry that were brought to Charlottesville by white nationalists" are "not who we are."[24] Former Deputy Attorney

General Sally Yates tweeted that the "poison spewed by Nazis, white supremacists, and the KKK is not who we are as a country."[25] House Speaker Paul Ryan asserted that "bigotry is counter to all this country stands for."[26] Kentucky Senator Rand Paul said in a statement that "This is not who we are, and we will not stand by while you divide us."[27] Senator John McCain of Arizona invoked the men of the revolutionary period to assert that white supremacist bigotry runs counter to American ideals. "Our Founders fought a revolution for the idea that all men are created equal," said McCain in a statement. "White supremacists and neo-Nazis are, by definition, opposed to American patriotism and the ideals that define us as a people and make our nation special."[28] Thomas Garrett, a Virginia Republican who represents Charlottesville's district in Congress, denounced the views and actions of the white supremacists as antithetical to "who we are as Americans."[29] To underscore his point, Garrett invoked Virginia's rich founding era history, noting both that Charlottesville is "the city where Thomas Jefferson lived when he drafted the Declaration of Independence and observed all people are created equal"[30] and that Virginia's first congressman was James Madison, the chief drafter of the Constitution.

While the sentiment that white male supremacy is "not who we are" is admirable, it is flatly contradicted by America's history. Jefferson and Madison would likely have been far more shocked at the sight of women and black men speaking and moving freely in public than by the sight of armed white men menacing them. Congressman Garrett's subtle paraphrase of Jefferson's statement that "all men are created equal" as "all *people* are created equal" artfully elides how Jefferson's vision of equality was restricted to men, and, as we know from his other writings and his personal life, to white men in particular. In Congressman Garrett's revisionist account, "we've worked since 1776 to erase horrible flaws like slavery and second-class citizenship,"[31] a claim that would no doubt have surprised the small group of white, wealthy, male founders, many of whom personally owned slaves and all of whom enjoyed political, legal, and economic domination over women. The men who drafted the Constitution did so in proceedings that were unauthorized, secret, and devoid of participation by women, nonwhite men, and white men without property. The Constitution may have begun with the words "We the People,' but it was a document that both reflected and perpetuated white male supremacy.

Of course, the Constitution is not the same document today as it was when it was drafted in 1787. In particular, the adoption of the Bill of Rights in 1791, the addition of the Reconstruction Amendments between 1865 and 1870, and the Nineteenth Amendment's recognition of women's right to vote in 1920 have changed the Constitution in significant ways. Constitutional interpretation, too, has become less hostile to gender and racial equality over time, and the Fourteenth Amendment in particular has been valuable in protecting the rights of women and nonwhite men.

But these changes were very late in coming, and they have at most *modified* white male supremacy, not dislodged it. The effects of decades, in some cases centuries, of exploitation and exclusion cannot be reversed in a few generations. As white men today enjoy the political, economic, and cultural privileges accumulated by their forebears over two centuries, women and nonwhite men contend with the deprivations accumulated by theirs.

Women and minorities have been denied rights to political participation far longer than they have been allowed to exercise them. Congress was entirely white until 1870 and entirely male until 1916. The Supreme Court was composed exclusively of white men until 1967, and of men until 1981. While women and nonwhite men today are not formally excluded from political participation the way they were in the past, their representation in government is still not even roughly proportional to their percentage of the population. The U.S. population has been around 50 percent female since 1790, and as of 2016, it was 38 percent nonwhite. The 115th Congress, which began its term in January 2017 and is the most diverse Congress to date, is 80 percent male and 81 percent white. Only two African Americans and four women have served on the Supreme Court in its entire history. Every American president except one has been white, and every American president has been male.

Their unequal status under the Constitution has also meant that women and nonwhite men have been excluded from economic, educational, and cultural participation longer than they have been included. Slavery did not just exploit the labor of black men and women; it also denied them basic education, broke up their families, and dissolved their community ties. Until the late 1800s, most women, regardless of race, were denied the right to own property, to make contracts, and to obtain education or paid employment. Well into the twentieth century, women and nonwhite men's access to housing, universities, and workplaces was denied outright or severely restricted. Their ability to participate in military service, athletics, journalism, and the arts was similarly curtailed, and they faced aggressive harassment when they ultimately did obtain entry into spaces that had been previously accessible only to white men.

White men have, in other words, maintained a near-absolute monopoly on the interpretation and enforcement of the Constitution for the entire history of the United States—from the drafting of the Constitution itself, to the body enacting legislation in its name, to the institution interpreting its commands, to its highest executive official, to the very rights it protects. That has remained true as the political pendulum has swung in favor of conservatism to liberalism and back again. That has remained true no matter how "progressive" the politics on the left or "compassionate" on the right.

While some of the beneficiaries of this constitutional cartel have, at momentous points in history, used their power to confer constitutional recognition on women and minorities, the creation, interpretation, and application of constitutional rights have all primarily served the interests of the Americans who most closely resemble the original founding fathers. The core of constitutional power and privilege in this country has never shifted dramatically—that is to say, democratically—away from white men.

The observation that both conservatives and liberals are susceptible to constitutional fundamentalism is not meant to suggest that there are no real differences in constitutional approaches or priorities. One of the main differences is that conservatives tend to take an "originalist" interpretive approach, considering the meaning of the Constitution to be fixed, while liberals are more frequently associated with the "living constitutionalist" interpretive approach, which considers the meaning of the Constitution to evolve over time in light of changing practices and mores of society.

But constitutional fundamentalism, like all fundamentalism, is inherently conservative. It seeks to preserve an idealized past and to rationalize inequality. This kind of conservatism transcends political affiliation. Instead of focusing on the objective reality of white male supremacy, both conservative and liberal constitutional fundamentalists focus on white men's subjective feelings of persecution. This phenomenon is particularly pronounced with regard to First and Second Amendment rights. Like religious fundamentalism, constitutional fundamentalism can easily slide into fanaticism, that is, the justification of violence in the name of sacred beliefs.

Despite the protestations of Republican leaders in the wake of Charlottesville, the conservative constitutional tradition has for decades demonstrated a strong attachment to gender and racial hierarchy. It has long been allied with Christian religious leaders and viewpoints; favors judges and scholars who adopt an "originalist" approach to the Constitution; overtly endorses a social order that prioritizes the interests of white, heterosexual men; and includes fringe movements that openly call for and use violence to defend their interpretations of constitutional rights.[32] Conservative constitutional energy has for many years focused heavily on advancing an extreme interpretation of the Second Amendment that taps into conservative anxieties about both gender and race. As Rosamond C. Rodman writes, "the renewed interest in the Second Amendment came on the heels of the 'ideological disarray of the post-Vietnam decade' in which the events of the Vietnam War, racial conflicts like Watts and Detroit, and the rise of second-wave feminism challenged long-standing cultural assumptions and ideas."[33] The National Rifle Association (NRA) has been enormously successful in advocating for a virtually unlimited right to bear arms in the courts, in legislatures, and in public discourse.

The liberal constitutional tradition, on the other hand, is often assumed to be the counterpoint of the conservative tradition. It largely avoids the open embrace of religious ideology; is associated with a dynamic and "living" approach to constitutional interpretation; expressly denounces sexism, racism, and homophobia; and is rarely used to justify physical violence. Liberals are for the most part critical of extreme interpretations of the Second Amendment. When liberals invoke the Constitution, they often do so on behalf of less powerful members of society: women, racial and sexual minorities, and the poor. Liberals have historically been the champions of free speech and have focused much of their constitutional energy on the First Amendment. The ACLU plays a similarly influential role in liberal constitutionalism as the NRA does in conservative constitutionalism.

In recent decades, however, conservative and liberal constitutionalism have converged in many respects. This convergence can be expressed as the triumph of civil libertarianism, that is, the triumph of the *civil liberties* approach over the *civil rights* approach to constitutional rights.[34] Though the terms are sometimes used interchangeably, they describe distinct and, in some cases, mutually exclusive concerns. The civil liberties approach to constitutional rights emphasizes individual rights and the need to protect them from the interference of the government; the civil rights approach emphasizes group rights and the need to ensure their equal protection by the government. As Christopher Schmidt explains,

> [A]dvocates of civil rights typically ask the government to do more: to implement more aggressive antidiscrimination regulations, to extend the equal protection norm, through legislative or judicial or administrative action, to new areas of society and to new groups. Civil libertarians generally believe that government power and individual freedom operate as a zero-sum game. Their basic demand is that the government do less.[35]

The turn to civil libertarianism is largely responsible for what legal scholar Mary Ann Glendon refers to disparagingly as "American rights talk," which

> is set apart from rights discourse in other liberal democracies by its starkness and simplicity, its prodigality in bestowing the rights label, its legalistic character, its exaggerated absoluteness, its hyperindividualism, its insularity, and its silence with respect to personal, civil, and collective responsibilities.[36]

Civil libertarianism, long associated with the political left, is often perceived as being distinct from economic libertarianism, which is more often associated with the political right. But the two share many characteristics.[37] The language of libertarianism, emphasizing "free markets" and "deregulation," allows the beneficiaries of the status quo to pretend that they have achieved their success through hard work and natural competition rather than historical privilege and systematic exploitation.

The right's civil libertarian tactics are vividly on display with regard to gun rights and the Second Amendment. The NRA warns that allowing any regulation of any gun rights will lead to mass disarmament and that the deadly consequences of firearm use must be tolerated to protect the right of self-defense for all.

The left's civil libertarianism on free speech closely resembles the right's civil libertarianism about guns. The ACLU warns that even the most modest regulation of any speech rights will lead to mass censorship and that the devastating effects of abusive speech must be tolerated to protect freedom of speech for all.

As free speech priorities have shifted from political speech to commercial speech, from vulnerable populations to powerful ones, and from individuals to corporations, civil libertarianism has become indistinguishable from economic libertarianism. This merging of the left and right was dramatically illustrated by the ACLU's decision to line up alongside the NRA to push for corporate interests in the controversial 2010 Supreme Court case *Citizens United*.

The convergence of liberal and conservative civil libertarianism, and its increasingly corporatized character, is perhaps no more apparent than in the structure and operation of the Internet as we know it today. It is no coincidence that the Internet—the dominant modern marketplace of both commerce and ideas—is controlled by a handful of multi-billion-dollar corporations with no incentive to distinguish between productive and destructive uses of technology. Thanks to the joint efforts of conservative and liberal advocates and lawmakers, companies like Google and Facebook are essentially immunized from liability for the activity they facilitate even as they are allowed to reap enormous profits from it.[38]

The effects of constitutional fundamentalism about guns, speech, and the Internet have become painfully clear in recent years. Like other forms of extremism, constitutional fundamentalism waxes and wanes over time, flaring up most violently in response to threats to the status quo. In 2016, America was poised to issue the most dramatic challenge to white male supremacy in its history. President Barack Obama's eight-year tenure was a great success by numerous objective measures, despite unprecedented obstructionist hostility from Congress. The Supreme Court had recognized the right of same-sex couples to marry; the Black Lives Matter protest movement had brought issues of racial inequality and police brutality into the mainstream; and women were closer than ever to achieving financial, educational, and professional equality. Perhaps most significantly, it was also the year that Hillary Clinton became the first female presidential candidate to be nominated by a major political party, despite being subjected to an unrelenting stream of misogynist attacks from both the right and left. The country was on the brink of breaking up the white male monopoly of power.

But 2016 was also the year that an openly misogynist, racist, and xenophobic billionaire reality star was selected as the presidential nominee for the Republican Party. It is hard to imagine a more obvious manifestation of the desperate attempt by white male supremacy to reassert itself than Donald Trump's candidacy for president. His lack of relevant experience or demonstrable skills did not matter, nor did his ostentatious wealth, his multiple business failures, his infidelities or multiple marriages, nor even his boast on tape about sexually assaulting women. The Republican Party—the party of "family values" and "personal responsibility" and "fiscal conservatism"—not only selected him as their candidate but rallied behind him as he mocked the disabled, called for a ban on Muslims, insulted the families of dead veterans, and made clear that he would use the presidency to enrich his own personal wealth. He was heralded by his supporters, and eventually by the conservative establishment, as a workingman's hero and a bold political leader who would, according to his catchphrase, "Make America Great Again."

From the perspective of principled conservatism, the choice of Donald Trump was confounding; from the perspective of preserving the white male monopoly on power, it made perfect sense. Trump's selection as the Republican Party nominee demonstrated the degree to which far-right extremism had moved into the conservative mainstream. Donald Trump did not need to be morally upstanding, financially responsible, or even minimally competent. He only had to reassure America that he would return it to "the good old days" of white male supremacy.

In many ways, Trump is the very embodiment of the domination/victimization paradox of white male supremacy. It was fashionable among Republicans in the latter part of the twentieth century to mock the very concept of victimization. People who were disturbed by racist abuse or sexual harassment or homophobic slurs were "bleeding heart liberals"; discrimination was just "rough talk" that hurt the feelings of "sheltered crybabies"; calls for civilizing political discourse were derided as political correctness intended to "sanitize the workplace" or to turn college campuses into "safe spaces"; accusations of "silencing" and "erasing" were hysterical overreactions to uncomfortable truths. When the political correctness debate re-emerged around 2008, the Internet provided conservatives with new slurs and memes to ridicule the sensitivities of liberal snowflakes. Conservatives and libertarians portrayed themselves, by contrast, as rough-and-tumble, tell-it-like-it-is brawlers, not afraid of giving offense and certainly never taking it.

But at least by 2016, conservatives and libertarians had become extremely comfortable identifying as victims. They no longer dismissed sexism, racism, intolerance, or discrimination as liberal fantasies; instead, they bemoaned the fearsome power of liberals to emasculate and silence white men, making them fearful of celebrating their masculinity, their racial heritage, or their belief in traditional gender roles. It is now commonplace for self-identified conservatives to cry censorship when they are criticized on Facebook or blocked on Twitter; an endless stream of books, news features, and think pieces are dedicated to the feelings of disaffected, conservative white men; and it is now possible for a Republican president to literally demand that the cast of a Broadway play ensure that the theater be a "safe space" for the vice president of the United States.

The Republican embrace of victim politics and its slide into extremism paid off handsomely in the 2016 election, with the result that in 2017 the White House, Congress, the Supreme Court, and the majority of state governments were all in the hands of not only white men, but of Republican white men. Within a few months of Trump taking office, the rights of women, minorities, and immigrants were being actively undermined; freedom of the press and of association were under attack; freedom of religion was increasingly being used as a pretext for discrimination; the nature of truth itself was called into question; and white men were freer than ever to endanger public welfare with their fetish for weapons.

That a barely literate, openly racist, pathologically dishonest sexual predator could be elected to the highest office in America in 2016 was a grave indictment of the state of constitutional culture in the United States. While many liberals and a number of moderate conservatives were horrified by Trump's election, and organizations such as the ACLU immediately challenged some of the Trump regime's most egregiously unconstitutional policies, liberals also played a role in Trump's success. Liberal constitutional fundamentalism helped pave the way for radical rightwing extremism and overt white male supremacy to take hold in the United States.

Trump's rise was fueled not only by the full-throated support of far-right extremists and the conservative gun lobby, but also by massive online harassment campaigns, foreign propaganda schemes targeting the news and social media, and public demonstrations by increasingly emboldened neo-Nazis—all of which were able to flourish because of the left's fanatical interpretations of the First Amendment.

Liberal constitutional fundamentalism created the free speech orthodoxy that allowed threats, conspiracy theories, defamation, and outright lies to flourish unchecked in the media and on the Internet. In the name of free speech, liberals helped eliminate nearly every potential standard and safeguard against violent rhetoric, false statements, and targeted harassment. Civil libertarianism helped distort the political landscape to such an extent that the most privileged members of society could present themselves as oppressed victims. The deregulated Internet, which the left and the right fought so hard for, removed any incentive on the part of giant tech corporations to take responsibility for the content they unleash into the world, no matter how destructive it might be.

The Trump era has exposed the hollowness of liberal free speech platitudes: the belief that truth will eventually prevail, that the best answer to bad speech is more speech, and that protecting the free speech rights of the worst people in society is necessary to protect the free speech of all. It is little wonder that in recent decades the right has found free speech orthodoxy more and more appealing, as it increasingly became a way for rich and powerful white men to drown out the voices of everyone else. The right has put the deregulatory, benefit-the-powerful strategy of the left's free speech orthodoxy to good use: to mobilize its base around the violent reassertion of white male supremacy.

It is hardly surprising, then, that the picture of who holds power today does not look that different from 1787: The government, the military, law enforcement, the financial sector, the tech industry, the entertainment industry, and the media are all dominated by white, wealthy men. This near-total retention of power is neither a coincidence nor the result of superior effort or talent. It is the completely predictable result of a political, economic, and cultural system that has excluded and exploited women and nonwhite men for generations.

Despite all of these advantages, the narrative of white male persecution persists. In Charlottesville in August 2017, white men from all over the country marched into a small college town with torches and guns to protest their perceived oppression. In their eyes, white men are victims, even though they are the only group in America that has never experienced systematic discrimination and has perpetually dominated the ranks of its ruling class. Conversely, in their view, women and nonwhite men are oppressors, despite having been denied equal rights throughout history and never holding more than a fraction of the country's political and economic power. To the demonstrators, the removal of a Confederate monument is an act of violence, while the celebration of treason in defense of slavery is an act of patriotism. According to these members of the alt-right, the suicide rate of white people is evidence of "white genocide,"[39] while the murder of an unarmed woman is "payback"[40] exacted against a "fat, childless slut."[41]

The Charlottesville protesters should not be dismissed as fringe extremists who do not represent "who we are." While their words and actions are extreme, they reflect sentiments that have long been cultivated by the right and allowed to flourish by the left. The demonstrators were only the latest in a long line of white men who have violently resisted every effort to make the fiction of constitutional equality into reality. From the Civil War to Jim Crow, from mob attacks on female suffragists to abortion clinic bombings, from the bloody civil rights struggles in the 1950s and 1960s to Charlottesville in 2017, there have always been white men willing to fight to keep women and nonwhite men from becoming part of "we the people," and there have always been constitutional fundamentalists to help them do so.

Charlottesville is who we are.

It is not, however, all we are.

During his speech at the 2016 Democratic National Convention, Khizr Khan, the father of a Muslim soldier who was killed in Iraq, held aloft a copy of the Constitution as he denounced then-Republican presidential candidate Donald Trump's proposed immigration ban against Muslims. "Have you even read the United States Constitution?" Khan asked from the podium, addressing Trump. "In this document, look for the words 'liberty' and 'equal protection of law.'"

Khan was of course referring to the Fourteenth Amendment, which provides that no state may "deprive any person of life, liberty, or property, without due process of law; nor deny to any person within its jurisdiction the equal protection of the laws." The Fourteenth Amendment, unlike the First or Second Amendments, is not a right in isolation, but a rule that applies to all rights and all laws. Like Immanuel Kant's categorical imperative, John Rawls's justice-as-fairness, or most simply the Golden Rule, the equal protection clause is an indispensable and irreducible moral obligation that underlies all rights and privileges. When we adhere to the imperative of equal protection, we are prohibited from making exceptions of ourselves, either to obtain privileges or to avoid punishments. The command to treat others as we would wish to be treated provides us with the only sure means of distinguishing our prejudices from our principles.

Constitutional fundamentalists, like religious fundamentalists, read sacred texts selectively. Like Christian fundamentalists who cherry-pick Bible passages that justify their personal views and ignore the ones that contradict them, constitutional fundamentalists focus on isolated amendments that validate their own interests while disregarding the parts of the Constitution that challenge them. As Khan publicly pointed out to Donald Trump, to do this is to betray the Constitution itself. The Fourteenth Amendment's equal protection clause makes clear that constitutional rights must be accessible to everyone or no one. It requires us to be concerned not only with *which* rights are being protected but *whose* rights are being protected. It requires that we ask whether privileging certain rights jeopardizes other rights and whether privileging certain people's rights jeopardizes other people's rights. The Fourteenth Amendment's equal protection clause is, in short, the test of constitutional fidelity and the antidote to constitutional fundamentalism.

This book endeavors to take the constitutional command of reciprocity seriously. It aims to dismantle the cult of the Constitution that has sustained an elitist and antidemocratic system of constitutional protection for more than two hundred years. It attempts to conduct a transparent accounting of the motivations, costs, and benefits of constitutional choices and the allocation of constitutional resources. While it focuses primarily on fundamentalist interpretations of the First and Second Amendments, the effects of constitutional fundamentalism can be observed in the interpretation of many constitutional provisions. First and Second Amendment fundamentalism have created particularly urgent and volatile dangers for our time, and it is hoped that the lessons that can be learned from studying these forms of constitutional fundamentalism can be usefully applied to other forms.

Chapter 1 describes how the cult of the Constitution was established in 1787 and how it has persisted to the present day. It explains how the founding fathers' original disavowal of white male supremacy allowed them to deceive themselves, and posterity, that the Constitution was a noble exercise in equality and democracy. This deception is kept alive through ritualized, idealized invocations of the founding fathers and the Constitution. Americans across the political spectrum are eager to proclaim their fidelity to the Constitution despite being largely ignorant of both the text itself and its interpretation by the courts. Though conservatives and liberals differ in their interpretive approaches to the Constitution, neither approach has dislodged the near-monopoly maintained by white men on political, economic, and social power.

Chapter 2 explores the specific appeal of the Second Amendment to conservative constitutional fundamentalists. The most ardent defenders of the individual right to bear arms tend to believe in strict social hierarchies reinforced by rigid gender roles, racial superiority, and distrust of government. Powerful gun rights organizations such as the NRA manipulate their followers into believing that they are always just one step away from being disarmed by the government, which cultivates a collective paranoia and persecution complex among gun owners that spills over into other social issues, from religious freedom to political correctness to women's reproductive rights. Second Amendment fundamentalists promote a view of self-defense that overprotects the powerful and underprotects the most vulnerable members of society, as exemplified by policies such as open-carry and stand-your-ground laws. Second Amendment fundamentalists rally behind neighborhood vigilantes and police officers, but not the victims of domestic violence, racial harassment, or police brutality.

Chapter 3 focuses on First Amendment fundamentalism. It assesses the historical influence of the ACLU in shaping political and social understandings of free speech and examines the rightward shift in contemporary First Amendment practice and application. The left–right First Amendment alliance has helped transform free speech doctrine from a shield protecting the most vulnerable to a sword wielded by the most privileged and powerful members of society. Liberal and conservative constitutionalist views have converged on topics ranging from revenge porn to commercial and corporate expression to campus speech. This convergence has deepened existing inequalities in the free speech and other constitutional rights of women and racial minorities.

Chapter 4 details the role of the Internet in pushing the worst excesses of constitutional fundamentalism in an increasingly violent and irrational direction. Constitutional fundamentalists are dangerously susceptible to being radicalized by false persecution narratives. The Internet, in bringing fundamentalists together and amplifying their shared feelings of grievance, helps turn fundamentalists into fanatics prone to justifying and employing violence to protect their identity and their beliefs. The law responsible for the Internet's diffuse and deregulated structure, Section 230 of the Communications Decency Act, allows online intermediaries to reap the financial and constitutional benefits of online speech while avoiding any responsibility for their costs. While Section 230 has played a vital role in the growth and development of the Internet's positive potential, it has also incentivized powerful corporations to engage in increasingly risky conduct that inflicts massive harms to privacy, security, and democracy.

The conclusion explains why, despite the dangers of constitutional fundamentalism, we can and should still have faith in the Constitution. This will require, however, an unflinching commitment to the principle of reciprocity expressed in the Fourteenth Amendment's equal protection clause.

The adherents of the cult of the Constitution would have us believe that "we" are facing an unprecedented erosion of our constitutional rights that can only be countered with "more" of everything: guns, speech, Internet. But we are not facing a sudden crisis of constitutional scarcity. We are facing a *continuing* crisis of constitutional inequality. For more than two hundred years, the lion's share of legislative, judicial, political, and social resources has been devoted to protecting the constitutional rights of white men above all others. It is long past time to stop pretending that white men are the primary victims of constitutional deprivation or that the protection of their constitutional benefits will trickle down to other groups. The health of our constitutional rights must no longer be measured in terms of effects on white men, but on the groups that have been historically excluded from constitutional protection.

Although women and minorities suffer earliest and most, the self-serving and irrational appropriation of constitutional principles to justify lies, harassment, discrimination, and outright violence endangers society as a whole and threatens to destroy democracy. We are all, as a society, less informed, less peaceful, less democratic, less stable, and less free because of constitutional fundamentalism. Constitutional rights cannot be defended unless they are defended for all, and conflicts among constitutional rights must be resolved according to the demands of equality. "We the people" must mean all of us, or none of us.

CHAPTER 1

THE CULT OF THE CONSTITUTION

"If miracles are men's wishes fulfilled, so with the miracle at Philadelphia."
—Catherine Drinker Bowen, *Miracle at Philadelphia*

THE FOUNDING OF THE CONSTITUTIONAL CULT

It is a story every American schoolchild knows, endlessly re-enacted in history books, somber oil paintings, and ponderous documentaries.[1] During the sweltering summer of 1787, fifty-five delegates from twelve[2] of the original thirteen states met in Independence Hall in Philadelphia to draft, debate, and produce a plan of government that became the Constitution of the United States. George Washington presided over the Constitutional Convention, and the delegates included such luminaries as Benjamin Franklin, James Madison, and Alexander Hamilton. Writing to John Adams from Paris, Thomas Jefferson admiringly described the delegation as "an assembly of demigods."[3] Madison's voluminous notes on the proceedings portray months of bitter conflict, impassioned speeches, and seemingly insurmountable divisions, so that the convention's ultimate success seemed to him to have been divinely assisted. Marveling "that so many difficulties should have been surmounted," Madison wrote that it is "impossible for the man of pious reflection not to perceive in it a finger of that Almighty hand which has been so frequently and signally extended to our relief in the critical stages of the revolution."[4] Washington expressed a similar sentiment to the Marquis de Lafayette in 1788, calling it "little short of a miracle" that delegates of states so varied "in their manners, circumstances, and prejudices, should unite in forming a system of national Government."[5]

That the framers regarded their handiwork as divinely inspired is notable enough, but even more remarkable is how this reverential view of the Constitution and its drafters has persisted through history. As Thomas C. Grey writes, the Constitution "has been, virtually from the moment of its ratification, a sacred symbol."[6] Constitutional reverence is apparent in the title of one of the most acclaimed accounts of the Constitutional Convention, Catherine Drinker Bowen's 1966 *Miracle at Philadelphia*. Bowen describes the framers' "spirit of compromise" in worshipful tones:

> Compromise can be an ugly word, signifying a pact with the devil, a chipping off of the best to suit the worst. Yet in the Constitutional Convention the spirit of compromise reigned in grace and glory; as Washington presided, it sat on his shoulder like the dove. Men rise to speak and one sees them struggle with the bias of birthright, locality, statehood— South against North, East against West, merchant against planter. One sees them change their minds, fight against pride, and when the moment comes, admit their error.[7]

In accounts like Bowen's, the framers are described as men with a godlike ability to transcend their individual differences for the sake of the common and enduring good. According to the traditional narrative, "we the people" are able to enjoy the blessings of liberty because of the framers' sublime wisdom and beatific selflessness.

In modern times, in certain circles, this idealized vision is sometimes accompanied by a perfunctory acknowledgment of the limitations or imperfections of the framers, generally followed by a reassertion of the exemplariness of their character and their labor. Consider a typical example:

> The Founders were imperfect men and the Constitution an imperfect document. But all things considered what happened at Independence

Hall was little short of a miracle. And for a group of fiercely proud and independent individuals to rise above such deep difference for the sake of the public good, to comprise [sic] in order to advance justice and human dignity, was a rare and wonderful thing.[8]

The "imperfect men" narrative is significant, first, for its euphemistic gloss of the bluntly racist and sexist reality of the Constitutional Convention. It does little to convey the outright exclusion of women and nonwhite men from the process of drafting America's foundational document. The convention was composed of white men with property—property that included, for many of the delegates, human beings. The men who wrote that the Constitution was intended to "secure the Blessings of Liberty to *ourselves* and *our* Posterity,"[9] meant exactly that: liberty for people like them, at the expense of those not like them.

The narrative of imperfect men is significant for another reason: It presents two competing visions of the framers. On the one hand, the framers are praised for their transcendent vision of equality and liberty; on the other, they are excused for excluding women and nonwhite men from that vision because they were, after all, merely men of their time. According to this view, prevailing eighteenth-century norms simply did not countenance equality of gender and race.

Of course, prevailing eighteenth-century norms also did not countenance the overthrowing of monarchy rule. The American Revolution dramatically repudiated long-held assumptions about political legitimacy and the nature of political representation. The British Empire had insisted that the interests of the colonists were "virtually represented" by members of Parliament, even though the colonists had not elected these representatives. Submission to monarchical rule was presented as the natural order; the colonists' revolt against "taxation without representation" was a decisive rejection of this narrative. The 1776 Declaration of Independence, boldly asserting the right of the people to "alter or abolish" governments that fail to protect fundamental rights, was enormously influential throughout the world, helping spark independence movements in several countries.

The Constitutional Convention continued the break with tradition and prevailing norms. The delegates had been authorized only to revise the

Articles of Confederation, the original governing document of the thirteen states. Led by James Madison, the delegates instead decided to devise an entirely new constitution. They also agreed to keep the proceedings of the convention secret until they were concluded.

Against this background, to describe the men of the revolutionary and founding eras as "products of their time" rings hollow. Their elevated status in American culture derives almost entirely from their radical rejection of dominant eighteenth-century political and social norms.

Nor can it be maintained that the framers were unaware of the contradictions between their egalitarian rhetoric and their continued commitment to gender and racial inequality. These contradictions were noted by many of the framers' contemporaries, often in direct communications to the framers themselves.

In a letter written in 1774 to her husband John Adams, then a delegate to the First Constitutional Congress, Abigail Adams wrote,

> I wish most Sincerely there was not a Slave in the province. It allways appeard a most iniquitious Scheme to me, fight ourselves for what we are daily robbing and plundering from those who have as good a right to freedom as we have. You know my mind upon this Subject.[10]

The Revolutionary War had prompted intense reflection regarding the practice of slavery and challenged long-held beliefs of racial inferiority. While slavery was a widespread practice, many high-profile statesmen and intellectuals of the time were strongly and vocally opposed to the institution. As the British author Thomas Day succinctly put it in 1776, "If there be an object truly ridiculous in nature, it is an American patriot, signing resolutions of independency with the one hand, and with the other brandishing a whip over his affrighted slaves."[11] Thomas Jefferson included a condemnation of slavery in his original draft of the Declaration of Independence, calling it a "cruel war against human nature itself, violating its most sacred rights of life and liberty." But delegates of the Constitutional Congress from both the South and the North objected to the passage, and it was taken out.

Jefferson's views on slavery were complex to say the least, as he himself owned slaves. In 1791, Benjamin Banneker, a former slave who had taught himself to read and write and became a prominent mathematician and astronomer, wrote Jefferson a letter urging him to abandon his hypocritical position on slavery:

> Sir, how pitiable is it to reflect, that although you were so fully convinced of the benevolence of the Father of Mankind, and of his equal and impartial distribution of these rights and privileges, which he hath conferred upon them, that you should at the same time counteract his mercies, in detaining by fraud and violence so numerous a part of my brethren, under groaning captivity and cruel oppression, that you should at the same time be found guilty of that most criminal act, which you professedly detested in others, with respect to yourselves.[12]

The decision to protect the institution of slavery in the Constitution is often characterized as a regrettable but necessary compromise between the slave-holding southern states and the antislavery northern states. Indeed, the notorious clause in Article I, Section 2 counting slaves as three-fifths of a free—that is to say, white—person for the purposes of apportioning representation in the House of Representatives is known as the Three-Fifths Compromise.

That section is not the only part of the Constitution that indulged the institution of slavery; Article I, Section 9 prevented Congress from prohibiting the importation of slaves until 1808, and Article IV, Section 2 (the fugitive slave clause) required the return of escaped slaves to their masters. As Justice Thurgood Marshall observed, the "compromise" on slavery in fact benefited the economic interests of the states as a whole:

> [T]he Southern states acceded to the demands of the New England states for giving Congress broad power to regulate commerce, in exchange for the right to continue the slave trade. The economic interests of the regions coalesced: New Englanders engaged in the "carrying trade" would profit from transporting slaves from Africa as well as goods produced in America by slave labor. The perpetuation of slavery ensured the primary source of wealth in the Southern states.[13]

As historian Charles Beard detailed in *An Economic Interpretation of the Constitution of the United States*, the framers were "immediately, directly, and personally interested in, and derived economic advantages from, the establishment of the new system."[14]

In any case, protecting slavery in the Constitution as a "compromise" is hardly deserving of the name. Compromises generally involve the sacrifice of one's own interests for the sake of another good. But slavery did not compromise the interests of wealthy white men, even antislavery ones: It compromised—in an absolute sense—the interests of the enslaved.

As unrest grew over British treatment of the colonies, questions had also arisen over the continuing subordination of women. In 1764, the influential Massachusetts statesman James Otis asked, "Are not women born as free as men? Would it not be infamous to assert that the ladies are all slaves by nature?"[15] while in 1773, Thomas Paine bemoaned the fact that "throughout most of history, women, almost without exception, had been 'at all times and all places, adored and oppressed.'"[16]

Women played an essential role in the Revolutionary War, both on the battlefield and off. They led boycotts and demonstrations against British tax policies; marched alongside the soldiers dependent on them for food, clothing, and medical treatment; took up wounded men's places at the cannon; disguised themselves as men and fought alongside them; and risked torture and death as spies and couriers.[17] Women took over men's tasks at home, learning how to run farms and shops and to defend themselves and their children from enemy forces.[18] In short, women actively participated in the politics, economics, and physical defense of the colonies throughout the revolutionary period. Their willingness and ability to perform traditionally masculine tasks, from public speaking to taking up arms to farm labor, refuted longstanding gender stereotypes of women's supposed physical and mental inferiority to men. As historian Carol Berkin writes, the postwar period was marked by a "lively debate" over "what changes in women's roles might prove necessary in the new republican society."[19]

In 1776, Abigail Adams famously beseeched her husband John Adams to "remember the Ladies," pointing out the hypocrisy and injustice of men fighting against tyranny by the British while maintaining their tyranny over women, long before the parallel was made explicit in the Declaration of Sentiments at the Seneca Falls Convention in 1848: "Do not put such unlimited power into the hands of the Husbands. Remember all Men would be tyrants if they could."[20]

Abigail's reference to the tyranny of men over women was not mere rhetoric. Under the British legal doctrine known as *coverture*, married women could not own property, enter contracts, or exercise basic civil rights. The legal existence of wives was literally subsumed—"covered"— under that of their husbands. As William Blackstone described it, "the very being or legal existence of the woman is suspended during the marriage, or at least is incorporated and consolidated into that of the husband, under whose wing, protection, and cover, she performs every thing."[21] Coverture also justified husbands' rights of physical chastisement and sexual access, which is to say, the right to beat and rape their wives. Consequently, women in eighteenth-century England and America endured the physical hardships of childbirth, household labor, and marital violence while enjoying little or no access to education, employment, public engagement, or basic civil and political rights.

While the framers engaged in exhaustive debate over the most effective means of checking governmental tyranny, they made no effort to address the unchecked power of men over women.[22] The founders were apparently untroubled by the contradiction, expressed so patiently by Abigail, that "whilst you are proclaiming peace and good will to Men, Emancipating all Nations, you insist in retaining an absolute power over Wives."[23] While women were subjected *to* the constitutional contract, they were not acknowledged as subjects *of* the constitutional contract.[24] Borrowing the language of the American revolutionaries, Abigail threatened, "If perticuliar care and attention is not paid to the Laidies we are determined to foment a Rebelion, and will not hold ourselves bound by any Laws in which we have no voice, or Representation."[25]

Less famous than Abigail's eloquent plea, however, is her husband's uncharacteristically patronizing reply, which ridiculed the idea of both gender and racial equality. John Adams, considered one of the most enlightened and progressive framers, responded that he could not "but laugh" at Abigail's "extraordinary code of laws":

We have been told that our struggle has loosened the bonds of government everywhere; that children and apprentices were disobedient; that
schools and colleges were grown turbulent; that Indians slighted their
guardians, and negroes grew insolent to their masters. But your letter was
the first intimation that another tribe, more numerous and powerful than
all the rest, were grown discontented.[26]

Adams clearly found the idea of women and nonwhite men being inspired
by the promise of fair representation and popular sovereignty ridiculous.
As Berkin writes, "Ready to rebel against the unlimited power of king and
Parliament, John Adams was not ready to see the hierarchy of gender de-
stroyed in the process."[27] Though the men of the revolutionary period had
rejected the concept of virtual representation by the British monarchy, they
apparently accepted the idea that women's interests could be adequately
represented by their male relatives.[28]

Adams's response to a fellow statesman's inquiry about the possibility of expanding the voting franchise to white men without property was
more respectfully articulated, but even more nakedly elitist. While he
conceded that "in theory, that the only moral foundation of government
is, the consent of the people," Adams asked, "to what an extent shall we
carry this principle?"[29]

Depend upon it, Sir, it is dangerous to open so fruitful a source of controversy and altercation as would be opened by attempting to alter the
qualifications of voters; there will be no end of it. New claims will arise;
women will demand a vote . . . and every man who has not a farthing,
will demand an equal voice with any other, in all acts of state. It tends
to confound and destroy all distinctions; and prostrate all ranks to one
common level.[30]

Adams, one of the most open-minded framers, plainly saw the contradiction
at the heart of the constitutional project. He was keenly aware that the rights
granted to himself and his fellow elites ought, logically, to be granted to other
groups. But instead of following this logic to its inevitable conclusion, he
recoiled from it—in effect recoiling from the principle of democracy itself.

In claiming rights for white men with property while denying them to others, Adams and the other framers also violated the basic moral principle of reciprocity. This principle, often called the Golden Rule, is older than Christianity and recognized by every major religious and ethical tradition,[31] from the New Testament command to "do unto others as you would have done to you" (Matthew 7:12) to Immanuel Kant's categorical imperative to "act only according to that maxim whereby you can at the same time will that it should become a universal law."[32] The Irish statesman Edmund Burke articulated a version of the reciprocity principle in 1777 in his rebuke of the British Parliament's selective suspension of the colonists' right of habeas corpus, writing that liberty "is a general principle, and the clear right of all the subjects within the realm, or of none."[33] In Burke's words, to give rights to some people and deny them to others is "a most invidious mode of slavery."[34]

In ancient texts, the principle of reciprocity was often expressed in terms of a prohibition. A papyrus from Egypt's Late Period (c. 664 BCE–323 BCE) reads, "That which you hate to be done to you, do not do to another."[35] In the *Analects*, written in 500 BCE, Confucius is asked by a disciple whether there was "any one word that could guide a person throughout life," and he responded "'shu' [reciprocity]: never impose on others what you would not choose for yourself."[36] According to a Talmudic passage written around the year 500, in response to a man demanding to have the Torah explained to him while he is standing on one foot, the rabbi says: "What is hateful to yourself, do not do to your fellow man. That is the whole Torah; the rest is just commentary."[37]

The *cri de coeur* of the American Revolution was "no taxation without representation," a rejection of their perceived exploitation by the British empire. Yet the framers of the Constitution imposed that evil and worse on women and nonwhite men. They enslaved black men and women, exercised quasi-monarchical rule over their wives, and taxed women and free black men with property—all while denying them even the most basic right of representation: the right to vote.[38] The American ruling elite extracted the reproductive, domestic, and agricultural labor of women and slaves even as it excluded them entirely from the political process. As the colonists threw off the yoke of tyrannical rule, they maintained it around women and slaves. The framers of the Constitution consigned women and black men to a condition they found intolerable for themselves.

That the most privileged members of a society banded together to consolidate their power over weaker groups is not a new or uncommon story. It may even be fair to say that this is how most nations were founded. What makes the Philadelphia convention extraordinary is not that it was an immoral coup d'état by a white, male, wealthy elite committed to gender, racial, and economic hierarchy. It is that it has been so convincingly presented, both at the time and for generations after, as precisely the opposite: as the heroic effort by noble and selfless men to establish the greatest democracy in the world. The beatification of the framers and the sacralization of the Constitution in the face of contradictory reality raise two questions: Why did the framers engage in this elaborately deceptive mythology about their actions, and why has it proven so seductive to future generations?

That is, why did the Philadelphia delegates not simply write a Constitution that told the truth: that an elite minority of white, wealthy men was seizing power and imposing its will upon the rest of the population? Perhaps, as some suggest, the framers' expression of noble ideals in the Declaration of Independence and the Preamble to the Constitution was an exercise in humility and aspiration. They may have been aware that they personally fell far short of these ideals but hoped that articulating them would help future generations achieve them. As George Washington himself wrote in 1787, the framers were not "more inspired," wiser, or more virtuous "than those who will come after us."[39] The decision to include an amendment process provides support for the idea that the framers believed the Constitution was "not perfect, but rather perfectible."[40]

There is likely some truth to this, but it is also likely not the full story. Philosophers, poets, and psychologists have long observed that while human beings are primarily motivated by self-interest, they are also deeply reluctant to confront this fact. The seventeenth-century mathematician and theologian Blaise Pascal wrote, "The nature of self-love and of this human Ego is to love self only and consider self only," but that man also "wants to be the object of love and esteem among men." When man learns that "his faults merit only their hatred and contempt . . . he devotes all his attention to hiding his faults both from others and from himself."[41] Acknowledging that one is acting out of naked self-interest conflicts with what psycho-analysts call the "ideal ego," or the idealized version of ourselves that we want to believe is our true self. The transcendental, universalizing rhetoric of the Constitution helped the framers deceive themselves as well as others about their motivations.[42]

Deceiving others was essential to maintaining the precarious legitimacy of the Constitutional Convention. The revolutionary message was that any government not based on equal representation and the consent of the governed was illegitimate; the revolutionary rallying cry of "no taxation without representation" explicitly acknowledged the immorality of benefit-ing from the labor of people while denying them political representation. If the masses were allowed to clearly see that the framers were repeating the sins of the monarchy, there was a real possibility that they might rise up against the framers just as they had previously risen up against colonial rule. The founders knew that white, wealthy men were greatly outnum-bered by women, slaves, and the poor, all of whose labor was essential to the survival of the nation. There is a glimpse of this in *Federalist* No. 10, in which Madison pondered the difficulty of keeping constitutional power from dissatisfied majorities while striving "to preserve the spirit and the form of popular government."[43] Madison understood that the masses had to be made to feel as though they were included and represented in their government even though they were not.

Whether the founders sincerely believed to some limited extent in the lofty, egalitarian sentiments of the Declaration of Independence and the Preamble to the Constitution, the texts themselves functioned as highly effective propaganda. As Max Lerner wrote in the *Yale Law Journal* in 1937, "one of the essential techniques of power-groups is to manipulate the most effective symbols in such a way that they become instruments of mass persuasion," and the Constitution served as one such symbol.[44]

Constitutional propaganda allowed the framers to launder their self-interest through a seemingly noble enterprise and to divert the attention of oppressed groups away from the material reality of their subordination and toward abstract concepts of equality. As described by the philosopher Louis Althusser, the point of the "beautiful lie" of ideological propaganda is to "assure the domination of one class over others, and the economic exploitation that maintains its pre-eminence." It does so by working "on the consciousness of the exploited to make them accept their condition as 'natural'" while simultaneously working "on the consciousness of members of the dominant class to allow them to exercise their exploitation and domination as 'natural.'"[45] In its profound distortion of reality, ideological propaganda impairs the ability of both the dominant and the exploited to perceive their own motivations clearly.

Women and slaves were encouraged to see themselves in "we the people," to identify with the white, wealthy, male heroes of the Revolution, and to accept any apparent injustices as ordained by a higher and natural order. The religious overtones of this constitutional propaganda, then and now, were no coincidence. Early American culture was steeped in Christian beliefs and practices, which long encouraged the acceptance of inferior roles of women and slaves as part of a divinely sanctioned, patriarchal order. As Lerner observes, "the very habits of mind begotten by an authoritarian Bible and a religion of submission to a higher power have been carried over to an authoritarian Constitution and a philosophy of submission to a 'higher law.'"[46]

The belief in a higher power that invests one's existence with a transcendent meaning is key to what psychiatrist Robert Jay Lifton calls "ideological totalism." According to Lifton, "where totalism exists, a religion, a political movement, or even a scientific organization becomes little more than an exclusive cult."[47] Lifton describes the three primary characteristics of cults as charismatic leadership, the use of "thought reform" or propaganda, and the "economic, sexual, and other exploitation of group members by the leader and the ruling coterie."[48]

The framers were influential and well-respected statesmen, including many heroes of the Revolutionary War, who were widely admired by the American public. The stirring, egalitarian rhetoric of the Declaration of Independence and the Constitution was simultaneously persuasive and coercive, extolling the virtue of consent of the governed even as such consent was never sought or obtained. The ruling system that they founded relied on the economic, sexual, and political exploitation of women, slaves, and the poor by a ruling elite. In other words, what was founded in Philadelphia in the summer of 1787 was not merely a constitution, but a cult.

CONTEMPORARY CONSTITUTIONAL FUNDAMENTALISM

The mystery remains, however, why the cult retains its power in the present day. That the founders managed to convince a small, war-weary, struggling nation that its new rulers were selfless and benevolent, when the options for resisting this narrative were extremely limited, is perhaps not surprising. The real miracle of Philadelphia is that worship of the framers and of the Constitution has persisted for over two hundred years. As Sanford Levinson and others have observed, the Constitution has been a key part of the American "civil religion" throughout history.[49] The culture of constitutional veneration is so powerful that anything less than fulsome praise for the Constitution and its framers is widely regarded as blasphemous even today. The fundamentalist attachment to the Constitution not only has not subsided over the centuries, but has, in many ways, become more widespread, more explicit, and more extreme in the present day.

Even in an era of intense political polarization,[50] Americans seem to be of one mind with regard to the Constitution. It is venerated by individuals across the political and cultural spectrum: Republicans and Democrats, politicians and pundits, billionaires and blue-collar workers. A 2010 national survey by the Center for the Constitution found that 88 percent of respondents think that the Constitution "still works," and 86 percent believe that the Constitution is important to their daily lives. The mission statements of the vastly influential National Rifle Association and the American Civil Liberties Union, two organizations frequently at opposite ends of the political spectrum, proclaim similar constitutional commitments: The NRA promises "to protect and defend the Constitution of the United States," while the ACLU promises "to defend and preserve the individual rights and liberties guaranteed to every person in this country by the Constitution and laws of the United States."

Reverence for the Constitution is also reflected in average Americans' increasing fondness for invoking the document in a wide range of conflicts and a wide range of contexts. Issues that might have once been understood as matters of personal preference, aesthetic taste, business practice, or cultural debate are now frequently imbued with constitutional meaning in the courts, in the political arena, and in popular culture. In our contemporary constitutional culture, everything from suspensions from social media platforms to restrictions on concealed-carry permits can be framed as attacks on constitutional rights; publishing sex tapes or preventing doctors from asking questions about gun ownership in the home can be characterized as exercises of constitutional freedom. These constitutional claims are advanced not only in courtrooms and congressional hearings but on college campuses, in town halls, and in social media.

This popular constitutionalism[51] not only influences public perceptions of constitutional rights but can also have dramatic effects on political and legal outcomes. As David Cole details in *Engines of Liberty: The Power of Citizen Activists to Make Constitutional Law*, "associations of committed citizens are central actors in the making of constitutional law—as important, if not more important, than the courts."[52]

Such widespread popular enthusiasm for the Constitution, especially across political and cultural lines, can be viewed as a reassuring sign of American patriotism: While Americans may be divided by political ideology, gender, race, or economic status, they are united in respect for the country's founding document. That the Constitution can be invoked by such diverse groups, in such diverse settings, and for such diverse interests can be viewed as a testament to its greatness.

On the other hand, the fact that ideologically opposed groups possessing incompatible views and values, as well as greatly varying degrees of constitutional literacy, all believe themselves to be equally devoted to the same text raises questions about the intelligibility of both the devotion and the text. While complex legal texts inevitably inspire contradictory interpretations, there is a limit to how many interpretations a text can sustain and still remain coherent. It is not possible that all interpretations of the Constitution can be correct, or even equally plausible. If the Constitution is meant to be more than a blank screen onto which various divided factions can project their personal or partisan desires, then the nature and quality of constitutional claims deserve careful scrutiny.

At a minimum, constitutional devotion should be grounded in knowledge of its text. On this point, the news is grim. In the words of historian Michael Kammen, the American relationship toward the Constitution is a "curious blend of reverence and ignorance."[53] Numerous surveys have demonstrated that the general public's knowledge of the Constitution is, for lack of a better word, dismal. A 2010 Center for the Constitution survey that found that although the majority of Americans admire the Constitution and believe it affects their daily lives, more than 70 percent of respondents had never read the Constitution in its entirety.[54]

A 2017 Annenberg Constitution Day Civics Survey found that only 26 percent of Americans could name all three branches of government and that 33 percent could not name a single one.[55] It also found that 37 percent of Americans could not name a single freedom guaranteed by the First Amendment and that more than half incorrectly believed that undocumented immigrants have no constitutional rights.[56] An Annenberg survey from 2015 found that more than a third of Americans believe that the Bill of Rights includes the right to own a home; 27 percent believe it guarantees "equal pay for equal work"; and 12 percent think it includes the right to own a pet.[57] A 1987 quiz administered by the Hearst Corporation found that eight in ten Americans believed that the Constitution includes the phrase "all men are created equal" and that nearly half thought that it also included the phrase "From each according to his ability, to each according to his need," an 1875 quote from Karl Marx.[58]

The level of public comprehension about the basic workings of the Supreme Court and the substance of its significant decisions is similarly low. According to a 2015 survey, nearly half of Americans do not know that when the Supreme Court rules 5–4 on a case, it means that the ruling is law and must be followed.[59] Public understanding of high-profile Supreme Court cases is muddy at best: For example, though the Supreme Court's 2012 Affordable Care Act ruling was highly publicized, the Pew Research Center found in 2012 that 45 percent of respondents either believed that the Supreme Court had rejected most provisions of the act or did not know what the Court did in that case.[60] Similarly, only 34 percent of respondents knew that the Court invalidated key provisions of the 1965 Voting Rights Act in 2013; 23 percent believed the Court had upheld the law, and 43 percent did not know what the Court had done.[61]

Low constitutional literacy in the general public might be less concerning if we could assume that the people responsible for interpreting, applying, and defending constitutional rights—the professional class of political leaders, legislators, judges, advocates, civil liberties groups, and the like—were more knowledgeable than the average citizen.

The 2016 presidential election did not provide much reason for optimism on this front. Both as a presidential candidate and as president, Donald Trump has demonstrated an extraordinary lack of even rudimentary knowledge about the Constitution. In 2015, he promised a police association that as president he would mandate the death penalty for anyone who killed a police officer, notwithstanding the fact that the Constitution does not afford the president the power to either make laws or impose punishments. Speaking at a rally in February 2016, Trump claimed that he would "open up those libel laws" so that he could sue the currently "totally protected" newspapers that criticized him, seemingly oblivious to the fact that a president does not have the power to change state tort law and that newspapers are already susceptible to libel actions. In June 2016, Donald Trump told a group of House Republicans he wanted "to protect Article I, Article II, Article XII" of the Constitution, despite the Constitution having only seven articles.[62] A few weeks after the election, President-Elect Trump asserted in a post on Twitter that "Nobody should be allowed to burn the American flag—if they do, there must be consequences—perhaps loss of citizenship or year in jail!" He was apparently unaware—or unconcerned—that the Supreme Court has ruled that the First Amendment protects flag burning and that the government cannot revoke citizenship except in rare circumstances.[63]

To be clear, the survey results about constitutional literacy and remarks by Trump outlined above are not illustrations of ideological differences in constitutional interpretation. They are examples of actual, factual ignorance concerning the text of the Constitution and significant Supreme Court holdings. They demonstrate that large numbers of Americans do not possess even basic knowledge about the Constitution and that the person elected in 2016 to "preserve, protect, and defend the Constitution of the United States" appears to know even less.

Thanks to the Constitution, the fate of constitutional rights and liberties does not lie solely in the hands of the president. The president is, first, surrounded by advisors and cabinet officials, and the legislative and judicial branches of the government are filled with individuals with constitutional expertise. Civil society includes plenty of lawyers, law professors, advocates, and civil liberties groups well versed in the text and application of the Constitution. But these experts frequently come to entirely different, and often predictably partisan, conclusions about what the Constitution means. The general public's constitutional illiteracy renders it unable to make informed assessments of constitutional claims and thus highly susceptible to partisan manipulation.

The picture is bad enough when it comes to objective awareness of what the Constitution says; it is far worse when it comes to what the Constitution *means*. Being able to name the rights afforded by the First Amendment is one thing; understanding the complexities of how they have been understood over time is another. Some people may know all the words of the first two amendments by heart but have no sense of the drastic difference between what those words mean today compared to what they meant at the time they were written. Even a cursory survey of constitutional history reveals that the most basic assumptions about our constitutional rights have changed over time.

There is almost no constitutional claim of substance that has not been intensely debated in oral arguments, judicial opinions, law review articles, and scholarly texts, and there is scarcely any assertion about the scope or meaning of constitutional rights that has not been challenged by lawyers, judges, and scholars. Beyond specific controversies, judges and scholars fiercely disagree even about *how to read* the words of the Constitution—whether with deference to the authors' intended meaning, to their commonly understood meaning at the time they were written, or to how they are understood today. Settled precedent on many constitutional questions exists, but understanding it requires close study of detailed and often convoluted Supreme Court opinions. Constitutional law, in short, is a remarkably complex subject.

"The Constitution" includes the Preamble, the articles, the Bill of Rights, and seventeen other amendments. Given the Supreme Court's role in interpreting and applying constitutional principles, real knowledge of the Constitution also requires a certain level of familiarity with more than two centuries of case law interpreting all of the above. If the majority of Americans have not even read the entire text of the Constitution, much less tackled Supreme Court jurisprudence, their claims to honor the Constitution cannot be taken at face value.

In a very public display of constitutional veneration on January 6, 2011, members of Congress took turns reading the Constitution from the floor of the House of Representatives. This was the first such reading in congressional history, and representatives of both parties expressed enthusiastic support for the exercise. Representative Gabrielle Giffords, a Democrat from Arizona, said that "[r]eflecting on the Constitution in a bipartisan way is a good way to start the year," while Representative Phil Gingrey, a Republican from Georgia, described the reading as "heartwarming."[64] According to Representative Bob Goodlatte (R-Va.), who organized the reading, "this is a very symbolic showing to the American people and reminder to the members of Congress that we are a government of laws not of men and that this Constitution is the foundation for all of our laws."[65] The recitation of the Constitution was widely reported in the mainstream media and hailed as a positive demonstration of bipartisan unity.

The reality was considerably more complicated. For one, the version of the Constitution that was read on the floor of Congress had been redacted. Notably, the organizers of the reading decided that passages in the Constitution referring to slavery, including the three-fifths clause and the fugitive slave clause, should be omitted.[66] The ostensible explanation was that these passages had been rendered obsolete by later amendments. Several members, including two African American representatives, Elijah Cummings (D-Md.) and Jesse L. Jackson Jr. (D-Ill.), objected to the omissions.[67] According to the statement by Representative Cummings,

> "To not read the full document, including all the text that was later amended, is to fail to acknowledge the struggle our nation has constantly fought, within and without, to 'keep' our Republic. . . . It is a failure to show Americans that while we seek a more perfect union, we do so from imperfect beginnings, through an imperfect history, with an imperfect government created by an imperfect document."[68]

Before the reading began, Rep. Jesse Jackson Jr. stated that the struggles of African Americans, women, and others "to create a more perfect document" shouldn't "be lost upon the reading of our sacred document."[69]

The question of race was spotlighted again as Rep. Frank Pallone Jr. (D-N.J.) recited the passage requiring the president to be a "natural-born citizen." A woman in the audience yelled out, "Except Obama, except Obama," before being escorted out.[70] Her outburst was a reference to the "birther" conspiracy theory that President Barack Obama was born in Kenya rather than the United States—a conspiracy that was most famously promulgated by President Obama's successor to the White House.

The congressional ritual came with a hefty price tag, costing the American taxpayers over a million dollars.[71] Its salutary effects were far from apparent, as the 112th Congress would prove to be one of the most polarized, most disliked, and least efficient in U.S. history.[72] Not only did it fail to pass almost any significant legislation to address pressing economic, environmental, or public safety issues, the legislative measures it did attempt were overwhelmingly targeted at undermining the welfare of the most vulnerable members of society. The Republican-led House voted to repeal the Affordable Care Act thirty-three times without a single proposal to replace it, a move that would disproportionately harm women, minorities, and the poor.[73] The House also voted fifty-five times for policies that would negatively impact women's reproductive rights and safety and allowed the Violence Against Women Act to expire.[74] It voted for a budget proposed by Paul Ryan that would have resulted in major cuts to Medicaid, Medicare, food assistance, and Pell grants for low-income students.[75]

What was touted as a unifying display of congressional commitment to the Constitution was actually a contentious, costly, partisan ritual. Its participants could not even agree which version of the Constitution they were dedicating themselves to, to say nothing of how such dedication should be expressed. Indeed, the reading's organizer, Representative Goodlatte, made clear from the beginning that he intended the reading to serve as a partisan rebuke, stating that "historic and symbolic reading" of the Constitution was necessary to demonstrate "that the *new majority* in the House"—that is, the Republican majority—"truly is dedicated to our Constitution and the principles for which it stands."[76] The obvious implication was that the Democratic Party, which had previously held the majority in the House, had not been sufficiently dedicated to the Constitution.

The 2011 reading of the Constitution from the House floor inadvertently exposed the hollowness of American constitutional veneration. Instead of carefully studying the Constitution in its entirety in order to discern the complex values that should guide our society, Americans tend to invoke the Constitution superficially and selectively to promote the values they already hold. As Louis Seidman observes, every side insists that its reading of the Constitution is the true and principled one, while the "other side's manipulation of text and history amounts to a cynical, politically motivated effort to distort the Constitution's meaning."[77] Goodlatte's comments illustrate Seidman's point that invoking the Constitution in disagreements is often a strategy designed to portray political opponents as traitors to the country itself.[78]

At the same time, there was something fitting about the spectacle of Congress reading the Constitution as a unified body. Though liberals and conservatives often differ in their interpretive approaches to the Constitution, and often allocate their constitutional resources to serve different goals, they are both capable of falling prey to constitutional fundamentalism.

The fundamentalist approach to the Constitution is easiest to discern among conservatives and originalists. As Morton Horwitz writes, "To the extent that Constitution worship is America's secular religion, and all religions have a tendency towards fundamentalism, originalism in constitutional discourse is the equivalent of religious fundamentalism."[79]

While there is considerable variation among the views of those who consider themselves originalists, they generally share three key beliefs: that the Constitution has a fixed meaning; that this meaning is readily apparent; and that interpretations of the Constitution that diverge from its fixed and apparent meaning are illegitimate.[80] In this sense, the originalist approach to the Constitution closely resembles the Christian fundamentalist approach to the Bible.[81] Originalists make claims about the Constitution that are similar to the claims Christian fundamentalists make about the Bible: "there is a single, 'true' method of constitutional interpretation"; all "[o]

ther approaches to interpretation are simply wrong."[82] Originalism "has
a natural affinity with some varieties of Protestantism," notes Jill Lepore,
further observing that while

> originalism is a serious and influential mode of constitutional interpreta-
> tion . . . it is also a political product manufactured by the New Right and
> marketed to the public by talk radio, cable television, and the Internet,
> where it enjoys a competitive advantage over other varieties of constitu-
> tional interpretation, partly because it's the easiest.[83]

Conservative hostility to gender and racial equality is obvious and
explicit in ways rarely associated with liberals. Conservative constitutional
fundamentalists are more likely than liberal constitutional fundamentalists
to be allied with Christian religious leaders and viewpoints, to defend a
social order that prioritizes white, heterosexual men, and to endorse the
use of violence to protect their worldview.

Conservative constitutional fundamentalism is not driven solely by
religious ideology, however. It is also driven by economic ideology, namely
libertarianism. Conservatives invoke the Constitution not only to defend
gun rights and to rail against progressive social values, but also to promote
tax breaks for the wealthy, corporate welfare, and other policies benefiting
the most economically privileged members of society.

In contrast to conservatives, liberals are more frequently associated
with the "living" approach to the Constitution, which espouses a dynamic
and evolving constitutional interpretation. The liberal constitutional tradition differs from the conservative in its avoidance of overt religiosity;
its concern for issues of social justice; and its comparative sensitivity to
the dangers of sexism, racism, and homophobia. When liberals invoke
the Constitution, they often do so on behalf of less powerful members of
society: women, racial and sexual minorities, and the poor. At its best,
liberal constitutional theory and practice confront the limitations of the
Constitution and endeavor to transform the fiction of constitutional equality into reality. Liberal constitutional commitments have been the drivers of the civil rights movement, the women's rights movement, and the
same-sex marriage movement. Liberal constitutionalism has served as

an important counterweight to the most radical excesses of conservative constitutionalism.

However, liberal constitutional theory and practice have also helped to reinforce the gender and racial hierarchy of American politics and culture, in part by failing to present direct challenges to it. While the Democratic Party has historically put forward more women and minority congressional candidates than the Republican Party, its efforts have never come close to proportionally reflecting the gender and racial demographics of the country. The Democratic Party has been associated with progressivism and social justice since 1912, but it nominated only white men as presidential candidates for nearly a hundred years. The first nonwhite man to receive the nomination was Barack Obama in 2008, and the first female candidate to do so was Hillary Clinton in 2016. The party failed to produce diverse political representation or shift power away from white male elites even during long periods of Democratic political domination, including the more than three decades when Democrats won the majority of presidential elections between 1930 and 1968 and the more than six decades when they retained almost exclusive control of the House of Representatives between 1930 and 1994.

As conservatives have used the Constitution to move the country farther to the right, liberals have not made corresponding moves to the left. Liberals have ceded much of the constitutional field to conservatives and united with conservatives in much of the rest. While most liberal constitutionalists object to the conservative Second Amendment fundamentalism, they have failed to challenge it in any meaningful way or even to effectively acknowledge its disruption of the constitutional ecosystem. Not only does the fundamentalist interpretation of the right to bear arms increasingly undermine the right to free speech—Second Amendment fundamentalists have attempted to prevent physicians from asking patients questions relating to firearms,[84] censor information regarding violent crimes,[85] and intimidate individuals on college campuses[86] and in public places[87] by openly carrying firearms—but it also jeopardizes the most basic rights to life and liberty, especially those of vulnerable groups.

On many vitally important issues, liberal constitutionalists continue to defend the rights of marginalized groups against conservative attack, fighting for women's reproductive rights, same-sex marriage, criminal justice reform, and protections for immigrants. In this, they are sharply distinguished from conservative constitutionalists. But over the last few decades, liberal and conservative constitutionalists have begun to sound increasingly similar with regard to the First Amendment right to free speech. The "civil libertarian" approach to constitutional rights has prevailed over the "civil rights" approach, privileging the defense of isolated individual rights against government interference over the demand for government to protect rights equally among all groups.

While liberal civil libertarianism may at one time have been distinguishable from conservative economic libertarianism—when liberals were still critical of the laissez-faire capitalist ideology that inevitably enriches the wealthy and privileged at the expense of the poor and marginalized—it no longer is. Civil libertarians, like economic libertarians, ignore the extent to which all markets—economic, cultural, or political—have been manipulated by powerful elites to ensure their continued domination. Like economic libertarianism, civil libertarianism allows the beneficiaries of the status quo to pretend that their achievements are the product of hard work and natural competition rather than historical privilege and systematic exploitation. Accordingly, civil libertarians attack the regulation of constitutional rights in much the same way that the economic libertarians denounce the regulation of economic rights.

It is no coincidence that civil and economic libertarianism have converged as the white male monopoly on power has begun to slip. It is not just conservative white men who experience anxiety and distress at the erosion of racial and gender hierarchies. Because the affinity for white male supremacy conflicts with the political and social identity of liberals, some liberals are even more deeply invested in constitutional fundamentalism than conservatives. Constitutional veneration provides a socially acceptable way to disguise the prioritization of white men's interests and to relieve liberal cognitive dissonance.

The fear of losing long-held power and privilege often runs deeper than political affiliation or even class, and members of a dominant group are prone to experiencing the loss of unearned privileges as oppression. The extent to which liberals have embraced white male grievance politics was made abundantly clear in the aftermath of the 2016 presidential election. As conservatives celebrated the election of Trump and the domination of the Republican Party, the left quickly became consumed by finger-pointing. In particular, a powerful liberal narrative emerged that asserted that the Democrats' loss could be attributed to an overreliance on "identity politics." Hillary Clinton's rival for the Democratic nomination, Senator Bernie Sanders, helped sow the seeds of this narrative. In a speech a few weeks after the election, Senator Sanders insinuated that Clinton lost because she relied on her gender to get elected:

> "It is not good enough for someone to say, 'I'm a woman! Vote for me!' No, that's not good enough. . . . [T]that is the fight we're going to have right now in the Democratic Party. The working class of this country is being decimated. That's why Donald Trump won."[88]

The myth that the majority of Trump supporters were working class or concerned about the plight of the working class has been repeatedly shown to be false. Trump, like most Republicans, was strongly supported by wealthy elites primarily interested in tax cuts, and racism and sexism played a large role in the decision to vote for Trump. What is more, when Sanders and others invoke the "working class" in contrast to women and minorities, they create the false impression that the working class is made up of white men and erase the existence of working-class women and minorities.

After endorsing a Democratic candidate in Nebraska who opposes abortion rights, Sanders made a point of saying that "you just can't exclude people who disagree with us on one issue." This sentiment was echoed by the chairman of the Democratic Congressional Campaign Committee in August 2017, who announced that the party would fund anti-choice candidates in order to build "a broad coalition" to win back Congress. According to Representative Ben Ray Luján, "There is not a litmus test for Democratic candidates."[89] For self-identified leftists to reduce a basic exercise of bodily autonomy—a constitutional right guaranteed by the Fourteenth Amendment—as "one issue" not worthy of constituting a "litmus test" is extraordinary. It is hard to imagine any serious politician on the left making a similar assertion about, say, the right to free speech, or the right to a fair trial, or indeed any right that does not have the distinction of primarily affecting women.

A little more than a week after the 2016 election, Mark Lilla, a Columbia University professor, wrote an op-ed for the *New York Times* titled "The End of Identity Liberalism." A self-proclaimed liberal, Lilla asserted that an outsized emphasis on diversity has been "disastrous" for liberal democratic politics. Lilla bemoaned "the identity politics of today" that have been projected "back onto the past, creating a distorted picture of the major forces and individuals that shaped our country." Lilla's fetish for the founding era was made even more explicit when he conceded, in a parenthetical, that the "achievements of women's rights movements . . . were real and important," but hastened to add, "you cannot understand them if you do not first understand the founding fathers' achievement in establishing a system of government based on the guarantee of rights."[90]

In a piece bluntly titled "Making White Supremacy Respectable. Again," law professor Katherine Franke, Lilla's colleague at Columbia, delivered a scathing takedown of Lilla's idealization of the founding fathers:

> [T]he founding fathers denied women the right to vote, the right to equal protection of the laws, indeed, even full rights of citizenship at the founding of this great nation. It was the women's rights movement that forced a correction in the liberal structure created by the founding fathers. Even worse, the founding fathers both countenanced and participated in the enslavement of black people, counting them as 3/5ths of a person in the Constitution, and building a modern liberal economy on the barbaric commodification of human life. But as Lilla tells it, this history, indeed the present facts of inequality, distort and degrade the noble purpose of American liberalism.[91]

Unfortunately, contemporary liberalism is increasingly dominated by voices like Lilla and Sanders, promoting a faux-universalism that somehow always manages to erase gender and racial inequality and center on the experiences of white men. In this respect, liberalism is becoming increasingly fundamentalist, and increasingly indistinguishable from conservatism.

THE PERPETUATION OF THE CONSTITUTIONAL CULT

It is precisely through empty rituals like the congressional recital of the Constitution that the constitutional cult is kept alive. Republicans and Democrats participate in performative constitutionalism to reinforce the founding fraud—that the drafters of the Constitution were committed to equality and democracy and that "we the people" included us all. This illusion assures both those at the top of the hierarchy as well as those at the bottom that their respective positions are natural and just. If we have always been equal, then we are solely responsible for our successes and our failures.

As the next chapters will describe in more detail, the hallmarks of constitutional fundamentalism include an outsized focus on a single right in isolation that is believed to be essential and superior to all other rights (a "superright"[92]); a simplistic and selective interpretation of that right; the pretense of principled absolutism in the application of that right; the conviction that this right is under constant attack; and the vilification of those who are perceived as a threat to this right. All of these strategies serve to justify the unequal allocation of constitutional benefits and burdens on women and minorities.

Because constitutional fundamentalists, like fundamentalists generally, are irrational, they appeal to intuition and emotion instead of reason and logic. They rely heavily on what Lifton termed "thought-terminating clichés." As Lifton explains, "simplified, cliché-ridden language can exert enormous psychological force reducing every issue in a complicated life to a single set of slogans that are said to embody the truth as a totality."[93] This language helps fundamentalists resolve the cognitive dissonance they experience when they inevitably "sense a conflict between what they are experiencing and what dogma says they should experience. The internalized message of the totalistic environment is that one must negate that personal experience on behalf of the truth of the dogma."[94] Fundamentalists also encourage the vilification of nonbelievers: "Those who have not seen the light and embraced the truth are wedded to evil, tainted, and therefore in some sense, usually metaphorical, lack the right to exist."[95]

Conservative and liberal constitutional fundamentalists use similar constitutional rhetoric, employ similar political and legal strategies, and, whether intentionally or not, produce similar results. These convergences underscore the point that though constitutional fundamentalists on the right and left may focus on different aspects of the Constitution and interpret them very differently, their self-proclaimed dedication to the text serves as a powerful form of kinship. Constitutional fundamentalism, whether of the right or left, sanctifies the men and the moment of the founding era: that is, an era in which the interests of women and racial minorities were subordinated to those of white, economically powerful men. This shared allegiance to the Constitution and its authors is allegiance to its original sins. The effect, even if not the explicit goal, of constitutional fundamentalism of any political stripe is to ensure that the America of the future looks much like the America of the past.

THE OTHER PHILADELPHIA CONVENTION

In May 1838, activists advocating the abolition of slavery and the recognition of women's rights opened Pennsylvania Hall, just a few blocks away from the famed Independence Hall. The building was intended to serve as a forum for free discussion of the evils of racial and sexual subordination. The first event scheduled to take place at the hall was the annual Anti-Slavery Convention of American Women. Unlike the Constitutional Convention, this convention's invitees included a diverse cross-section of American society: men and women, whites and blacks.

In the weeks preceding the convention, notices were posted around Philadelphia encouraging those "who cared about their jobs and the Constitution to attend and protest this convention of 'amalgamators.'"[96] As the convention opened, several thousand protesters descended upon Philadelphia Hall, outraged by the sight of black men and white women mingling. As the female speakers attempted to open the meeting, protesters flooded into the hall, hissing, shouting, smashing windows, and threatening the speakers with bricks and rocks. The organizers pleaded with the mayor to intervene and instill order; the mayor refused on the grounds that they "had brought this chaos on themselves." Ultimately, the mobs took over the hall, "opened the gas jets, and set the auditorium on fire.[97] At least one newspaper account of the event defended the actions of the mob, condemning the "abominations" of the activists, which included "Negro fellows" accompanying "white 'ladies'" in the street and sitting together with them on the same benches. The newspaper account declared,

> "Such practices, outraging the moral sense of the community, and if continued, tending inevitably to throw society into confusion, and to engender immorality and vice, it could not be expected, that any people, having respect for themselves or affection for their children, would permit to endure."[98]

Fifty years after the "miracle at Philadelphia," women and black men attempted to take the Constitution at its word. They gathered in a peaceful assembly to be recognized as part of "we the people" upon whom the Constitution's legitimacy depended. For this, they were violently attacked by a mob claiming to defend the Constitution. Government officials not only failed to intervene, but essentially sided with the mob, blaming the participants for bringing the violence upon themselves.

While the first Philadelphia convention's "assembly of demigods" is lovingly re-created in American memory through schoolbooks, artistic renderings, and patriotic celebrations, the racist, sexist, violent mob attacking the second convention is barely known. This is how fundamentalism thrives: through selective remembering and selective forgetting. Successive generations of Americans have rationalized, downplayed, or ignored the founders' original sins, with the Orwellian result that words like "democracy," "liberty," and "equality" are used to describe a legacy of exclusion and exploitation of women and nonwhite men. Refusing to confront the reality of white male supremacy perpetuates the cult of the Constitution, leaving America at the mercy of extremists who will not hesitate to use violence to reassert their domination.

CHAPTER 2

THE CULT
OF THE GUN

AMENDMENT II

A well regulated Militia, being necessary to the security of a free State, the
right of the people to keep and bear Arms, shall not be infringed.

"The only thing that stops a bad guy with a gun is a good guy with a gun."
                                    –Wayne LaPierre, National Rifle Association

On December 15, 2012, the day after twenty children and six adults were shot
to death at Sandy Hook Elementary School, the *New York Review of Books*
published a piece by journalist Garry Wills titled "Our Moloch."[1] Moloch,
Wills wrote, was an Old Testament god who demanded sacrifices of living
children. Wills quoted John Milton's description of Moloch in *Paradise Lost*:

> . . . horrid king, besmear'd with blood
> Of human sacrifice, and parents' tears,
> Though for the noise of Drums and Timbrels loud
> Their children's cries unheard, that pass'd through fire
> To his grim idol.[2]

These images, wrote Wills, "give the real meaning of what happened at
Sandy Hook Elementary School." The killings must be understood not

only as the murderous actions of a single individual, but "the sacrifice we as a culture made, and continually make, to our demonic god" of the gun.[3]

In the six years since Sandy Hook, there have been more than 200 school shootings, leaving more than 400 dead.[4] Following the Parkland, Florida, school shooting that killed seventeen people and the Santa Fe, Texas, school shooting that killed ten, newspaper headlines noted that more people had been killed in 2018 at schools than had been killed in military service so far that year.[5] As Wills wrote in 2012,

> Adoration of Moloch permeates the country, imposing a hushed silence as he works his will. One cannot question his rites, even as the blood is gushing through the idol's teeth. . . . "It is not the time" to question Moloch. No time is right for showing disrespect for Moloch.[6]

Of course, the Americans who believe in an absolute right to bear arms no matter how many children are murdered in schools, movie theaters, churches, and homes do not literally worship the god Moloch. Instead, they worship the Constitution, or at least one part of it. In the wake of the 2014 Isla Vista rampage that left six college students dead, failed Tea Party candidate and conservative activist Joe Wurzelbacher (known as "Joe the Plumber") wrote an open letter to the victims' parents that stated "your dead kids don't trump my constitutional rights."[7] Following a mass shooting at Umpqua Community College in Oregon in 2015, former Republican presidential candidate Ben Carson took to Facebook to write, "I never saw a body with bullet holes that was more devastating than taking the right to arm ourselves away."[8] After fifty-eight Americans were gunned down in Las Vegas in October 2017, former Fox News host Bill O'Reilly referred to the massacre as "the price of freedom."[9]

GUNS, GOD, AND THE CONSTITUTION

In January 2016, a group calling itself the Citizens for Constitutional Freedom began what would become a month-long armed standoff at the Malheur National Wildlife Refuge in Harney County, Oregon. The group, led by a man named Ammon Bundy, claimed to be protesting what they considered to be the unconstitutional control of local lands by the federal government. During their occupation of the federal facility, members of the group stockpiled firearms and explosives; commandeered government vehicles; broke into safes to steal money, cameras, and computers; and damaged tribal artifacts. The occupation is estimated to have cost taxpayers at least $9 million dollars.[10]

Ammon Bundy is the son of rancher Cliven Bundy, who famously led his own armed standoff with the federal government over grazing rights in Nevada in 2014. When the Bureau of Land Management attempted to seize the cattle that the elder Bundy had been illegally grazing on federal land, the elder Bundy and his supporters met them with assault weapons and sniper rifles. Cliven Bundy asserted that the Constitution gave him the right to engage in violence against the government: "The only peaceful resolution to all this is for [the federal authorities] to obey the Constitution. . . . Read it, understand it, abide by it. There doesn't have to be violence. None of that has to happen if they would just abide by the Constitution."[11]

The Bundys are Mormon and believe they are fulfilling the prophet Joseph Smith's 1840 prophecy, which speaks of "the Staff upon which the Nation shall lean" that will "bear the Constitution away from the very verge of destruction."[12] Cliven Bundy told the *Los Angeles Times* in 2016 that he keeps a copy of the Constitution in his pocket at all times: "It's something I've always shared with everybody and I carry it with me all the time. . . . That's where I get most of my information from. What we're trying to do is teach the true principles of the proper form of government."[13] In an interview with the *New York Times*, Cliven Bundy described his understanding of the Constitution's origins: "'Don't we believe that Jesus Christ is basically the author of the Bible? Well, if the Constitution is inspired, who is the author? Wouldn't that author be Jesus Christ again?'"[14]

The Bundys are not alone in the belief that the Constitution was inspired or written by God, a belief that writer Chris Zinda has dubbed "theo-constitutionalism."[15] One of the most influential theo-constitutionalists is the Mormon author W. Cleon Skousen, the founder of a far-right foundation called the National Center for Constitution Studies (NCCS), formerly known as the Freeman Institute. The NCCS publishes a best-selling pocket-sized version of the Constitution annotated by Skousen[16]—the version that

Cliven Bundy keeps in his pocket—as well as Skousen's history book *The Making of America*. When that book was chosen by California's Bicentennial Commission in 1987 to raise funds for the state's bicentennial celebration, it came to light that it "characterized African-American children as 'pickaninnies' and described American slave owners as the 'worst victims' of the slavery system."[17] Skousen was also a staunch defender of the far-right John Birch Society and a conspiracy theorist; he believed, for instance, that Dwight D. Eisenhower was a Soviet agent and that a cabal of international bankers was conspiring to establish a "one-world government."[18]

Skousen died in 2006, but his legacy is very much alive. Skousen's wide contemporary following includes not only the Bundy family but many prominent conservatives. These include several high-profile Republican politicians, including Utah Senator Orrin Hatch, former governor of Massachusetts and presidential candidate Mitt Romney, and former presidential candidate and Secretary of Housing and Human Development Ben Carson. Former Fox television personality Glenn Beck was largely responsible for bringing Skousen's work out of obscurity in 2006, at which point it became influential in the Tea Party movement.[19]

At a 2010 Tea Party rally, former vice presidential candidate Sarah Palin engaged in some light theo-constitutionalism when she declared that "[w]e'll keep clinging to our Constitution, our guns, and our religion and you can keep the change."[20] The remark was a delayed riposte to a 2008 comment by then-presidential candidate Barack Obama about white working-class voters who "cling to guns or religion."[21] Palin's addition of "the Constitution" was a slyly dignifying move; it suggested that fidelity to guns and God was inextricably connected to fidelity to the Constitution itself. The Tea Party movement helped bring the guns-and-God constitutionalism of the far-right fringes into the conservative mainstream.

Thus, it was not particularly surprising that the 2014 Nevada standoff with the federal government earned Cliven Bundy effusive praise from Republican leaders and pundits. Fox News personality Sean Hannity invited Cliven Bundy onto his show twice for sympathetic interviews.[22] Senator Dean Heller of Nevada referred to Bundy and his supporters as "patriots." In an interview with Fox News, Senator Rand Paul (R-Ky.) expressed the view that the Nevada standoff raised "a legitimate constitutional question."

Senator Ted Cruz (R-Tex.) agreed with the Bundys that "we have seen our constitutional liberties eroded under the Obama administration."[23]

Conservative leaders' open embrace of the Bundy family did not last long, however. On April 23, 2014, the *New York Times* reported that Cliven Bundy had engaged in a racist diatribe during one of the daily news conferences he held for his supporters. Describing an experience he had while driving by a housing project in Law Vegas, Bundy said,

> "I want to tell you one more thing I know about the Negro. . . . In front of that government house the door was usually open and the older people and the kids . . . they didn't have nothing to do. . . . And because they were basically on government subsidy, so now what do they do? They abort their young children, they put their young men in jail, because they never learned how to pick cotton. And I've often wondered, are they better off as slaves, picking cotton and having a family life and doing things, or are they better off under government subsidy? They didn't get no more freedom. They got less freedom."[24]

In a maneuver that would be repeated following the "Unite the Right" rally in Charlottesville in 2017, the Republican leaders and pundits who had previously expressed support for Cliven Bundy and his views scrambled to distance themselves from his overtly racist remarks. Senator Heller issued a statement through his spokesman that he "completely disagree[d] with Mr. Bundy's appalling and racist statements, and condemns them in the most strenuous way." A spokesperson for Senator Cruz stated that the senator found the comments "completely unacceptable." Senator Paul characterized Bundy's remarks as "offensive" and proclaimed that he "wholeheartedly disagree[d] with him." Even rightwing firebrand Sean Hannity condemned Bundy's comments as "beyond repugnant. . . . beyond despicable . . . . beyond ignorant to me."[25]

The modern Republican political establishment has been careful, at least since the "Southern strategy" era, to avoid overt expressions of white male supremacy and to avoid the explicit endorsement of violence to further it. As Jason Sattler observed in the wake of Charlottesville, most Republican leaders understand that "they must reject public displays of bigotry" in order to maintain their political respectability.[26] So-called dog-whistle politics relies on coded language and euphemisms rather than blatant expressions of racism and misogyny.[27] Mainstream conservatives prefer genteel euphemisms like "protecting life," "states' rights," "the free market," and "law and order" to crude sexism and racial epithets. The discomfort many establishment conservatives experience with Donald Trump has less to do with substantive disagreement than with Trump's seeming obliviousness to this need to disguise conservative attachment to white male supremacy. "[T]hey're aware of the dirty deal their party has made," writes Sattler, which makes them "eager for the president to shut his mouth before he blows the whole scam up."[28]

This "dirty deal" includes the longstanding and intimate relationship between conservatives and violent extremists. Conservatism has stoked the narrative of white male persecution that has fueled domestic terror-ism for decades, at least since the founding of the first Ku Klux Klan around the end of the Civil War. The KKK's constitution promises "to protect and defend the Constitution of the United States of America";[29] its Ku Klux Kreed "avows the distinction between the races of mankind as decreed by the Creator" and swears "to be true to the maintenance of White Supremacy and strenuously oppose any compromise thereof."[30] The KKK's explicit interweaving of white male supremacy, religion, and the Constitution has prompted mainstream Republicans to deny the group's close historical ties to rightwing politics, sometimes going so far as to claim that the KKK began as a leftist organization.[31]

The civil rights movement in the United States served as a catalyst for the white supremacist movement. The National States Rights Party (NSRP) was founded in 1958 to counter the successes of the civil rights movement and to advance the goals of white supremacy and anti-Semitism. For nearly three decades, its members organized demonstrations, incited riots, and bombed houses of worship. One of the group's most notorious members, Charles "Connie" Lynch, was infamous for stirring up crowds with diatribes about race, religion, and the Constitution. Racial violence frequently followed Lynch's speeches. In one instance, Lynch told a crowd in Baltimore, "I represent God, the white race and constitutional govern-ment, and everyone who doesn't like that can go straight to hell. I'm not inciting you to riot—I'm inciting you to victory!" After this speech, "stirred-up white youths headed for the city's slums, attacking blacks with fists and bottles." Lynch later told a crowd in Alabama that "[i]f it takes killing to get the Negroes out of the white man's streets and to protect our constitutional rights, I say, 'Yes, kill them!'" A group of men departed from that rally and shot a black man on the highway.[32]

One strain of rightwing extremism is known as the "patriot" or militia movement. The Bundy family are members of this movement. The patriot movement took off in the 1970s as part of the backlash to the modest social progress of the post–World War II period and the social unrest of the 1960s. Like the KKK, these groups' defense of the Constitution is inextricably tied to the violent assertion of white male supremacy. The movement offered a way for white men to express their fear and anxiety about social change under the guise of defending the Constitution.

The founder of the influential paramilitary group Posse Comitatus, William Potter Gale, told followers in a 1982 radio broadcast that they were "either going to get back to the Constitution of the United States in your government or officials are going to hang by the neck until they're dead,"[33] Gale made clear that "getting back to the Constitution" required patriotic militants to "mobilize against blacks, Jews, and other . . . enemies of the Republic."[34]

Desegregation and abortion rights in particular generated fears that women and nonwhite men might someday be able to compete with white men in education and employment, which would in turn threatened to destabilize centuries of white male domination of politics, economics, and culture. Those who felt that white men's domination was the result of natural order, superior merit, or both viewed the advancement of women and nonwhite men's equality as an assault on their rightful position at the top of the American hierarchy.

Conservative ideologues stoked this resentment by encouraging white men to attribute their misfortunes to the advancement of women and nonwhite men. If white men struggled to get jobs or to gain admission to universities, they were being oppressed by "affirmative action" handing opportunities to unqualified minorities and women. If white men felt they could no longer openly tell racist jokes or engage in sexualized commentary about women, they were being silenced by a culture of "political correctness." Even as white men retained the bulk of their unearned political, social, economic, and cultural privileges, conservative leaders, pundits, and media figures insisted that their "traditional" values and freedoms were under constant assault.

The rightwing militia movement used the rhetoric of patriotism and constitutional rights to advance a violent, paranoid, and bigoted worldview. Its leaders focused on the Second Amendment in particular, literally weaponizing the Constitution around white male grievance.

SECOND AMENDMENT FUNDAMENTALISM

Rightwing extremists' call for violent uprisings against the government was embraced by groups devoted to "Second Amendment absolutism," who "interpreted the Constitution as conferring an unfettered right to gun ownership."[35] In the 1980s, these groups found their values powerfully vindicated by the National Rifle Association (NRA). By 1992, the NRA had transformed itself from a sportsmen's organization supporting modest firearms regulation into a powerful special interest lobby denouncing all forms of gun control as government tyranny. In 1995, NRA CEO and Executive Vice President Wayne LaPierre wrote in a fundraising letter that the federal Assault Weapons Ban "gives jackbooted government thugs more power to take away our constitutional rights, break in our doors, seize our guns, destroy our property, and even injure or kill us."[36] In speeches, letters, interviews, and videos, the NRA encouraged its base of conservative white men to perceive danger around every corner—from liberals, from minorities, from feminists, from socialists, and most of all from the government. The NRA urged its followers to fight back against these devious, godless, totalitarian forces in one specific way: by exercising their God-given, constitutional right to bear arms.

The NRA's propaganda relies on a potent mix of white male grievance, antigovernment sentiment, paranoia, and constitutional fundamentalism. It has courted and encouraged rightwing militant groups, who have in turn eagerly embraced the NRA's ideology. As one NRA member and budding militant warned in 1993,

"Once you take away the guns, you can do anything to the people. You give them an inch and they take a mile. I believe we are slowly turning into a socialist government. The government is continually growing bigger and more powerful and the people need to prepare to defend themselves against government control."[37]

Two years later, that NRA member would carry out what would be the deadliest terror attack on American soil until September 11, 2001. In a letter to a friend in 1994, Timothy McVeigh warned that those "who betray or subvert the Constitution . . . are domestic enemies and should and will be punished accordingly."[38] McVeigh was a great admirer of *The Turner Diaries*, a white nationalist novel often described as the Bible of the radical right. *The Turner Diaries* are the fictional diary entries of Earl Turner, who helps lead the "Great Revolution" to overthrow the race-mixing, pro-feminist, liberal government led by Jewish politicians and enforced by African Americans.

Less than a year later, McVeigh parked a truck filled with 5,000 pounds of explosives in front of the Alfred P. Murrah Federal Building in Oklahoma City and lit the fuse. The blast killed a total of 168 people, including 19 children.

When he was apprehended following the bombing, McVeigh was wearing a T-shirt emblazoned with a Thomas Jefferson quote popular with far-right extremists: "The tree of liberty must be refreshed from time to time with the blood of patriots and tyrants." The quote is one of many taken out of context to suggest that the founders approved of antigovernment violence. It was frequently invoked by Tea Partiers during the Obama administration and remained popular among conservative leaders even after the Tea Party label faded. The Republican governor of Kentucky, Matt Bevin, alluded to the quote in a speech at the Values Voters Summit two months before the 2016 election as he contemplated the possibility of a victory by Hillary Clinton:

"Somebody asked me yesterday . . . 'Do you think it's possible, if Hillary Clinton were to win the election, do you think it's possible that we'll be able to survive, that we'd ever be able to recover as a nation?' . . . I do

think it would be possible, but at what price? At what price? The roots of
the tree of liberty are watered by what? The blood of who? The tyrants,
to be sure, but who else? The patriots.

Whose blood will be shed? It may be that of those in this room. It might
be that of our children and grandchildren."[39]

The remarks were understood by many to be calling for armed insurrection in the event of a Republican loss in the presidential election, though
Bevin later denied this. Bevin's comments drew comparisons with sentiments expressed in 2010 by Tea Party candidate Sharron Angle, who
was then facing Democrat Harry Reid in the Arizona senatorial election.
In an interview with a conservative radio show host, Angle said, "if this
Congress keeps going the way it is, people are really looking toward those
Second Amendment remedies and saying my goodness what can we do
to turn this country around? I'll tell you the first thing we need to do is
take Harry Reid out."[40]

In August 2016, Donald Trump made a similar statement regarding his
political opponent, Hillary Clinton. After falsely claiming at a campaign
rally in Wilmington, North Carolina, that Clinton wanted to "abolish
the Second Amendment," Trump warned the audience that there would
be "nothing you can do, folks," before suggesting '[a]lthough the Second
Amendment people, maybe there is, I don't know."[41]

The conservative obsession with the Second Amendment displays all
the hallmarks of constitutional fundamentalism: an outsized focus on an
absolute "superright" believed to be both essential and superior to all
other rights; a simplistic, selective, and self-righteous interpretation of
that right; the conviction that this right is under constant attack; and the
encouragement of active, even violent resistance to perceived threats to it.
Second Amendment fundamentalists frequently engage in "rights talk," to
use Mary Ann Glendon's term, which "promotes unrealistic expectations
and ignores both social costs and the rights of others."[42]

Joseph Blocher writes that gun rights talk "is not just about rights, has
even less to do with the Constitution, and may not even be about guns.
It is, at root, a debate about culture and values."[43] This is a culture that

relies on a fundamentally inverted view of reality: Even as white men as a group enjoy more unearned political, social, and economic privileges than any other group in America, they see themselves as persecuted victims whose efforts to protect themselves and their families are under constant attack. The sources of persecution are everywhere—the government, criminals, terrorists, feminists, affirmative action, diversity initiatives, the LGBT "agenda," political correctness—fueling the conservative desire for righteous, retaliatory violence. To those who fear physical and symbolic disempowerment, of being literally un-manned in a changing world, guns promise a reassuring, talismanic power.

The Role of the NRA

The gun lobby has been so successful in associating the Second Amendment with an individual right to use guns for self-defense that it is difficult to remember that this interpretation breaks with more than two hundred years of legal, political, and social consensus about what the Second Amendment protects. The Second Amendment consists of a single, grammatically tortured sentence that mentions neither guns nor self-defense: "A well regulated Militia, being necessary to the security of a free State, the right of the people to keep and bear Arms, shall not be infringed." Tellingly, the version of the amendment emblazoned on the façade of NRA headquarters in Fairfax, Virginia, omits the entire first half of the text, so that only "the right of the people to keep and bear arms, shall not be infringed" remains. As Michael Waldman details in *The Second Amendment: A Biography*, the NRA is almost singlehandedly responsible for the now-dominant view that the Second Amendment protects a personal right to use guns for self-defense rather than the right of militia to guard against government tyranny.[44] The NRA, which bills itself as "America's longest-standing civil rights organization," has played a key role in promoting Second Amendment fundamentalism.

Wayne LaPierre has been the executive vice president of the NRA since 1993. In 2003, he published a book titled *Guns, Freedom, and Terrorism*. The book is a textbook example of constitutional fundamentalism. It is replete with pious invocations of the founders; assertions of the uniquely important nature of the Second Amendment; fearmongering, vilification, and patriotic platitudes, all intertwined with a narrative of persecution.

LaPierre uses the September 11, 2001, terrorist attacks as the moral grounding of his book. "The forces of evil" behind the 9/11 attacks were "waging war on the very 'idea' of America," LaPierre writes, but they will be defeated by "the overwhelming force of what makes America, America—the U.S. Constitution and its Bill of Rights." The founders "sought, fought for, and cherished freedom. . . . [T]his is precisely why they insisted on leaving us freedom's legacy, our Bill of Rights."[45] LaPierre not only fails to note that the founders only sought freedom for people who looked like them, but also either does not know or does not care that the founders only reluctantly included the Bill of Rights as a concession to the states that were fearful that the Constitution gave the federal government too much power.

While he concedes that all of the Amendments in the Bill of Rights are important, LaPierre insists that "some rights are more important to the whole than others." The Second Amendment is the "First Freedom," "the one right that all the others lean on the most. . . . [N]othing precious can be held for long unless we have the ability to defend against its being taken from us—and the Second Amendment guarantees each one of us that ability." In one of the book's most purple passages, LaPierre writes, "The Constitution provides a doorway for freedom of speech and of religion and of assembly. And that doorway to freedom is framed by the muskets that first defended liberty at a place called Concord Bridge."[46]

As Waldman has demonstrated, there is no evidence to support the claim that the founders considered the right to bear arms to be of particular importance. When Madison outlined the twenty proposed amendments to the Constitution (it would only later be narrowed to ten) to the House of Representatives in 1789, this right almost completely slipped his mind until the end: "O. I had forgot, the right of the people to bear Arms." Those genuinely interested in the founding fathers' constitutional preferences might be surprised to learn that the one amendment Madison believed to be "the most valuable" was one that forbade Congress and the states from violating "the equal rights of conscience, or the freedom of the press, or the trial by jury in criminal cases."[47]

LaPierre confidently asserts that "there can be no denying that there is no such thing as a free nation where police and military are allowed the force of arms but individual citizens are not."[48] But the founders themselves likely would have denied this. As Adam Winkler has explained, the founders believed that it was permissible to deprive citizens of their guns if "pressing public necessity demanded it," "even if those citizens were left without guns to defend themselves from a criminal attack"—making them, to use the gun lobby's parlance, the original "gun grabbers."[49] What is more, of the twelve congressmen who debated the amendment regarding the right to bear arms on the House floor in 1789, "[n]one mentioned a private right to bear arms for self-defense, hunting, or for any purpose other than joining the militia."[50]

The NRA itself did not advance a fundamentalist interpretation of the Second Amendment until fairly recently. Founded in 1871 by Union officers who had been disturbed by their soldiers' poor marksmanship during the Civil War, the NRA was for years mostly focused on firearms training, safety education, recreational shooting, and hunting. The NRA supported the National Firearms Act of 1934 (NFA), which placed a tax on machine guns and sawed-off shotguns and required the sale of such firearms to be recorded in a national registry. During congressional hearings on the NFA, the NRA president at the time, Karl Frederick, stated, "I have never believed in the general practice of carrying weapons. . . . I do not believe in the general promiscuous toting of guns."

The NRA also supported the Gun Control Act of 1968 (GCA), which was passed in the wake of several high-profile assassinations (including of President John F. Kennedy, civil rights leader Martin Luther King Jr., and Senator Robert Kennedy) and growing concern over armed black nationalist movements. The executive vice president of the NRA at the time, Franklin Orth, said in testimony before Congress that "We do not think that any sane American . . . can object to placing into this bill the instrument which killed the president of the United States."[51] While the NRA objected to some of the provisions originally proposed in the GCA, including the creation of a national firearms registry, it endorsed the more modest version of the GCA that was ultimately adopted by Congress.

The NRA and other gun rights groups began claiming that the Second Amendment protects the personal use of guns for self-defense in the 1960s. The first law review article to argue for this interpretation of the Second Amendment was published in 1960, inspired by an article in the NRA publication *American Rifleman*. A cascade of scholarship promoting the individual right interpretation of the Second Amendment, much of it funded by the NRA, appeared in the following decades. The NRA sponsored essay contests, book review grants, and academic endowments to entice legal scholars to advance the individual right view of the Second Amendment.

Around the same time, some members of the NRA were becoming dissatisfied with what they viewed as the leadership's complicity in undermining gun rights. In the 1970s, these members began pushing for the organization to promote a hardline stance on gun rights and to become more involved in politics. The NRA established its lobbying arm, the Institute for Legislative Action (NRA-ILA), in 1975. During the 1977 NRA annual convention, ILA director Harlon Carter seized control of the organization's leadership. The "Revolt at Cincinnati," as it became known, made Second Amendment rights the primary focus of the organization, and Harlon Carter became the NRA's new executive vice president. The revolt was symptomatic of a broader conservative backlash against government regulation during the 1970s.[52] Within the gun rights community, this hostility to government often blossomed into outlandish conspiracy theories. To take just one example, Carter's influential lieutenant, Neal Knox, believed that the assassinations of John F. Kennedy, Bobby Kennedy, and Martin Luther King were "part of a plot to advance gun control."[53]

Under Carter's leadership, the NRA's membership tripled in size, and its annual budget increased to more than $60 million. But the organization's public image began to decline in the late 1980s and early 1990s. The NRA's opposition to what many considered to be sensible and modest firearms regulations, such as a ban on armor-piercing bullets, struck many of its own members as too extreme. The NRA's influence weakened enough for Congress to pass the Brady Handgun Violence Prevention Act in 1993 (imposing background checks and a five-day waiting period for handgun purchases) and the Violence Crime Control and Law Enforcement Act in 1994 (prohibiting the possession of several types of assault weapons). LaPierre's continued use of aggressive antigovernment rhetoric after the 1995 Oklahoma City bombing drew criticism from many quarters, including from the former president, George H. W. Bush, who resigned his NRA membership in protest. By 1996, writes Reva Siegel, "the organization's membership had declined by twelve percent, and its contributions to political action committees had dropped by more than a fifth."[54]

The organization soon regained its influence, however. The man who deserves the most credit for rehabilitating the NRA's image and for providing its firearms fetish with a "constitutional pedigree" was the actor Charlton Heston,[55] perhaps best known for his portrayal of Moses in the film *The Ten Commandments*. Heston served as the president of the NRA from 1998 until 2003. At the 2000 annual NRA convention, Heston famously raised a rifle over his head and addressed what he characterized as presidential candidate Al Gore's desire to restrict Second Amendment rights: "I want to say those fighting words for everyone within the sound of my voice to hear and to heed, and especially for you, *Mr. Gore*: 'From my cold, dead hands!'" Heston would conclude with the words "From my cold, dead hands" every year that he addressed the NRA convention until his retirement.

Siegel explains that while Heston gave the NRA "a new, more family-friendly public image," he also succeeded in persuading gun owners to view themselves as persecuted victims of the "cultural war."[56] According to Heston, the truly oppressed class in America was white, Christian, straight, working-class men:

> "Heaven help the God-fearing, law-abiding, Caucasian, middle class, Protestant, or—even worse—Evangelical Christian, Midwest, or Southern, or—even worse—rural, apparently straight, or—even worse—admittedly heterosexual, gun-owning or—even worse—NRA-card-carrying, average working stiff, or—even worse—male working stiff, because not only don't you count, you're a downright obstacle to social progress."

Heston tapped directly into the deep vein of white male resentment and gave it a seductive constitutional gloss:

> "The Constitution was handed down to guide us by a bunch of those wise old dead white guys who invented this country. . . . [W]hy should I be ashamed of white guys? Why is 'Hispanic pride' or 'black pride' a good thing, while 'white pride' conjures up shaved heads and white hoods?"

Heston identified the "enemies" of the Constitution as "the feminists who preach that it's a divine duty for women to hate men, blacks who raise a militant fist with one hand while they seek preference with the other." Heston explained that the attack on firearms was really an attack on the Constitution and America itself:

> "As I have stood in the crosshairs of those who target Second Amendment freedoms, I've realized that firearms are not the only issue. No, it's much, much bigger than that."[57]

According to Heston, nothing less than a "cultural war" against white men was "raging across our land." As Scott Melzer writes, the NRA's "culture wars" framing proved very effective in bringing together diverse conservative groups, united by "their sense of victimization at the hands of a liberal culture run amok. In their eyes, immigrants, gays, women, the poor, and other groups are (undeservedly) granted special rights and privileges."[58]

Heston's performances as NRA spokesperson were a master class in conservative constitutional propaganda. The visuals alone were compelling: the tall, rugged figure of Heston, evoking his famous role as Moses, the bearer of God's law, lighting the path for a world that has lost its way. His speeches artfully wove together references to God, whiteness, maleness, persecution, and heroism—all tied to guns and the Constitution. Heston's status as a wealthy, famous, Hollywood celebrity who represented a multi-billion-dollar special interest lobby did not interfere with his ability to reassure working-class white men that their problems were the result of a loss of respect for whiteness, Christianity, heterosexuality, maleness. Though Heston was vague about the nature of those problems, beyond allusions to being made to feel "shame" for expressions of white pride, he was very clear about identifying their source: women and blacks.

Despite conservatives' performative disparagement of identity politics and victimhood, Heston and the NRA appeal not only to identity politics, but, as Deborah Homsher calls it, "victim identity group politics."[59] In the contemporary conservative narrative, white, straight, Christian men—despite being the one group in America that is not targeted for physical violence or sexual assault; denied employment or educational opportunities;

excluded from political participation; or kept from exercising basic rights to bodily autonomy on the basis of gender, race, religion, or sexual orientation—are victims. Michael Dorf describes gun rights advocates as "angry white men" whose sense of victimization is largely delusional: "[T]he movement for gun rights does not pit an oppressed group against an oppressive majority. . . . [S]upporters of gun rights are not, by any reasonable measure, oppressed."[60]

This is not to say that white, straight, Christian men do not experience hardship. Many Americans of all backgrounds struggle to maintain jobs, pay for health insurance, buy a home, and provide for their families. But none of these problems are caused by or exacerbated by being white, straight, Christian, or male. Instead of feeling solidarity with women and minorities who suffer the same hardships and more at the hands of the same elites, working-class white men hold them responsible for the undeserved hardships of working-class people. As David C. Williams writes,

> When the people feel betrayed by government and compelled to take up arms, they look for the cause of their felt disempowerment. In an old American tradition, rather than looking for the cause of their distress in an increasingly complex world, they seek out the enemies of the people that have betrayed them. Too often, they find these enemies in outgroups who, in fact, have even less power than they.[61]

It is always in the best interest of the ruling elite to set exploited classes against each other, and the well-financed gun lobby has done an excellent job of accomplishing this aim.

The Corporate Connection

In 2015, the annual revenue of the firearms and ammunition industry was $13.5 billion, the annual revenue of gun and ammunition stores was $3.1 billion, and the estimated overall economic impact of the firearms and ammunition industry in the United States was $42.9 billion.[62]

The industry thrives on dark warnings about gun control that the NRA and other gun rights groups inevitably circulate after mass shootings. After every high-profile gun massacre, NRA representatives rush to assure the public that the problem is not too many guns, but too few. At the same time, they warn Americans that such tragedies will be "exploited" as a means of passing gun control legislation, encouraging them to buy firearms and ammunition while they still can. "Gun and ammo sales spike as consumers rush to buy what they believe will soon be harder to obtain. This, in turn, often has a buoying effect to gun-and-ammo company stocks."[63] Smith & Wesson's stock went up more than 132 percent in 2015 while Sturm Ruger's increased by 75 percent.[64] In 2016, after several high-profile gun massacres were followed by promises by the Obama administration to implement more effective firearms regulation, Smith & Wesson reported that its revenue had grown 31 percent in its last fiscal year, a record-breaking total of $733 million. The company's CEO James Debney attributed its success to "increased orders for our handgun designed for personal protection."[65]

The NRA benefits directly from the largesse of the firearms industry. While the NRA presents itself as a grassroots organization, it received much of its more than $300 million revenue from donors in the firearms industry. The Violence Policy Center (VPC) reports that the NRA's Corporate Partners Program is "targeted at raising revenue directly from the gun industry." The promotional brochure for the program states that it "is geared toward your company's corporate interests." Though the NRA does not reveal the specific amount it has received from gun industry contributions, the VPC estimated that it is as much as $60 million, including eight "corporate partners" that the NRA itself boasts have given cash gifts of 1 million or more.[66] Among these contributors were "Beretta, Smith & Wesson, Brownells, Pierce Bullet Seal Target Systems, and Springfield Armory."[67] Since 1992, the online ammunition retailer MidwayUSA has participated in a program that allows customers "to round up their purchases to the nearest dollar and donate the difference to the N.R.A," a program that has "helped build an N.R.A. endowment balance of more than $14 million."[68]

Corporate donations have helped LaPierre bring home nearly $1 million per year in salary as the NRA's vice president. The exception was 2015, when LaPierre was given a retirement plan payout that resulted in a total salary amount of over $5 million.[69]

Boosted by this corporate funding and by Heston's leadership, the NRA in the late 1990s again became one of the most powerful lobbying organizations in the United States, exerting enormous power over legislation, litigation, and public opinion regarding the Second Amendment. The NRA plays a key role in perpetuating the political dominance of the Republican Party,[70] using its very deep pockets and its massive influence to boost the political campaigns of the candidates who toe the organization's party line and to attack candidates who do not.

"In state legislatures across the country," notes one commentator, "the NRA has earned a reputation as the lobbying group that lawmakers, especially Republicans, are least eager to cross. The organization demands absolute loyalty, and moves quickly to punish politicians who defy its wishes."[71] The NRA's influence is not limited to the Republican Party. In 1982, the NRA informed Democrat Bill Clinton, then running for a second term as the governor of Arkansas, that his answers to their political preference questionnaire were unsatisfactory. Clinton changed them immediately. He contacted the NRA vice president directly to tell him that he was "in support of the NRA position on gun control," at which point the NRA gave him an "A" rating.[72]

Since 1998, the NRA has donated millions of dollars to members of Congress, including 44 senators and 249 representatives in 2016.[73] Senate Majority Leader Mitch McConnell indicated in 2016 that Republicans would never confirm a Supreme Court nominee opposed by the National Rifle Association.[74] The NRA spent $52 million in political elections in 2016, a record for the group. In five of the six congressional races to which the NRA devoted significant funds, the organization's favored candidate prevailed.[75]

But the bulk of the NRA's generosity in 2016—a whopping $30.3 million—was devoted to supporting Donald Trump's presidential bid. After winning the election, Trump repeatedly demonstrated his eagerness to return the favor. Speaking at the group's annual convention in 2017, the first president to do so since Ronald Reagan, Trump vowed, "You came through big for me, and I am going to come through for you. . . . The eight-year assault on your Second Amendment freedoms has come to a crashing end."[76] The *Wall Street Journal* noted that Trump's NRA address "represents a major victory for the organization and a symbol of its pull with the new administration."[77]

The NRA has succeeded not only in focusing conservative constitutional energy on the Second Amendment but also in establishing its idiosyncratic and historically unsupported individual gun rights interpretation as Second Amendment orthodoxy. The percentage of Americans who supported banning handguns dropped from 60 percent to 24 percent between 1959 and 2012, and by 2008 nearly two-thirds of Americans believed the Second Amendment "'guaranteed the rights of Americans to own guns' outside the militia."[78] This view of the Second Amendment was famously denounced by no less than former U.S. Supreme Court Chief Justice Warren Burger, a conservative appointed to the Court by Richard Nixon, who called it "one of the greatest pieces of fraud—I repeat the word 'fraud'—on the American public by special interest groups that I have ever seen in my lifetime."[79]

The NRA's individual rights interpretation of the Second Amendment is fraudulent in three ways. First, the holders of the right morphs from the "militia" into "private individuals." Second, the object of the right morphs from "arms" into "guns." Third, the purpose of the right morphs from the "security of a free State" into "self-defense." In the 2008 case *District of Columbia v. Heller*, the Supreme Court largely validated this NRA-championed interpretation of the Second Amendment.

The Role of the Supreme Court: District of Columbia v. Heller

The NRA was, to the surprise of some, opposed to the *Heller* litigation. It went so far as to try to get Congress to repeal the Washington, DC, law under attack in *Heller* so that the case would be rendered moot. The NRA's lack of enthusiasm for *Heller* is understandable in light of how enormously successful the NRA had been in pushing for expanded gun rights in state legislatures, exerting influence over political leaders, and changing public perception without the Supreme Court's help.

For years, the NRA had invoked its peculiar interpretation of the Second Amendment to call for easing restrictions on "concealed carry" (often referred to as "constitutional carry"), challenging "gun free zones" and other regulations affecting where firearms could be brought and fired, and broadening the legal concept of self-defense through stand-your-ground laws. It had accomplished all this without a formal judicial endorsement of its interpretation of the Second Amendment from the Supreme Court. From the NRA's perspective, *Heller* was not worth the risk. A negative ruling could jeopardize its successes, and a positive ruling might be even worse.

Winkler explains that the NRA had "thrived over the years thanks to crisis-driven fund-raising appeals warning members that the government was coming to take their guns. Every time a new gun control law was proposed, the NRA sent out mass mailings telling members that they needed to send money right away to stop the law" or risk losing the right to bear arms altogether.[80] The NRA's business model depended on convincing its members that they were always one step away from losing their constitutional rights. If the Supreme Court definitively pronounced the Second Amendment as protecting the right of personal gun ownership, the NRA's ability to capitalize on the uncertainty of gun rights would be severely diminished.

Heller's ruling was a substantial, though not complete, endorsement of the NRA's extremist view of the Second Amendment. Justice Antonin Scalia, writing for the majority in *Heller*, held that the Second Amendment protects "an individual right to use arms for self-defense"[81] and that handguns in particular, as "the quintessential self-defense weapon," must be afforded protection under the Constitution.[82]

The decision was peculiar in many ways. First, as many legal scholars have observed, *Heller*'s "originalist" endorsement of the theory that the Second Amendment guarantees a personal right to use arms for self-defense directly conflicts with the longstanding and textually intelligible interpretation of the amendment as guaranteeing the right of militias to keep arms to guard against government tyranny. Historians roundly derided Justice Scalia's claim that his holding was faithful to the original meaning of the Constitution:

> [T]he originalist interpretation of the Second Amendment as guaranteeing a right to be armed for personal, non-militia purposes receives virtually no support among professional historians. Of the sixteen academic historians who joined briefs amicus curiae in *Heller*, fifteen argued for the militia purpose view.[83]

For many, Justice Scalia's opinion exposed the hollowness of the conservative originalist approach to the Constitution. Far from engaging in an objective, historically sensitive analysis of the plain meaning or understanding of the Second Amendment, the Court's holding in *Heller* essentially projected the views of modern-day gun rights activists onto an eighteenth-century document—precisely what originalists accuse "living constitutionalists" of doing with regard to abortion and LGBT rights. As Reva Siegel writes, while the *Heller* Court "claims to derive its authority to enforce the Second Amendment solely from epochal acts of constitutional lawmaking in the eighteenth century," it

> takes guidance from the lived experience and passionate convictions of Americans in times since the founding—convictions and experience the majority is prepared to elevate over the considered views of "hundreds of judges" in the twentieth century.[84]

Heller's outcome was harshly criticized not only by liberals and progressives, as might have been expected, but by prominent conservatives as well. These included Circuit Judge J. Harvie Wilkinson III, a Reagan appointee, who compared *Heller*'s regrettable "judicial activism" with that of *Roe v. Wade*. As tempting as it may be to read an individual right to self-defense into the Constitution, Wilkinson maintains, it betrays originalist principles to do so. "After decades of criticizing activist judges for this or that defalcation," he wrote, "conservatives have now committed many of the same sins . . . read[ing] an ambiguous constitutional provision as creating a substantive right that the Court had never acknowledged in more than two hundred years since the amendment's enactment."[85]

The interpretation of the Second Amendment as an individual rather than a militia right created other odd effects. Justice Scalia held that while the government could not constitutionally prohibit citizens from using popular weapons of self-defense, it could constitutionally prohibit civilians from possessing "dangerous and unusual weapons." As Siegel writes, it is "striking that an *originalist* interpretation of the Second Amendment would treat civic republican understandings of the amendment as antiquated, and refuse to protect the arms a militia needs to defend against tyranny."[86]

The twists of *Heller* did not stop there. Not only did the "originalist" Justice Scalia fail to provide an originalist analysis of the Second Amendment, a "progressive" justice, John Paul Stevens, did provide such an analysis, one that reached the same conclusion as the majority of constitutional historians: The original public meaning of the Second Amendment was that it protected the right of the people to be armed while serving in a state militia.

In *Heller*, Justice Scalia claimed that "the American people have considered the handgun to be the quintessential self-defense weapon." He provided no evidence for this assertion, instead expressing his own views about the superiority of handguns to long guns:

> It is easier to store in a location that is readily accessible in an emergency; it cannot easily be redirected or wrestled away by an attacker; it is easier to use for those without the upper-body strength to lift and aim a long gun; it can be pointed at a burglar with one hand while the other hand dials the police.[87]

Though the outcome in *Heller*—along with the Supreme Court's holding in *McDonald v. City of Chicago* two years later that the individual right to keep and bear arms apply to the states as well as the federal government—was celebrated by the gun rights lobby, the Court's interpretation of the right to bear arms is narrower than the lobby's own view. The NRA and other gun rights organizations have insisted for decades that the Second Amendment demands the loosening or elimination of restrictions on concealed carry and open carry, the expansion of the legal definition of justifiable use of deadly force, and the overturning of laws that restrict the ability of certain groups—for example, domestic violence offenders, the mentally ill, and felons—to obtain or keep firearms. The Court has not yet indicated a willingness to expand the understanding of the Second Amendment beyond the right of an individual to possess a handgun for protection inside the home. The gun lobby's multiple challenges to various gun control laws in the wake of *Heller* and *McDonald* have mostly failed.

A significant passage in Scalia's *Heller* opinion emphasized that the right to bear arms was not absolute:

Like most rights, the Second Amendment right is not unlimited. It is not a right to keep and carry any weapon whatsoever in any manner whatsoever and for whatever purpose: For example, concealed weapons prohibitions have been upheld under the Amendment or state analogues. The Court's opinion should not be taken to cast doubt on longstanding prohibitions on the possession of firearms by felons and the mentally ill, or laws forbidding the carrying of firearms in sensitive places such as schools and government buildings, or laws imposing conditions and qualifications on the commercial sale of arms.[88]

But whatever restraint the Supreme Court, or any court, might demonstrate in its formal decisions interpreting constitutional rights has limited impact in a culture of constitutional extremism. Courts do not make laws; legislatures do. If there is no political will to regulate firearm use and access, then it is cold comfort that courts might uphold such regulations.

What is more, if there is strong political will to interpret constitutional rights far more broadly than courts would be inclined to, there is very little that courts can do to stop them. As the saying goes, the Constitution is a floor, not a ceiling: Courts can intervene when laws interpret constitutional rights too narrowly, but there is little they can do about laws that interpret them too expansively. Recall the NRA's lack of enthusiasm and even apprehension about the *Heller* litigation: An official interpretation of the Second Amendment from the Supreme Court was unnecessary to the gun lobby's tremendously successful agenda to expand gun rights, and indeed potentially undermined it.

The Supreme Court's selective, ahistorical, and illogical interpretation of the Second Amendment did advance the agenda of constitutional fundamentalists. On its own, however, its rulings to date do not prevent state and federal governments from passing sensible firearm regulations; or require that Americans civilians with no weapons or firearms safety training be allowed to carry loaded weapons into malls, churches, bars, and daycare centers; or encourage men to attend crowded protests with assault rifles strapped to their backs; or allow armed vigilantes to shoot unarmed black teenagers walking home in the rain.

The roots of Second Amendment fundamentalism and its influence on American culture run much deeper. The blame for the current unconscionable state of affairs lies not only with the Supreme Court, but also with the gun lobby and with every elected official that does its bidding.

HOW THE GUN LOBBY HIJACKED SELF-DEFENSE

It is a testament to the propaganda power of the gun lobby that discussions of the Second Amendment invariably become discussions of self-defense and guns. Conflating guns with the constitutional right of self-defense means that laws promoting gun use will be viewed as protecting the constitutional right to self-defense, while laws restricting gun use will be viewed as attacking the constitutional right to self-defense. In the name of the Second Amendment, the gun lobby can push for the use of firearms by more people in more places, relaxing restrictions on open carry, and aggressively modifying the concept of self-defense through stand-your-ground laws, while portraying gun control advocates as enemies of self-defense and the Constitution itself.

Second Amendment fundamentalists believe that the Constitution guarantees (1) an individual right (2) to use guns (3) in self-defense—even though none of these terms appear in the text of the amendment itself. As detailed above, the individual right theory of the Second Amendment is roundly disparaged. But the underlying assumption that guns are an effective form of self-defense has been less scrutinized. There are many reasons to reject this assumption.

All credible empirical evidence supports the conclusion that firearms are highly unreliable and ineffective tools of self-defense. In addition to endangering public safety, the equation of the right to self-defense with gun rights distorts the concept of self-defense, obscures racial and gender disparities in the right to use deadly force, and reinforces the ideology of white male supremacy.

The Right of Self-Defense

The right to self-defense has long been acknowledged as a fundamental and natural right. It is not, however, an absolute or unlimited right. If every individual in a community had the right to use force whenever he felt entitled to do so, that community would quickly disintegrate into what philosopher John Locke called a "state of war." In a state of war, any person could be deprived of life, liberty, and property merely on the whim of another person.

According to classic social contract theory, individuals give up some "natural rights," including the absolute right to determine when and how to use force against other individuals, to avoid this state of chaos. In exchange, the state provides protections of these rights. This principle of social contract is reflected in the Declaration of Independence, which states that governments are established in order to secure the "unalienable rights" of mankind, "deriving their just powers from the consent of the governed." As George Fletcher writes, ordered societies depend on the state's monopoly of force to avoid chaos and to regulate disputes. "When private individuals appeal to force and decide who shall enjoy the right to 'life, liberty and the pursuit of happiness,'" they undermine the rule of law.[89]

Thus, using the Second Amendment to justify absolutist views of self-defense is self-contradictory. The Second Amendment, as a part of the Constitution, is also part of the social contract made between the American people and their government. That contract explicitly commits the people to submit to the authority of government, with only limited exceptions. To call for the right of individuals to have ultimate authority over when and how to use deadly force is to call for a state of war. The belief in absolute rights—self-defense or otherwise—is incompatible with a commitment to the Constitution.

It is true, of course, that individuals are entitled to use force if the state fails to live up to the social contract. The Declaration of Independence proclaims "the Right of the People to alter or to abolish" government that has failed to secure their rights or attempts to "reduce them under absolute Despotism." Far-right militant groups are fond of using this revolutionary rhetoric to justify their calls for armed insurrection against the government and to denounce "government tyranny." But the Declaration also makes clear that revolution is justified only under the most extreme circumstances, not "for light and transient causes." Revolt against an existing government is only justified where there is "a long train of abuses and usurpations" attempting to establish "an absolute Tyranny."

The question then becomes whether the state has engaged in such tyrannical oppression. The answer is yes, at least against certain subordinated groups. Women and nonwhite men have been repeatedly subjected to direct, state-sponsored violence as well as systematically denied protection against private violence. The institution of slavery imposed a regime of state-supported violence against black men and women, including forced labor, beatings, rapes, and murders. The law provided virtually no opportunity for slaves to exercise a right of self-defense against their white owners; indeed, beating and rapes of slaves were not even classified as crimes.

After slavery was formally abolished, the state continued to sanction violence against black men and women through the Black Codes and discriminatory application of criminal laws and self-defense laws. When they were not actively participating in mob violence against black individuals, Reconstruction-era state officials were turning a blind eye to the beatings, lynchings, and rapes of black men and women. In the present day, the state continues to exert disproportionate violence against the black community through lethal policing and mass incarceration while failing to protect black communities from private violence.[90]

American common law granted husbands a "right of chastisement"—a right to inflict corporal punishment—over their wives, which persisted in some form until the mid-nineteenth century. American law also allowed for a "marital rape exemption" according to which husbands could not be found guilty of raping their wives. The last state to remove the marital rape exemption did so only in 1993, and marital rape is treated as a less serious crime than other sexual assaults in most jurisdictions even today. High rates of domestic violence and sexual assault persist in part because the state fails to adequately define, investigate, and punish these crimes, and it grants perpetrators a wide range of defenses to excuse or mitigate their actions.[91]

Yet the cry for armed insurrection against the government does not come from women and nonwhite men. Second Amendment fundamentalists are overwhelmingly white and male, members of the one group that has never experienced systematic victimization by either the state or by private citizens. Their race and gender have never made them the target of state violence, whether through enslavement, sexual subordination, or formal discrimination. They do not suffer higher rates of crime than other groups, nor have crimes against them and their property been routinely unacknowledged or unaddressed by the state. They are the one group that has not only never been excluded from government power but also the one group that has retained a monopoly on government power throughout America's entire history. White men have, in short, the weakest claim of any group to engage in self-defense against the government.

It is a testament to the depth of the white male victim complex that some white men believe they have the right to overthrow a government that has served their interests above all others. In the conservative narrative of white male persecution, so skillfully promoted by charismatic figures such as Charlton Heston, white men—particularly heterosexual, Christian, white men—are constantly under attack not only by society, but by the government. Not only do they have to remain eternally vigilant against "criminals," "terrorists," and "illegal immigrants"—who are inevitably coded as nonwhite and non-Christian—but also against the state's constant attempts to strip them of their rights. Remarkably, the far-right's rabidly antigovernment sentiment has not only largely escaped being labeled as treasonous and anarchic, but has in fact frequently been framed as patriotic.

The fetishization of the Second Amendment as the bulwark against government tyranny relies on the false narrative of white male persecution. This proclaimed fidelity to constitutional rights has nothing to do with acknowledging actual oppression by the state; rather, it serves as a pretext for the continued and increased over-protection of white men's interests.

Individuals are entitled to use self-defense against other citizens when it is not possible to defer to the state's monopoly on violence. As George Fletcher explains, "When individuals are threatened with immediate aggression, when the police cannot protect them, the monopoly of the state gives way."[92] Individuals may act in self-defense if they face a serious threat of irreparable injury, and there is no time to wait for the state's intervention. As Locke writes,

[T]he law, which was made for my preservation, where it cannot interpose to secure my life from present force, which, if lost, is capable of no reparation, permits me my own defence, and the right of war, a liberty to kill the aggressor, because the aggressor allows not time to appeal to our common judge, nor the decision of the law, for remedy in a case where the mischief may be irreparable.[93]

But even when individuals are entitled to use self-defense, there are restrictions on how they can exercise this right. According to the common law right of self-defense, individuals are only justified in using *necessary and proportional* force against imminent and unlawful aggression. The right of self-defense is not synonymous with the right to use *deadly* force; many common self-defense situations do not pose a risk of serious bodily injury or death. As guns are inherently lethal, their use is disproportionate except when it is the only available means of responding to an imminent and unlawful threat of severe physical injury or death. Less lethal threats must be met with less lethal force. There are numerous methods and tools of self-defense that can be used in a nonlethal manner, including shoving, slapping, strangling, punching, kicking, restraining, and the use of implements such as knives, bats, brass knuckles, pepper spray, Tasers, and the like.

An exclusive focus on guns is not justified even for the limited category of self-defense situations that do call for deadly force, as firearms are far from the only available tools of deadly force. Certain martial arts and hand-to-hand combat techniques can deliver lethal blows, as can a wide range of weapons, including machetes, axes, hand grenades, rocket launchers, and cannons.

In short, a gun is a tool solely of deadly force, and only one such tool among many. The vast array of potential self-defense scenarios calling for varying levels of responsive force, stark differences among individuals in the probability and nature of the need for self-defense, and tremendous variations (of size, strength, physical ability, and skill) among the general population all underscore the general unsuitability of guns for self-defense.

According to traditional concepts of self-defense, the deadly force of firearms can only be justifiably used in situations when there is no time to appeal to law enforcement, and there is no other reasonable option available to avoid an unlawful and imminent threat of serious physical injury or death. This is an exceedingly narrow category of self-defense scenarios.

And yet the gun lobby/*Heller* interpretation of the Second Amendment focuses *solely on* the *right to use firearms in self-defense.* This focus justifies expanding access to and use of firearms by more people in more places, for relaxing restrictions on open carry, and for aggressively modifying the concept of self-defense through stand-your-ground laws. At the same time, it ignores other approaches and other tools of self-defense, no matter how much more effective they might be.

Gun-Centered Self-Defense

This interpretation would be arbitrary and troubling enough even if gun use were, as the gun lobby claims, a superior means of self-defense. But the reality is that firearms are impractical and ineffective tools for self-defense, and they do far more to endanger than to protect individual and general welfare. Of the multiple methods and tools available for self-defense, firearms stand out in several negative ways.

First, guns are inherently and intentionally lethal. They are designed solely to kill, making them particularly ill suited to the proportionality and imminence requirements of lawful self-defense. Second, safe and effective use of firearms requires extensive knowledge and training that average gun owners, to say nothing of those around them, simply do not have.

Third, the groups that are most likely to be victimized by crime generally—adolescents, the disabled, and the poor—are least likely to be able to use guns in self-defense. Adolescents are more than twice as likely to be victimized by crime as adults;[94] the rate of violent victimization of the disabled population is three times the rate of the non-disabled population;[95] and poor households are more likely to experience criminal victimization than more well-off households.[96] But guns are legally unavailable to minors, unusable or inaccessible to many disabled individuals, and prohibitively expensive for impoverished individuals.

Fourth, the use, storage, and transportation of firearms creates risks not only to gun owners but to everyone around them, including children, cohabitants, bystanders, and the general public. The presence of guns tends to escalate aggression,[97] create a false sense of security,[98] and encourage violence as a first resort.[99] Experts estimate that gun violence cost the United States $229 billion in 2012,[100] including "medical and mental health care costs, criminal justice costs, wage losses, and the value of pain, suffering and lost quality of life."[101]

There are more guns in the U.S. civilian population than any other country in the world. Americans make up only 5 percent of the world's population but own nearly half of the world's guns—more than 300 million firearms.[102] If it were true that guns were an effective means of self-defense, then the United States should be one of the safest countries in the world. But Americans are ten times more likely to be killed by firearms than people in other developed nations, and its firearm homicide rate is twenty-five times higher than other high-income nations.[103] The firearm suicide rate in the United States is eight times higher than other high-income nations.[104] The United States experiences more public mass shootings than any other country in the world, four times as many as the Philippines, the country with the next highest rate.[105]

Gun violence kills 33,000 Americans every year,[106] including 1,300 children,[107] and injures more than 70,000. That translates to more than 300 people killed or injured by guns a day.[108] Americans' lifetime odds of being killed by a gun (excluding suicides and accidents) are 1 in 370, far higher than the odds of death by drowning (1 in 1,188), death by fire (1 in 1,498), or death by sharp object (1 in 2,325).[109]

According to the gun lobby, this carnage can only be answered with one solution: more guns. The more gun violence there is, the more people fear gun violence, and the more they fear gun violence, the more the gun lobby tells them that the only answer to bad gun violence is good gun violence.

The NRA and other lobbyists claim that guns are law-abiding citizens' only hope to defend themselves.[110] But there is broad consensus among gun researchers that defensive gun uses are rare, especially compared to unlawful and socially undesirable uses. Terrorist groups such as the Islamic State take advantage of America's lax gun laws to arm their fighters.[111] Guns "are used to threaten and intimidate far more often than they are used in self defense. Most self-reported self defense gun uses may well be illegal and against the interests of society."[112] According to the Violence Policy Center, "for every justifiable homicide in the United States—for every lethal shooting in defense of life or property—guns are used to commit 34 murders and 78 suicides, and are the cause of two accidental deaths."[113] Researchers have found no evidence that guns are more effective than other forms of self-defense.[114] A 2014 study of 160 mass-casualty shootings between 2000 and 2013 found that only seven were ended by armed civilians, including off-duty policemen, shooting at the gunman.[115]

The belief that untrained, average citizens possess the skill to use guns effectively against unlawful violence is dangerous wishful thinking. There is ample evidence that guns are dangerously ill suited for most self-defense situations. Even trained professionals, such as soldiers and law enforcement officers, have low firearm accuracy rates. Factors such as stress, overconfidence, lighting, and racial bias interfere with the judgment and skills of those with years of training in conflict situations. The highly trained New York Police Department's "average hit rate during gunfights was just 18 percent. When suspects did not return fire, police officers hit their targets 30 percent of the time."[116]

The average untrained civilian is even more likely to harm himself or others than to prevent a crime. According to David Chipman—a former Alcohol, Tobacco, and Firearms agent—"the presence of a firearm is a greater risk, especially in the hands of an untrained person."[117] According to a 2015 expert report on firearms and self-defense, "Citizens with little or no training are foolish to think that they will have the focus and presence of mind to respond calmly and appropriately when under duress."[118] Access to a firearm makes a person almost twice as likely to become a homicide victim and three times more likely to commit suicide.[119] A 2009 study showed that people with guns in their possession were more than four times more likely to be shot than those without.[120] The presence of guns increases the likelihood of accidental death across all age groups.[121]

In his 2003 book, NRA Vice President LaPierre writes, "[T]he Founders and an army of scholars dating from the republics of Plato and Rome to modern-day America agree: self defense works—criminals fear armed citizens and so do terrorists."[122] LaPierre's claim contains three common gun fallacies. First, as noted above, the founders believed that the government had the right to confiscate weapons when demanded by public necessity, and regulations regarding the storage and carrying of firearms and ammunition have existed since colonial times. During the revolutionary period, free men of eligible militia age were required to present themselves at "musters," or public gatherings, to have their weapons inspected and registered. In some colonies, gun ownership was contingent upon swearing loyalty oaths. Strict regulations about where gunpowder could be stored and where loaded weapons could be brought were common throughout the original states in the late 1700s. The founders also found it appropriate to forcibly disarm "slaves, free blacks, and people of mixed race out of fear that these groups would use guns to revolt against slave masters." As Winkler writes, while guns were privately owned, they were considered "assets to be used if necessary for the public good." The founders endorsed "the basic idea that gun possession must be balanced with gun safety laws."[123]

LaPierre's second fallacy is that criminals and terrorists "fear" armed citizens. This presumes that criminal and terrorists are both aware of and deterred by the presence of other armed individuals. But the entire point of concealed carry is that only the carrier knows he is armed, and there is no evidence showing that the mere possibility of armed bystanders deters criminals or terrorists. Contrary to the NRA's claim that more guns lead to less crime, overwhelming scholarly and expert research demonstrates that increased gun ownership and permissive gun laws have no deterrent effect on crime.[124]

Eliminating restrictions for concealed-carry permits, for example, have no effect on crime "[b]ecause beliefs over the distribution of firearm carriers are impervious to permitting policies and do not respond positively to the true distribution of carriers."[125] The 2011 shooting of Arizona Congresswoman Gabrielle Giffords provides one illustration of this point. Arizona eliminated permit requirements for concealed carry in 2010. In the NRA's theory, making it easier for people to obtain concealed-carry permits will lead to fewer crimes, as criminals will fear the higher likelihood of armed citizens. But the possibility of armed bystanders clearly did not deter Jared Loughner from opening fire in a crowded parking lot.

The converse of the "more guns, less crime" claim is the claim that "gun-free zones" attract crime and violence. This too is a myth. The vast majority of firearm violence occurs in private, not public, and is triggered by factors such as arguments and personal grudges. As the *New York Times* noted in 2015,

> [R]ampage killings are not the typical face of gun violence in America. Each day, some 30 people are victims of gun homicides, slain by rival gang members, drug dealers, trigger-happy robbers, drunken men after bar fights, frenzied family members or abusive partners. An additional 60 people a day kill themselves with guns.[126]

Mass shootings are exceedingly rare: "Less than one percent of gun murder victims recorded by the FBI in 2012 were killed in incidents with four or more victims."[127] Of the mass shootings that took place between 2009 and 2016, 69 percent "took place wholly in private residences," and no more than 13 percent "took place entirely in public spaces that were so-called gun-free zones." Of the tiny fraction of mass shootings that did occur in "gun-free zones" over the last three decades, "not a single case includes evidence that the killer chose to target a place because it banned guns. To the contrary, in many of the cases there was clearly another motive for the choice of location."[128] What is more, the NRA itself raises no objection when weapons are prohibited for high-profile events, such as the Republican National Convention[129] or its own events.[130]

Multiple studies have shown a correlation between permissive gun laws and *increases* in crime, injuries, and suicides, as well as injuries and death caused by accidental discharges.[131] States that have passed laws expanding right-to-carry[132] and stand-your-ground laws[133] experience *more*, not fewer, robberies, rapes, assaults, and murders. A 2011 study showed that firearm deaths "are significantly lower in states with stricter gun control legislation."[134] As Daniel Webster and Jens Ludwig have succinctly concluded, "the best science indicates that more guns will lead to more deaths."[135]

The campus-carry movement starkly illustrates the dangers of these gun lobby myths. Colleges and universities have long been gun-free zones with rates of violence far lower than the country's average. "The overwhelming majority of the 4,400 colleges and universities in the United States prohibit the carrying of firearms on their campuses. These gun-free policies have helped to make our postsecondary education institutions some of the safest places in the country."[136] The risk of sexual assault for students is 1.2 times lower than that of nonstudents.[137] While the criminal homicide rate in the United States is around 5 per 100,000 persons overall and 14 per 100,000 for those aged 17 to 29, "the overall homicide rate at post-secondary education institutions was 0.07 per 100,000 students."[138]

Nonetheless, in 2009 the NRA began to support the campus-carry movement that aimed to allow students and faculty to carry loaded weapons into universities and colleges. As of March 2017, ten states have passed campus-carry laws, and many more are considering them. There is no evidence that the passage of these laws has reduced crime rates, and sexual assault rates have actually risen in states that have passed campus-carry laws. Colorado provides one case in point: "Since all public colleges in Colorado have been forced to allow campus carry (2012–2013), the rate of rape has increased 25% in 2012 and 36% in 2013," while the "national average over the past ten years has been slowly decreasing at a rate of approximately 3% per year."[139]

LaPierre's third fallacy is the false dichotomy between armed criminals on the one hand and armed law-abiding citizens on the other. One week after a man shot and killed twenty children and seven adults (including his mother) in Newtown, Connecticut, LaPierre stated in an interview that "the only thing that stops a bad guy with a gun is a good guy with a gun."[140] There is a Schroedinger's cat-like problem at work in this assertion: It is impossible to know whether the guy with the gun is good or bad until he starts shooting. In a world in which people with assault rifles can roam freely into churches, nightclubs, and elementary schools—the world that gun rights activists are agitating for—there is no legitimate basis for stopping them, or even calling the police to report them, up until the moment they decide to fire that rifle through the brain of an elderly parishioner, a club-goer on the dancefloor, or a 6-year-old child. In many situations, it will not even be clear whether the first one to fire is a bad guy, or whether the one to return fire is a good guy, even after the smoke has cleared.

The Giffords shooting is instructive on this point as well. An armed bystander named Joe Zamudio heard the shots and came running onto the scene with his gun out. He saw a man holding a gun and, believing him to be the shooter, almost decided to shoot him. Instead, he grabbed the man and pushed him against a wall. Bystanders shouted at him that the man with the gun had wrestled it away from the actual shooter. Zamudio had come a hair's breadth away from shooting a good guy because he thought he was a bad guy. One reason Zamudio had decided not to fire was because "he didn't want to be confused as a second gunman." As William Saletan wrote in *Slate*,

> That's what happens when you run with a firearm to a scene of bloody havoc. In the chaos and pressure of the moment, you can shoot the wrong person. Or, by drawing your weapon, you can become the wrong person—a hero mistaken for a second gunman by another would-be hero with a gun. Bang, you're dead. Or worse, bang bang bang bang bang: a firefight among several armed, confused, and innocent people in a crowd.[141]

If the NRA truly believed its own claims that gun use enhances rather than endangers public safety, it would welcome comprehensive empirical research into the issue. Instead, the group has been extremely hostile to rigorous, scientific inquiry into firearms use. After a 1993 study funded by the Centers for Disease Control and Prevention's National Center for Injury Prevention found that the presence of a gun in the home more than doubled the inhabitant's risk of homicide and more than quadrupled the risk of suicide, the NRA attempted to have the center shut down. While it did not succeed in doing so, the organization did succeed in getting Republican Congressman Jay Dickey of Arkansas, the NRA's self-proclaimed "point person in Congress,"[142] to sponsor a bill that "cut $2.6 million from the CDC's budget—the exact amount the CDC had invested in research on firearm injuries the previous year." In 1996, the Republican-controlled Congress passed the "Dickey Amendment," which dictated that "[n]one of the funds made available for injury prevention and control at the Centers for Disease Control and Prevention may be used to advocate or promote gun control." While the bill did not expressly ban gun violence research, the deliberately vague wording—combined with an onslaught of harass-ment of researchers—had a chilling effect on scientific progress, effec-tively ending all federal research programs related to gun violence. As Dr. Mark Rosenberg, former director of the CDC's National Center for In-jury Control and Prevention, put it: "The scientific community has been terrorized by the NRA." [143]

In the face of overwhelming evidence of unlawful death and destruc-tion, the gun lobby takes refuge in its most despicable cliché: "Guns don't kill people, people kill people." When all else fails, the gun lobby washes its hands of the bloodshed caused by guns by insisting that guns are merely neutral tools that can be used for good or evil purposes. But such a position is entirely incompatible with the linchpin of the gun lobby's pro-firearms propaganda, namely, that guns—not people—re-duce crime and save lives.

What is more, a firearm is not a tool like any other. Comparisons to automobiles and swimming pools and other products that are also capable of causing injury or death are inapposite because such products are not designed, as firearms are, *exclusively* to cause injury or death. And indeed, products that have the realistic potential to cause serious injury or death are extensively regulated, from automobiles to swimming pools to chain-saws and opioids. Firearms are one of the deadliest products in the world and yet are virtually unregulated. They come with no warning labels, no instruction manuals, and no directions for safe storage and use. In most states, thanks in large part to the NRA, people can obtain, use, and carry lethal weapons without so much as an hour of firearms instruction or training. While gun manufacturers and sellers could easily take measures to make guns less susceptible to theft and misuse, the gun lobby helped ensure that they have no incentives to do so.

The NRA has gone so far as to retaliate against manufacturers who do make attempts to adopt safety standards. Beginning in the late 1990s, several lawsuits were brought against gun manufacturers and sellers for negligent practices and the harmful effects of gun violence, including many by the mayors of several large cities. These suits did not often succeed, but as with other industries, civil litigation encouraged the firearms industry to adopt improved safety measures and to take other precautions. For example, as part of a settlement agreement with the Clinton administration to end several lawsuits in 2000, Smith & Wesson agreed to implement a range of safety practices, including establishing a code of conduct for authorized dealers and distributors, limiting the number of rounds in magazines, installing internal locks on firearms, and adding a hidden set of serial numbers on new guns.

The CEO of Smith & Wesson at the time, Ed Schultz, was interested in developing a so-called smart gun that could only be fired by its owner. The day the settlement was announced, the NRA harshly criticized Smith & Wesson as being "the first gun maker to run up the white flag of surrender." The organization publicized Schultz's phone number and encouraged its members to express their disapproval; Schultz began receiving threats. The NRA helped organize a boycott of the company. The boycott led to Smith & Wesson's sales dropping by 40 percent and to the closure of two factories. In less than a year, Smith & Wesson's stock had lost 95 percent of its value, and the company's British owner sold it to an American buyer for a fraction of what it had been worth a few years before.

The company was able to regain its status as one of the country's top firearms manufacturers by completely repudiating the terms of the Clinton-era settlement—a decision eased by the Bush administration's decision not to enforce the terms of the agreement—and introducing its first assault-style rifle.

In 2005, the NRA lobbied hard for the Protection of Lawful Commerce in Arms Act, a federal bill that prohibited lawsuits against firearms manufacturers, distributors, and dealers for harms "resulting from the criminal or unlawful misuse" of their products. The PLCAA had a massive chilling effect on litigation against the firearms industry, effectively eliminating any incentive for the firearms industry to make its products safer. It has resulted in what Andrew Jay McClurg has termed the "Second Amendment right to be negligent":

> Subject to some narrow exceptions, the PLCAA bars all actions against
> gun manufacturers for harm caused by the criminal misuse of a firearm,
> including negligent marketing and distribution claims for failing to act
> reasonably to monitor, train, or terminate corrupt or negligent dealers,

even though they are known to be the principal conduits of guns used in crimes, or "crime guns." The PLCAA also precludes products liability design defect claims arising from volitional acts that are classified as unlawful, even in cases of accidental shootings that could have been prevented by a feasible alternative design. Because no federal gun safety design regulations exist, the absence of a threat of tort liability leaves gun manufacturers with little incentive to implement safer gun designs, such as personalized gun technology that would prevent unauthorized users from operating a firearm.[144]

In 2011, the CEO of the gun manufacturer Sturm, Ruger, & Co., stated that the PLCAA is "probably the only reason we have a U.S. firearms industry anymore."[145]

Who Gets to Use Guns?

Guns are far more likely to be used to inflict unlawful violence than to protect against unlawful violence, and these risks are not evenly distributed across society. Far from being an equalizer, gun use worsens existing disparities in the ability of individuals to protect themselves. The groups most vulnerable to violence are also the groups least able to protect themselves using guns. As discussed above, when it comes to the right of self-defense, the state overprotects white men and underprotects women and nonwhite men. Conflating the right to self-defense with access to and willingness to use firearms undermines rather than enhances the ability of women and black men to protect themselves. While guns are poor tools of self-defense for everyone, they are especially impractical and dangerous tools for women and nonwhite men.

Women and black men have different self-defense needs than white men, needs that are particularly poorly served by firearms. Women and black men are also held to a very different standard than white men when they do engage in deadly force. Self-defense laws were written with the primary goal of protecting white men's prerogative to use violence both inside and outside the home.[146] The law has historically discouraged both women and black men from engaging in defensive violence and treats them harshly when they do.

In early America, a woman who killed her husband would be guilty of petty treason; in modern-day America, women face lengthy prison sentences for shooting abusive partners. Throughout America's history, gun laws were used to prevent black men from carrying weapons; today, black men who carry or use weapons are frequently met with suspicion, harassment, and violence.

Women face far greater risks of sexual assault and intimate partner violence than men do. According to a study by the Centers for Disease Control and Prevention, there were nearly 1.3 million rapes of women in the United States in 2010. The vast majority of women (80 percent) are sexually assaulted by men they know, in situations that would make it highly impractical or dangerous to have access to a weapon (such as on a date, in bed, drinking at a party). While it is possible that a woman could in some situations use a gun to ward off a sexual assault, there is no indication that this happens frequently enough to balance the vast increase of risk and injury that gun access creates.[147]

Women account for 84 percent of domestic violence victims.[148] In the United States, more than three women a day are murdered by current or former intimate partners.[149] Nearly one in three women has experienced violence by a current or former intimate partner.[150] A woman is killed every 16 hours by an intimate partner with a gun.[151] "About 4.5 million have had an intimate partner threaten them with a gun and nearly 1 million have been shot or shot at by an intimate partner."[152] The violent confrontations women are most likely to face involve people whom the victims love and trust, in situations in which few women are likely to have weapons at the ready.

When guns are available in the home, they are statistically far more likely to endanger rather than protect women. The presence of a gun in a domestic violence situation increases a woman's chance of homicide by 500 percent.[153] As discussed in more detail below, women who use deadly force to defend themselves against abusive partners are treated extremely harshly by the law. "Most battered women who kill in self-defense end up in prison. . . . There is a well-documented bias against women [in these cases]."[154]

Blacks experience more crime victimization than any other racial group,[155] and yet their ability to defend themselves—with guns or otherwise—is severely curtailed by racial bias in the general public, law enforcement, and the criminal justice system as a whole. Black men's attempts to exercise self-defense—or even merely to stand up for themselves—are often perceived as displays of unlawful force, with deadly results. The role of racial bias, both explicit and implicit, in the perception of threats is at least one factor in the extraordinarily high rates of extrajudicial killings of black men, which one study reports as occurring once every 28 hours.[156] While white open-carry activists can march unmolested through town squares and grocery stores with loaded rifles slung across their backs, black men and boys with toy guns (and sometimes no guns at all) are gunned down by police officers and neighborhood watchmen.[157]

According to one study of race and firearms,

> Race stereotypes can lead people to claim to see a weapon where there is none. Split-second decisions magnify the bias by limiting people's ability to control responses. Such a bias could have important consequences for decision making by police officers and other authorities interacting with racial minorities. The bias requires no intentional racial animus, occurring even for those who are actively trying to avoid it.[158]

As one scholar put it, "law-abiding men of color are . . . more likely to be harassed simply for choosing to carry a gun."[159]

In 2014 in Ohio, an open-carry state, a black man named John Crawford was shot dead by police in a Walmart aisle after he picked up an air rifle from a display; a few months later, police shot and killed a black 12-year-old boy named Tamir Rice after he was seen carrying what turned out to be a pellet gun. In 2016 in Minnesota, a state that allows concealed-carry permit holders to open carry, police shot and killed Philando Castile after Castile informed them that he had a permit and a lawful weapon in the car he was driving. One might reasonably expect that the NRA would condemn Castile's murder, especially when one recalls NRA Vice President LaPierre's professed outrage in 1995 that "if you have a badge, you have the government's go-ahead to harass, intimidate, *even murder* law-abiding citizens," but the NRA said nothing.[160]

The NRA has not encouraged black people to engage in armed insurrection in the face of continuing brutalization at the hands of government.
It has offered no criticism of the militarized response to African Americans
assembling to protest police brutality and other injustices. When Black
Lives Matter protesters are met with SWAT teams, armored shields, and
even tanks, the NRA suddenly has nothing to say about the government's
use of force against citizens.[161]

The gun lobby's racial double standard has a long history:

> White Second Amendment advocates . . . are often framed as patriots, but
> black activists with guns have historically been perceived as insurgents. In
> fact, modern gun control was spurred in part by the Black Panther Party
> for Self-Defense's embrace of firearms in the late 60s, with conservatives
> like California governor Ronald Reagan signing bills restricting the rights
> of gun owners. Later, this group was eviscerated by local and federal law
> enforcement through assassination, surveillance, and covert sabotage.[162]

The equation of self-defense with gun use is reductive and dangerous
to the general welfare. But the harms it imposes are not shared equally
across all groups. The people who are most in need of a robust right to self-
defense are the ones least well served by Second Amendment fundamentalism. The gun rights agenda increases the vulnerability of these groups and
undermines their ability to exert their right to self-defense. The hijacking
of self-defense by the gun rights narrative further entrenches sexist and
racist inequality and reinforces the use of force as a white male privilege.

Who Gets to Stand Their Ground?
Given this background, a constitutional commitment to self-defense—one
that seeks to protect the rights of all groups equally—should be primarily
concerned with addressing the denial of women and minorities' rights to
protect themselves. The conservative interpretation of the Second Amendment as the right to gun use has done just the opposite. The triumphs of
Second Amendment fundamentalism serve the interests of only one group:
white men. The gun rights lobby opposes prohibitions against bringing
loaded weapons into bars, churches, daycares, and colleges; fights training

requirements for permit holders; helps domestic abusers retain access to deadly weapons; demands that people be allowed to walk around public parks and streets with assault rifles slung across their backs; and has modified the concept of self-defense through stand-your-ground laws that encourage people to shoot their way out of avoidable disputes. None of these accomplishments make women or minorities safer; in fact, these actions increase women and nonwhite men's vulnerability to violence. They do, however, serve the interests of gun owners, the majority of whom are white and male and apparently terrified of being in any situation without a gun immediately at hand.

Florida passed the first so-called stand-your-ground law in the United States in 2005. Within ten years, thirty-three states had followed Florida's lead, transforming the concept of self-defense and use of deadly force in the United States.

As discussed above, the lethality and volatility (both intended and unintended) of firearms make them poor tools for self-defense, particularly in the hands of untrained individuals. Predictably, then, stand-your-ground laws have not only failed to deter crime, but have been instrumental in promoting and defending escalation to deadly force in situations that do not call for it. Homicide rates increased in states after they passed stand-your-ground laws, and states with stand-your-ground laws have higher homicide rates than states without them.

Moreover, the disastrous effects of stand-your-ground laws are not equally distributed across the population: The laws encourage the use of deadly force by those with the least need for it against those with the greatest. In particular, these laws exploit the racial biases underlying Americans' exaggerated fear of crime as well as rolling back the modest protections that victims of domestic violence—a group uniquely in need of a robust right to self-defense—have achieved after decades of reform efforts.

While proponents of Florida's stand-your-ground law like to claim that the legislative reform was the result of public demand, it was actually the product of NRA lobbyists and the American Legislative Exchange Council (ALEC), "the shadowy Koch brothers-funded network that brings together right-wing legislators with corporate interests and pressure groups to craft so-called 'model legislation.'"[163] The language of the bill was drafted by Marion Hammer, a former president of the NRA, founder of one of the NRA's Florida affiliate organizations, the Unified Sportsmen of Florida,[164] and, as the *New Yorker* put it, "the National Rifle Association's Florida lobbyist."[165] "There is no single individual responsible for enacting more pro-gun legislation in the states than Marion Hammer," according to Richard Feldman, a former political organizer for the NRA.[166]

Hammer's powerful advocacy for the stand-your-ground bill was built on what the *Rolling Stone* characterized as a "convenient tale": "Hammer claimed to have been stalked in a parking garage by six men, one of whom wielded a 'long-necked beer bottle' before she pulled out her .38 and aimed."[167] Hammer did not file a police report, but, she asserts, a police chief told her that had she shot the men, she could have been arrested.[168] One could hardly have invented a more compelling story to illustrate the need for stand-your-ground laws.

In 2005, Hammer gave an interview with the Center for Individual Freedom about the recently enacted law. In this interview, Hammer claimed that before 2005, the duty to retreat in Florida meant that

> if someone had tried to drag a woman into an alley to rape her, the women [sic]—even though she might be licensed to carry concealed and ready to protect herself, the law would not allow her to do it. It required her to try to get away and run and be chased down by the perpetrator before she could then use force to protect herself.[169]

Several years later, after the shooting of Trayvon Martin prompted scrutiny of the law, Florida politicians Don and Matt Gaetz (father and son) railed against critics of the stand-your-ground law by parroting Hammer:

> Consider an elderly woman in a dimly lit parking lot or a college girl walking to her dorm at night. If either was attacked, her duty was to turn her back and try to flee, probably be overcome and raped or killed. Prior to stand-your-ground, that victim didn't have the choice to defend herself, to meet force with force.[170]

It is notable, first, how the examples used by stand-your-ground proponents so often focus on confrontations with violent strangers, and in
particular stranger rape. This is striking not only because conservative
politicians tend to ignore or downplay the existence of sexual assault in
almost every context other than armed self-defense,[171] but also because
sexual assault is overwhelmingly a crime perpetrated in private by people
known to the victim.[172] Similarly, the "active shooter in the mall" scenario
is incredibly rare,[173] and one that does not readily lend itself to resolution
by an individual "standing his ground."[174]

Regardless, the claim that stand-your-ground laws are essential to an
effective right of self-defense and that the "duty to retreat" is practically
a death (or at least a rape) sentence bears closer examination. There are
considerable variations in the stand-your-ground laws of the thirty-three
states that have them, but their common characteristics are the elimination
of the "duty to retreat" from confrontations anywhere a person has the
right to be—hence the reference to "standing one's ground"—and broad
immunity provisions for those who successfully claim the defense.

Prior to the rise of these laws, traditional self-defense doctrine in the
United States and England included a "duty to retreat" from confrontations
outside the home. By emphasizing that deadly force should only be used as
a last resort, the duty to retreat rule reflected the value of preserving human
life. The duty to retreat is not absolute, however. First, the duty to retreat
generally did not apply inside the home—an exception known as the "castle
doctrine."[175] Second, the duty to retreat was generally considered to apply
only when an individual could retreat in "complete safety." That is, a person
was not required to retreat from a confrontation if she did not reasonably
believe she could do so without risking serious injury or death. In Florida
specifically, a person was only required, before 2005, to use "every *reasonable* means" to avoid danger before resorting to deadly force: "[A] person
may not resort to deadly force without first using every reasonable means
within his or her power to avoid the danger, including retreat."[176]

These longstanding qualifications of the duty to retreat rule are significant because they contradict the narrative that the rule condemned
law-abiding citizens to being shot down or raped in alleyways. A "college girl" attacked on her way to her dorm would not have been forced,

pre-2005, to "turn her back and try to flee, probably be overcome and raped or killed." If a victim reasonably feared that she would be raped or killed, and that fleeing would not prevent her from being raped or killed, then fleeing would not be a "reasonable means" of avoiding danger. Such a victim would have been within her rights before 2005 to stand and fight.

Proponents of stand-your-ground laws claim that citizens using justifiable force are required to languish in legal limbo, but there is scant evidence to support this assertion. A 2014 report by the American Bar Association Task Force noted that "proponents of Stand Your Ground laws could point to no examples of cases wherein traditional self-defense law would not have protected a law-abiding individual operating in justified self-defense."[177] As Pennsylvania District Attorney Edward Marsico Jr. characterized it, stand-your-ground "is a solution looking for a problem."[178]

Florida's stand-your-ground law was sold to the public as a necessary measure to protect "innocent people."[179] But like other states with stand-your-ground laws, Florida has seen an increase in homicides since passing the law.[180] The *Tampa Bay Times'* review of over a hundred fatal stand-your-ground cases in Florida found has seen that nearly half of individuals invoking the self-defense law had been arrested at least three times—many for violent offenses—before they killed someone.[181] More than a third had previously threatened someone with a gun or illegally carried a weapon. Far from having a deterrent effect on crime, the law appears to benefit repeat criminals.

The *Tampa Bay Times* study also revealed that a defendant who killed a black victim had a 73 percent chance of getting a dismissal based on stand-your-ground, compared to a 59 percent chance for those who killed white victims.[182] In short, the effects of Florida's stand-your-ground law have been an increase in homicides, protection for repeat criminals, aggravated racial and gender disparities, and heightened confusion created by the immunity provisions for the use of justifiable force.

Stand-your-ground laws have had similar effects across the nation. A white shooter killing a black victim is 350 percent more likely to be found justified than if the same shooter killed a white victim.[183] Studies show that the laws have no deterrent effect on crime and encourage escalation in confrontations.[184] Other studies demonstrate that states experienced a 7.1 percent increase in homicides after adopting stand-your-ground laws.[185] Experts note that stand-your-ground laws in some states allow individuals more freedom to use deadly force than soldiers in combat situations:

> U.S. service members operating in the most hostile environments . . . must consider the feasibility of less than lethal action when confronting threats on today's nonlinear battlefield. It is troubling that under Stand Your Ground, there are less restrictions imposed on US service members using deadly force when they return to the United States than when they are deployed in a combat environment.[186]

Moreover, the destructive influence of stand-your-ground cannot be fully captured only by the outcomes of specific cases. The promotion of a shoot-first mentality has deadly consequences even if individual defendants fail to raise or succeed on a specific stand-your-ground claim.

Consider the case of Joe Horn, a Texas stand-your-ground incident from 2007. Horn, 61, observed two men burglarizing his neighbor's home. In his 911 call, he suggested that he should go out and shoot the men. The operator advised him repeatedly to stay inside, telling Horn that "property isn't worth killing anyone over." Horn responded, "The laws have been changed in this country since September the first, and you know it," referring to the Texas version of the stand-your-ground law, which had passed on September 1, 2007.[187] Horn left his house with his shotgun; in the 911 call he is heard confronting the suspects, saying, "Move and you're dead," immediately followed by the sound of three shotgun blasts. When Horn got back on the phone with the operator, he shouted, "They came in the front yard with me, man, I had no choice!" A plainclothes police detective who had arrived at the scene saw Horn shoot both men in the back but did not arrest Horn. Police later identified the dead men as Colombian nationals with criminal records. A grand jury was convened in Horn's case, but no charges were brought against him.[188] Horn was hailed as a hero by many in Texas and elsewhere.[189]

More notoriously, the law came under fire in Florida following George Zimmerman's shooting of unarmed black teenager Trayvon Martin,[190] followed only a few months later by Michael Dunn's shooting of unarmed black teenager Jordan Davis.[191] Proponents insisted that such unpopular cases had "nothing to do" with stand-your-ground.[192] But the mere fact that a defendant might not raise a stand-your-ground claim—or may not prevail in doing so—does not mean the case does not implicate stand-your-ground. Laws should be assessed based not only on particular legal outcomes but also on the impact they have on human behavior. It is quite clear that many people *believe* that stand-your-ground laws give them the right to use deadly force in a wide variety of situations and act accordingly.

A less famous stand-your-ground case than Zimmerman's, and one with very different results, made it abundantly clear that the law has done nothing to improve the lot of women who use defensive force against abusive partners.[193] While promoters of stand-your-ground and gun rights rhetoric have tried to use women and domestic violence victims as poster children for their campaigns, Marissa Alexander's case is an illustration of how hollow these claims really are.

Alexander, an African American woman, was estranged from her husband, Rico Grey, and had previously obtained a protection order against him because of his physical abuse. Shortly after giving birth to their child, however, she invited him to their home to see some pictures of the baby. Grey brought along two of his other children to the house. When Alexander went to the bathroom, Grey started looking through her phone and found some text messages that he did not like. Enraged, Grey blocked her from leaving the bathroom, accusing her of cheating on him and telling her she could not leave. Alexander managed to break away and flee to her truck in the garage, but then realized that the garage door opener would not work. Before she went back to the house, she took the gun that she lawfully owned from the truck. Upon re-entering the house, Alexander told Grey, "You have to go," and he replied, "I am not going anywhere." She fired what she characterized as a warning shot to try to get him to leave, and he left unharmed with his two children.

Alexander's case seems to be exactly the kind of scenario stand-your-ground laws are meant to address. Alexander was defending herself in her own home from someone she knew—not merely presumed—was a threat, because he had in the past threatened to kill her if she ever cheated on him and had beaten her seriously enough on a prior occasion to put her in the hospital. But not only did the police arrest her on the spot after Grey called 911 (compared to the two months it took for Zimmerman to be arrested, and that only after extensive media attention), but Alexander was denied stand-your-ground immunity at a special hearing because, the judge indicated, Alexander was angry, not afraid, when she shot at Grey and had other options to exit the situation.

Alexander was convicted and sentenced to twenty years. As Florida Congresswoman Corrine Brown wrote in response to the verdict,

> The Florida criminal justice system has sent two clear messages today. One is that if women who are victims of domestic violence try to protect themselves, the Stand Your Ground law will not apply to them . . . the second is that if you are Black, the system will treat you differently.[194]

Alexander was later granted a retrial because of an error in the trial court jury instructions, but she was again denied stand-your-ground immunity. She eventually accepted a plea deal of three years in prison, which she had already served, as well as two years of house arrest.[195] Alexander's case should have outraged the stand-your-ground supporters who claim to care about victims being forced to helplessly submit to violent attacks, and yet the NRA and other stand-your-ground proponents were silent.[196]

When women like Alexander do use deadly force against abusive partners, they face precisely the kind of legal uncertainty and punishment that stand-your-ground proponents purport to criticize. But not only do stand-your-ground proponents fail to advocate on behalf of domestic violence victims upon whom an unreasonable duty to retreat has historically been imposed, but they explicitly single out this group as uniquely unable to avail themselves of protection under the law.

Marion Hammer, the chief architect of stand-your-ground, has made it abundantly clear that the law was not meant to aid domestic violence victims. When asked whether stand-your-ground laws should apply to domestic violence situations, Hammer responded, "You can't simply take action against an estranged spouse who breaks into the home if they own the home. You have to be under attack in those situations." In other words, a man can presume that a stranger trying to open his door intends to do him harm and is thus presumed to be justified in using deadly force, but a battered wife cannot presume that her abusive husband breaking down the door intends to harm her. She cannot presume this even if he has promised to kill her if she locks him out one more time, or if he has told her he would beat her to death if she ever tried to leave him. She is supposed to wait until the moment he comes at her with a gun or a knife before she is allowed to use deadly force—notwithstanding the fact that such force will almost certainly come too late.

The right to self-defense, if it means anything, must mean more than a single-minded focus on blunt instruments of death. It should take into account and evaluate the actual realities of violence: who uses it, how, and why.

The average American has statistically very little reason to fear crime, and those at the top of the current social hierarchy have even less. Wealthy white men have never been the primary targets of violent crime, and yet it is their interests and their view of the world that now dominate not only the legal but the social understanding of self-defense. The right to self-defense has been hijacked by the gun rights movement, which in turn has been hijacked by the most privileged members of our society. The NRA promotes stand-your-ground laws because it wants to keep Americans in a constant state of fear. A fearful population is a consumer population, and the insistence that only guns can save us keeps the bullets and the money flowing.

THE COSTS OF SECOND AMENDMENT FUNDAMENTALISM

On July 19, 2016, Chris W. Cox, the executive director of the National Rifle Association's Institute for Legislative Action, delivered an address at the Republican National Convention that was a textbook illustration of Second Amendment fundamentalism. It trotted out all of the gun lobby's favorite clichés: "We live in dangerous times"; "government has failed to keep us safe"; we all need a "good guy with a gun." The 2016 election, according to Cox, was no less than a referendum on the Second Amendment, which was in turn no less than "your right to protect your life." Calling the NRA "the largest and oldest civil rights organization in America," Cox claimed that the organization "fight[s] for the rights of all

Americans, regardless of race, religion or sexual orientation . . . because the right to protect your life is the most precious right you have." Cox closed by gravely intoning "The only way we save [this freedom] is by electing Donald Trump the next president of the United States."[197]

At a campaign rally in Iowa just a few months before, Donald Trump had bragged, "I could stand in the middle of 5th Avenue and shoot somebody and I wouldn't lose voters."[198] Responsible gun owners—good guys with guns—should have recoiled at such a statement coming from anyone, least of all a candidate for the highest office in the land. This was not a statement that indicated serious respect for guns or a principled commitment to the Second Amendment. A presidential candidate joking about being entitled to engage in random gun violence when 33,000 people are killed by guns every year should have drawn criticism from organizations claiming to promote the responsible use of firearms. Not only did the NRA not criticize Trump's comments, but it went on to throw its full support behind him.

A couple of months later, in September 2016, the man the NRA called the only hope for saving the Second Amendment advocated "taking guns away" from people on the street. Trump stated in an interview with *Fox and Friends* that if police officers

> see a person possibly with a gun or they think may have a gun, they will see the person, and they will look, and they will take the gun away. . . . They will stop, they will frisk, and they will take the gun away, and they don't have anything to shoot with.[199]

The statement raised eyebrows, though again, the NRA was silent. In stark contrast to the organization's repeated claims that Hillary Clinton wanted to take citizens' guns away based on her criticism of the *Heller* decision, the NRA said nothing about Trump's explicit call for the confiscation of weapons. Rather than criticizing Trump, it poured $30 million into helping him get elected.

Trump "clarified" his statement about gun confiscation a few days later, saying that he was "really referring to Chicago." This clarification seems to be nothing other than a barely coded reference to race: "Chicago" implies black men and black crime. Trump's maneuver was reminiscent of Ronald Reagan's selective support of gun control in 1960s California, aimed at neutralizing the threat of the Black Panthers and armed African American resistance.

The NRA's silence on Trump's statement—along with its silence on the militarized response to African American protesters, the murders of gun-carrying African Americans, and the denial of stand-your-ground defenses for women who use guns in self-defense—makes plain that the Second Amendment right it claims to defend for "all Americans" is in fact reserved exclusively for white men.

The cult of the Second Amendment allows the most powerful groups in society to promote and reap the benefits of the false narrative of white male persecution. The claimed constitutional commitment to self-defense is in reality a cover for perpetuating and monetizing white men's monopoly on deadly force. The costs of encouraging this force are not equally borne across society. The propaganda churned out by the NRA and other members of the gun lobby convinces many white men that guns assure not only their safety but their status.

In addition to endangering public safety and increasing gender and racial inequalities in the exercise of self-defense, Second Amendment fundamentalism also jeopardizes other constitutional rights. An isolated and radical focus on one right compromises the entire constitutional ecosystem. In particular, the transformation of the right to bear arms into a superright that trumps all other rights has dramatic consequences for the right of free speech. Second Amendment fundamentalism has served as a justification for varied attempts to literally stifle speech—from preventing physicians from asking about guns in the home to expunging the records of people granted stand-your-ground immunity.

The display of loaded weapons allowed by open-carry laws directly infringes upon the First Amendment freedom of expression. People cannot express themselves freely when they fear grave bodily injury or death. A person in possession of a loaded gun has the capacity to inflict imminent and fatal injury, which necessarily chills freedom of expression of those around them. This chilling effect, like other pernicious effects of gun use, is felt most acutely by the least powerful members of society.

Open-carry proponents have recently begun to claim, however, that the display of firearms in public is, in addition to being justified by the Second Amendment, also an exercise of the First: "Open carrying a firearm is an action; it is symbolic speech because it is a public statement. As history has shown us, actions and public statements, are protected by the First Amendment under symbolic speech," argues Tyler Yzaguirre, co-founder and president of the Second Amendment Institute.[200]

Not for nothing does the right refer to the unregulated carrying of weapons, concealed or openly, with permits or without, as "constitutional carry." In the cult of the gun, firearms are not just a part of the Constitution: They are the Constitution. When Second Amendment fundamentalism and First Amendment fundamentalism combine, constitutional rights become even more inextricable from white men's privileges.

CHAPTER 3

THE CULT OF FREE SPEECH

AMENDMENT I

Congress shall make no law . . . abridging the freedom of speech, or of the press; or the right of the people peaceably to assemble, and to petition the government for a redress of grievances.

"The best cure for bad speech is more speech."
        –ACLU of Nevada, Challenging the UNLV Hate Speech Policy

On May 26, 2017, Jeremy Joseph Christian boarded a local light rail train in Portland, Oregon. On the train were two teenage girls, one of whom was wearing a hijab, a traditional Muslim head covering for women. Christian began screaming at the two girls: "Go home, we need Americans here!" "I don't care if you are ISIS," "Fuck Saudi Arabia!" and "Free speech or die!" As the girls moved away from Christian, three passengers—Taliesin Myrddin Namkai-Meche, Rick Best, and Micah Fletcher—attempted to intervene. Christian stabbed each of the men with a knife he had concealed in his hand, killing Namkai-Meche and Best and severely wounding Fletcher.[1]

A month before the killings, Christian had attended a "March for Free Speech" rally organized by rightwing groups in Portland, where he had been seen giving Nazi salutes, using racial slurs, and making violent threats.[2] At his arraignment, Christian yelled out "Free speech or die, Portland. You got no safe place. This is America—get out if you don't like free speech."[3]

FIRST AMENDMENT FUNDAMENTALISM

Three days before alt-right demonstrators descended upon Charlottesville in 2017, *The Hill* published an op-ed that urged advocates of open carry to use the First Amendment as a justification for their position. "The First Amendment has historically been much more difficult to limit than the Second, so extending Freedom of Speech to encompass the open display of firearms needs to be addressed," wrote Tyler Yzaguirre, the co-founder and president of the Second Amendment Institute.[4] That this argument is not immediately implausible is an indication of the expansiveness of contemporary free speech doctrine and an illustration of the similarities between First and Second Amendment fundamentalists.

While their political loyalties may not often be aligned, First Amendment fundamentalists share many characteristics with Second Amendment fundamentalists. They are both deeply invested in a social identity that claims to value autonomy, expression, and individual independence, and both characterize the harm they impose on unwilling members of society as necessary for the greater good. They both tend to speak in absolutist terms about constitutional commitment yet read the Constitution selectively to favor their preferred rights—expanding when it comes to the interests of white men and contracting when it comes to the interests of women and minorities.

Both First Amendment and Second Amendment fundamentalists make use of constitutional propaganda that inverts power dynamics, portraying privileged individuals as vulnerable and vulnerable individuals as privileged. Ever-expanding definitions of what counts as "free speech" give constitutional cover to practices that disproportionately harm women and minorities, while attempts to ensure women and minorities' equal exercise of freedom of expression is labeled "censorship." Threats, harassment, and stalking that endanger the physical safety, psychological health, employment opportunities, educational experiences, and intimate relationships of women and minorities are left unregulated in the name of protecting "everyone's" right to free speech, while meaningful attempts to limit the impact of these forms of abuse are denounced as attacks on constitutionally protected expression. Fundamentalists transform the right to free speech, like the right to bear arms, into a sword as well as a shield to be wielded against women and minorities.

While conservative First Amendment fundamentalists are often gleeful about the potential to use the Constitution to limit the rights of women and minorities, liberal First Amendment fundamentalists often express regret that their high-minded free speech principles result in harsh consequences. Regardless of how its adherents feel about the outcomes, free speech fundamentalism has devastating effects on historically subordinated groups.

Today, conservative and liberal positions on political correctness, corporate speech, censorship, and academic freedom are often indistinguishable. The left–right First Amendment alliance, fueled in large part by the increasing corporate libertarianism of the ACLU and the Supreme Court, has helped transform free speech doctrine into a tool of the most privileged and powerful members of society.

The Role of the ACLU

Civil liberties groups play an important role in constitutional fundamentalism, whether liberal or conservative, by helping shape the narrative of constitutional rights and promoting solidarity—-or groupthink—among likeminded individuals. The NRA and the ACLU, while often perceived as political polar opposites, both claim to be nonpartisan organizations dedicated to upholding the Constitution. The NRA calls itself "the nation's largest and oldest civil rights organization," while the ACLU identifies itself in almost identical terms: "the nation's largest and oldest civil liberties organization."[5] The NRA claims "to fight for the rights of all Americans, regardless of race, religion or sexual orientation,"[6] and the ACLU claims to fight for "Native Americans and other people of color; lesbians, gay men, bisexuals and transgender people; women; mental patients; prisoners; people with disabilities; and the poor."[7]

The NRA does predate the ACLU—it was founded in 1871, nearly fifty years before the ACLU was founded in 1920—but it is doubtful that many people outside of its own membership would associate the group with either civil rights or civil liberties.[8] By contrast, the ACLU's longtime advocacy on issues such as desegregation, voting rights, criminal justice, immigration, law enforcement abuses, and reproductive rights has firmly established its reputation as a defender of the vulnerable.[9]

The ACLU's early free speech activism reflected an explicit concern for social justice, taking up the causes of laborers and political dissidents. But as Laura Weinrib details in *The Taming of Free Speech*, the ACLU's championing of free speech and other constitutional rights gradually became untethered from its social justice underpinnings.[10]

In recent decades, the ACLU has devoted considerable free speech resources to neo-Nazis, gun rights groups, the KKK, the North American Man/Boy Love Association (NAMBLA), the porn industry, the tobacco industry, and Donald Trump. The distastefulness of many of these beneficiaries supposedly underscores the high-mindedness of the ACLU's commitment to free speech. Those who sense less pure motives are dismissed as prudish or fainthearted, incapable of understanding the civil libertarian wisdom that protecting the worst among us is the only way to protect the best, that the cure for bad speech is more speech, and that no matter how much actual harm bad speech causes, any regulation of that speech would be infinitely worse.

Like the NRA, the ACLU invests heavily in the narrative of white male persecution. That narrative distorts the right to free speech in much the same way that the it distorts the right to bear arms: The mere *possibility* that white men's speech might be slightly curtailed is regarded as an unimaginable horror while the systematic silencing of women and minorities is dismissed as mere inconvenience. The ACLU's free speech alarmism mirrors the NRA's gun alarmism, warning the faithful that any number of nefarious forces—the government, social media platforms, universities—are waiting to strip them of their constitutional rights at the first lapse in vigilance. Indeed, the ACLU has on multiple occasions openly joined forces with Second Amendment fundamentalists, helping gun rights groups sue public libraries,[11] assisting gun owners in recovering firearms,[12] and vowing to defend "the individual's right to bear arms subject to constitutionally permissible regulations . . . as it defends other constitutional rights."[13] Like the NRA, the ACLU wields great influence over political leaders, has deep ties to major corporations, and supported the expansion of First Amendment rights to corporations in the Supreme Court case *Citizens United.*

According to the ACLU's website, "In many ways, the ACLU is the nation's most conservative organization." Though the statement was meant to underscore the organization's protection of "America's original civic values," it reveals an unintentional truth. In its prioritization of white men's free speech rights and its ties to corporate interests, the ACLU is, indeed, a deeply conservative, and fundamentalist, organization. According to Richard Delgado and David Yun,

> [T]he ACLU and conservative bigots are hand-in-glove. Like criminals and police, they understand each other's method of operation, mentality, and objectives. There is a tacit understanding of how each shall behave, and how each shall gain from the other. Indeed, primarily because the Ku Klux Klan and similar clients are so bad, the ACLU gets to feel romantic and virtuous—and the rest of us, who despise racism and bigotry, are seen as benighted fools because we do not understand how the First Amendment really works. . . . Sometimes, defending Nazis is simply defending Nazis.[14]

Today, the ACLU's approach to the First Amendment is thoroughly fundamentalist. What the NRA has done for the Second Amendment, the ACLU has done for the First: It promotes a simplistic orthodoxy built around the narrative of white male victimhood, the mythology of the free market, and populist and often patronizing clichés to ensure that the interests of white, male, often extremely wealthy men are protected above all others.

Free Speech Clichés

Self-proclaimed free speech defenders are fond of the expression "I disagree with what you say, but I will defend to the death your right to say it." While this platitude is often attributed to Voltaire, these are actually the words of Evelyn Beatrice Hall, who wrote a book on Voltaire more than a century after his death.[15] A similar sentiment is expressed in the phrase "freedom for the thought that we hate," which originated with Supreme Court Justice Oliver Wendell Holmes and served as the title of Anthony Lewis's influential book on the First Amendment. In his dissenting opinion in the 1929 case *United States v. Schwimmer*, Holmes wrote that "if there is any principle of the Constitution that more imperatively calls for attachment than any other, it is the principle of free thought—not free thought for those who agree with us but freedom for the thought that we hate."[16] The point is intuitively compelling: It is easy to fight to protect expression we agree with, but the true test of our commitment to the principle of free speech is if we are willing to fight for expression that we not only disagree with, but might actively despise.

Perhaps the most famous case illustrating the concept of "freedom for the thought that we hate" is *Collin v. Smith*, which involved a proposed Nazi march in Skokie, Illinois, in 1976. Members of the National Socialist Party of America (NSPA) announced their intention to march in Skokie, a Chicago suburb, wearing Nazi-style uniforms, displaying banners with swastikas on them, and holding placards reading "Free Speech for the White Man." Members distributed flyers and made unsolicited phone calls promoting the march to Skokie residents with Jewish-sounding names. At the time, around half of Skokie's population was Jewish, including hundreds of Holocaust survivors. The town of Skokie passed a series of ordinances to prevent the march from happening, which the NSPA, represented by David Goldberger of the ACLU, challenged in court. Eventually, the ordinances were found to violate the First Amendment, and the NSPA was given permission to march.

The NSPA march in Skokie never took place. The group had been threatening multiple marches in various suburbs after they were temporarily blocked from their usual rally site in Chicago's Marquette Park in 1976. Skokie was one of the few towns that responded to their provocation by passing ordinances to prevent them from making good on their threat. By the time the Skokie case was resolved, the group was cleared to hold their rally in Marquette Park, which it proceeded to do. According to Aryeh Neier, who served at the time as the ACLU's executive director, the lesson of Skokie is that "[i]n a country where free speech generally prevails, it is best to take hate speech in stride. Ignoring it sometimes works, as does overwhelming it with the peaceful expression of contrary views."[17]

The ACLU faced outrage from many in the Jewish community and experienced a significant drop in membership following the Skokie case, especially among Jewish members. David Goldberger, who is Jewish, faced particularly harsh criticism for his role in defending the NSPA. The Skokie case is only one of a number of unpopular cases the ACLU has taken on throughout its history, helping to cement its reputation as an organization willing to do the right thing even at great cost. This is a familiar point of civil libertarian rhetoric: Freedom is not free, and to enjoy the benefits of liberty, one must be willing to bear the costs.

The Skokie case thus seems to provide an elegant illustration of several revered and related free speech fundamentals: that the right of free speech must be defended absolutely, even when—or especially when—the speech or the speaker is hateful; that doing so protects the vulnerable as well as the powerful; that to restrict speech even for noble purposes has a "chilling effect" on freedom of expression; and that the best answer to bad speech is more speech. These are the cornerstones of the "marketplace of ideas" theory of free speech: When all ideas, even deeply offensive ideas, are allowed to freely circulate in the marketplace, the best ones will win out, and the truth will ultimately prevail. From this perspective, the gravest threat to freedom of speech is regulation, no matter how well intentioned.

The marketplace metaphor is, of course, an economic one, and a free-market capitalist one in particular. According to the free-market view, competition, not regulation, is the best way to maximize both individual and general welfare. Trying to forbid or violently confront hate speech not only violates established American constitutional principles, but is also counterproductive. Prohibition or violence may even elicit sympathy and support for hateful causes, and these tactics give groups like the Chicago Nazis the attention they crave, and without which they cannot survive.

Freedom for the thought we hate, the danger of chilling effects, and the merits of the marketplace of ideas are all settled tenets of First Amendment orthodoxy. As such, their validity is frequently assumed rather than demonstrated. Under close examination, however, these articles of faith do not prove to be deserving of such confidence.

The Thought We Hate?

"Hate" is a term that tends to generate more heat than light in the context of free speech. The mutually exclusive assertions that "the First Amendment protects hate speech" and "the First Amendment does not protect hate speech" are made with nearly equal frequency and confidence; both statements are essentially meaningless. "Hate speech" is not a legally recognized category, at least not by the Supreme Court. If what is meant by hate speech is merely unpleasant, unpopular, or crude expression, then it is true that the First Amendment protects hate speech. If what is meant by hate speech is true threats, incitement, defamation, obscenity, fighting words, or certain kinds of discriminatory expression, then it is not true that the First Amendment protects hate speech. "Hate" and "hatefulness" are subjective, vague, and arbitrary terms.

The meaning of "freedom for the thought we hate" is further obscured by the ambiguity of the word "we." All speech can be hateful to someone. Who is the "we" who must bear the speech they hate? The implications vary considerably depending on whether "we" are the general public, the Supreme Court, the Jewish community, or a neo-Nazi organization. What guidance, then, does the principle really provide? Does it mean that the Supreme Court should protect the speech hateful to Jews, the speech hateful neo-Nazis, or something else entirely?

As constitutional scholars know, the more vague and subjective a concept, the more susceptible it is to being interpreted in arbitrary and capricious ways. This is an accurate description of the concept of the "thought we hate." In explaining its solicitude toward hateful speech and why it so often defends "controversial and unpopular entities" such as neo-Nazis and the KKK, the ACLU states,

> We do not defend them because we agree with them; rather, we defend their right to free expression and free assembly. Historically, the people whose opinions are the most controversial or extreme are the people whose rights are most often threatened. Once the government has the power to violate one person's rights, it can use that power against everyone. . . . [W]e subscribe to the principle that if the rights of society's most vulnerable members are denied, everybody's rights are imperiled.[18]

This is an illuminating answer, though probably not in the way the ACLU intends. The professed animating principle—that the rights of the vulnerable should be protected not only for their sake but for the sake of the general welfare—is unimpeachable. It echoes the social justice insights of Kimberlé Crenshaw's intersectional scholarship and Mari Matsuda's concept of "looking to the bottom." But the way the passage actually defines vulnerability distorts the principle beyond recognition.

Notice the rhetorical slippage from "unpopular entities" to "controversial or extreme" opinions to "threatened rights" to "society's most vulnerable members." It is a skillful sleight of hand: *Unpopular entities* with *controversial and extreme opinions* are *vulnerable people* whose *rights are threatened*. But whether a group is unpopular or an opinion is controversial is, of course, in the eye of the beholder. Even more importantly, being unpopular is not the same as being vulnerable, and being disliked is not the same as being threatened.[19]

By equating being disliked with being vulnerable, the ACLU is able to argue that they protect groups like Nazis, KKK members, and pornographers because they are the most vulnerable members of society. This is perverse for two reasons. First, these groups are neither universally disliked nor vulnerable in any objective sense; they enjoy considerable popularity and power. Second, classifying these groups as vulnerable erases truly vulnerable groups who are often exploited by the very groups that the ACLU is spending its considerable resources to protect.

What unites many of the groups that the ACLU protects is that they are dominated by white, often wealthy men who espouse white male supremacist ideology. White male supremacy can hardly be considered a "controversial" or "unpopular" view in a country that was literally founded on the concept. Overtly racist and anti-Semitic views, while waxing and waning over time, have become increasingly mainstreamed in the last decade. A 2017 poll found that more than a third of Americans "strongly or somewhat agreed that 'America must protect and preserve its White European heritage,'" and nearly 40 percent agreed with the statement that "white people are currently under attack in this country."[20]

Far from being persecuted, KKK members have exerted considerable political and cultural influence throughout America's history, including serving in law enforcement and on the Supreme Court. The man elected president in 2016 ran on a platform of white male supremacy and is widely viewed by the KKK and the alt-right as a champion of their worldview. If opinions routinely voiced by the president, the attorney general, and many others in the White House—broadcast incessantly on media outlets such as Fox News and Breitbart and featured prominently on major social media platforms and websites—can be considered "controversial" and "extreme," then those words have lost all meaning. The ACLU's equation of white male supremacy with vulnerability plays directly into the false and dangerous narrative of white male persecution.

Chilling Effects

One of the most common justifications for aggressive interpretations of the First Amendment is the concern about "chilling effects." In Leslie Kendrick's description, a chilling effect "is a concern that an otherwise legitimate rule will curb protected expression outside its ambit. This phenomenon generally arises when would-be speakers, faced with the uncertainties of the legal process, refrain from making protected statements."[21] In other words, restrictions of even *unprotected* speech are dangerous because of their potential to discourage *protected* speech.

When courts strike down laws for "overbreadth" or "vagueness," they often do so for reasons relating to chilling effects. Overly broad laws restrict not only unprotected speech but protected speech, whereas vague laws make it difficult for people to know what speech is restricted and what is not. According to the theory of chilling effects, both kinds of laws create the risk that citizens will self-censor or be otherwise deterred from engaging in protected speech.

The Supreme Court has also used the concern about self-censorship to invalidate laws that are neither overly broad nor vague. In *New York Times v. Sullivan* (1964), the Court held that a public official suing for defamation must prove that the speaker or publisher of the statement acted with "actual malice," which the Court defined as either knowing that the statement was false or acting with reckless disregard to its truth or falsity. Defamation is not protected by the First Amendment; nonetheless, the Court held that because "erroneous statement is inevitable in free debate . . . it must be protected if the freedoms of expression are to have the 'breathing space' that they 'need to survive.'" The case in effect used the First Amendment to grant an affirmative right of negligent defamation with regard to public officials, a right later extended to all public figures.

The concern about chilling effects is not limited to government action. Like all the rights enumerated in the Bill of Rights, the First Amendment is a restraint upon government or "state" (in the general sense) action. Private citizens do not have First Amendment rights against each other, and private companies, with limited exceptions, have no First Amendment responsibilities. For example, a private citizen has no First Amendment obligation to listen to a religious proselytizer or a political lobbyist on her doorstep; she can shut the door in anyone's face without running afoul of the First Amendment. "Censorship," in the strict legal sense, refers only to actions taken by the government to restrict speech.

However, civil liberties organizations such as the ACLU and the Electronic Frontier Foundation (EFF) (discussed in more detail in the next chapter) argue that the actions of private companies can also create chilling effects. The EFF is a co-founder of a project called Onlinecensorship. org, which tracks and critiques the content moderation policies of major social media companies. According to Jillian York, EFF's director for International Freedom of Expression, these "companies by and large do not consider their policies to constitute censorship. We challenge this assertion, and examine how their policies (and their enforcement) may have a chilling effect on freedom of expression."[22]

Many social media users seem to share in this perspective. It has become increasingly commonplace for users to characterize suspensions or other penalties imposed by social media platforms as censorship, some of whom have even attempted (unsuccessfully so far) to sue private companies like Twitter for violations of their First Amendment rights. Some users have even complained that being blocked or muted by other users is a form of censorship, implying that the right of free speech is not only a right to speak, but to demand a particular audience.

First Amendment fundamentalists' concern about chilling effects and censorship perpetuates the idea that the right to free speech is both incredibly fragile and under constant attack. This closely tracks the tactics of Second

Amendment fundamentalists regarding the right to bear arms. Just as the gun lobby warns that even seemingly innocuous regulations are a slippery slope to the confiscation of law-abiding citizens' guns, the free speech lobby sees the threat of censorship in every attempt to regulate any form of expression in any way. Like their Second Amendment counterparts, First Amendment fundamentalists rarely offer concrete evidence for their gloomy speculations. As Kendrick writes, "the Supreme Court has founded the chilling effect on nothing more than unpersuasive empirical guesswork."[23] Rumors of the fragility of the First Amendment, like the fragility of the Second Amendment, appear to be greatly exaggerated.

As Second Amendment fundamentalists have done with the right to bear arms, First Amendment fundamentalists have transformed the right to free speech into a superright with no sensitivity to context or to corresponding responsibilities. The overwrought fear of chilling effects has produced what could be called a "hothouse effect": an excessively solicitous approach to free speech that cultivates the right in an unnaturally isolated environment, one that has been stripped of all risk of competition or challenge.

While the chilling effects of free speech regulations are almost completely speculative, the chilling effect of unfettered harmful expression is not. It is undeniable that certain forms of speech can silence other speech.[24] The primary targets of silencing speech—harassment, threats, genocidal rhetoric, hate speech, revenge porn—are women, nonwhite men, and sexual minorities.

Empirical evidence of how harassment chills expression, mobility, and association is abundant. Cynthia Bowman observes that "the continuation and near-general tolerance of street harassment . . . inflicts the most direct costs upon women, in the form of fear, emotional distress, feelings of disempowerment, and significant limitations upon their liberty, mobility, and hopes for equality."[25] According to a 2014 study on street harassment, women's responses to street harassment include no longer visiting certain places alone; changing the way they walk, behave, or dress; giving up on outdoor activities; quitting jobs, or moving.[26] Mari Matsuda writes that victims of racist speech "have had to quit jobs, forgo education, leave their homes, avoid certain public places, curtail their own exercise of speech rights, and otherwise modify their behavior and demeanor."[27]

The Myth of the Marketplace

There are three main theories about why protecting free speech is important: the democracy theory, the autonomy theory, and the marketplace of ideas theory. According to the democracy theory, freedom of speech is vital to the exercise self-governance. The autonomy theory maintains that being able to speak freely is essential to the development and flourishing of the individual human personality. The marketplace of ideas theory posits that open debate of ideas will ultimately produce truth. The rise of First Amendment fundamentalism has coincided with a falling away of the first two theories in favor of an aggressive embrace of the third.[28]

According to the marketplace of ideas theory, unfettered competition will eventually lead to truth. The belief that unregulated "free" markets will produce optimal results derives from laissez-faire economics. Early versions of the concept can be found in some form in John Milton, John Stuart Mill, and Thomas Jefferson, but it was a passage from Justice Oliver Wendell Holmes, again, that brought the concept firmly into First Amendment jurisprudence. Dissenting in the 1919 case *Abrams v. United States*, Holmes wrote,

> But when men have realized that time has upset many fighting faiths, they may come to believe even more than they believe the very foundations of their own conduct that the ultimate good desired is better reached by free trade in ideas—that the best test of truth is the power of the thought to get itself accepted in the competition of the market, and that truth is the only ground upon which their wishes safely can be carried out. That, at any rate, is the theory of our Constitution.[29]

According to Thomas Joo, the marketplace metaphor rose to prominence in the period following World War II, which "saw a revolution in civil rights and civil liberties, as well as a revival of market fundamentalism, both of which contributed to a shift in focus from government authority to individualism."[30]

As noted previously, the defense of free speech was a somewhat partisan affair for much of the twentieth century. Conservatives were rarely as eager as liberals to defend speech when the speech in question favored

communism, civil rights, atheism, and antiwar sentiment. This was an era
in which free speech was still closely tied to concepts of democratic self-
governance and individual autonomy as well as the marketplace of ideas.

But the landscape of First Amendment advocacy has changed dramatically in the last few decades. Beginning around the 1970s, civil libertarianism began to resemble economic libertarianism more and more. This was
in many ways a strange turn, as liberals have historically been critical of
the concept of free-market fundamentalism, noting that the economic free
market is not truly free and that the antiregulatory impulses of libertarians tend to stack the deck in favor of the wealthy and privileged at the
expense of the poor and marginalized. Nonetheless, liberals increasingly
adopted free-market mythology with regard to civil liberties, and liberal
free speech priorities began to shift from political speech to commercial
speech, from vulnerable populations to powerful ones, and from individuals to corporations.

As they did so, conservatives became newly interested in free speech. By
the 1980s, conservatives were making aggressive use of the First Amendment to both promote discriminatory speech and to advance corporate
interests. As Wayne Batchis writes, conservatives moved "from unabashed
skepticism and First Amendment minimalism to a passionate libertarianism
and free-speech free-marketism," turning the First Amendment into an "affirmative tool for advancing mainstream conservative policy objectives."[31]
Soon, liberal and conservative civil libertarians were speaking the same
language: emphasizing the importance of competition and debate to free
speech, extolling the virtues of "counter-speech," criticizing regulations
of harmful speech as nefarious government interference, and portraying
the systematic privileging of the most powerful groups in society as the
natural product of unfettered market forces.

In the marketplace mythology, competition, not regulation, is always
the answer to conflict; the unregulated marketplace will provide the most
beneficial outcomes for the general welfare. Just as Second Amendment
fundamentalists insist that the best response to gun violence is more guns,
First Amendment fundamentalists insist that the best response to bad
speech is more speech. In the context of free speech, competition is often
couched in terms of "counter-speech" and beneficial outcomes in terms of

"truth." In Justice Louis Brandeis's famous formulation, "If there be time to expose through discussion the falsehood and fallacies, to avert the evil by the processes of education, the remedy to be applied is more speech, not enforced silence."[32] The optimistic embrace of counter-speech as the cure for falsity and injury is, however, unfounded.

The first problem is that there is no such thing as a "free" market, economic or otherwise. Economic markets are subjected to extensive regulation, from corporate structuring to securities regulation to quality and safety standards. As Joo writes, "equating 'markets' with unregulated competition ignores the fact that markets require, and receive, some degree of regulation in order to operate properly. Regulation and markets are complementary, not antithetical, institutions."[33] The marketplace of speech is similarly subject to extensive regulation; indeed, many economic regulations are also speech regulations. Contrary to the claims of First Amendment fundamentalists, it is not true that the vast majority of speech is constitutionally protected against regulation. In addition to explicitly unprotected categories such as obscenity, true threats, incitement, defamation, speech integral to criminal conduct, child pornography, and fighting words, the government also regulates the marketplace of ideas through trade secrets law, products liability, antitrust law, copyright, trademark, privacy law, antidiscrimination law, perjury, evidence law—and the list goes on.[34]

Second, markets do not produce truth or objectively optimal outcomes; they merely reflect consumer preferences. While those preferences might favor the general welfare or truth, they equally might not. The only conclusion one could draw about an idea that has triumphed in the marketplace is that many people like it, or at least the people with the most power in the marketplace like it.

Third, even if people had strong preferences for the truth, there is no reason for confidence that the marketplace would help them discover it. As the "fake news" epidemic has amply demonstrated, Americans are neither necessarily interested in nor particularly gifted at discerning truth from falsity or fact from opinion. Short attention spans, lack of education, and confirmation bias lead many people to believe things that are demonstrably false. Being constantly plugged into the Internet, a medium allowing nearly unfettered and instantaneous exchange of information, has worsened, not improved, this situation. It is important to recall that Justice Brandeis's praise of counter-speech was contingent, not absolute: "*If there be time* to expose through discussion the falsehood and fallacies, to avert the evil by the processes of education, the remedy to be applied is more speech, not enforced silence."[35] In an age of instantaneous transmission, there often is literally *no time* to correct falsehoods before they go viral.

Even when truth does emerge in the market, it often does so too late to correct first impressions or undo harm. As the expression goes, "a lie can get halfway around the world before the truth has a chance to get its pants on."[36] What is more, Joo writes,

> [M]arket correction not only takes time, it is not unidirectional. Incorrect notions in economic markets and in the "marketplace of ideas" do not simply rise and then permanently fall. They rise and fall and rise and fall in endless repetition: truths and falsehoods alike come and go.[37]

Attempts to correct untruths can actually backfire, due to what psychologists call "the illusory truth effect." Repeated exposure to false information, even in a corrective context, increases the likelihood that the false information will be remembered as true. Recent studies have confirmed that when people view false headlines, they are more likely to accept them as true when they counter them again.[38]

Finally, there are many forms of speech that simply cannot be countered in any meaningful way. Justice Brandeis spoke of "falsehood and fallacies" that can be averted by "processes of education." But it is not only false information that can inflict great injury, as Brandeis himself knew well. In 1890, Brandeis and his friend Samuel Warren wrote a groundbreaking article titled "The Right to Privacy," arguing that every person had the right to keep truthful, intimate information out of public view. In contrast to the law of defamation, which involves the right "to prevent inaccurate portrayal of private life," the law of privacy protects the right to "prevent its being depicted at all."[39] There is no "counter-speech" to the publication of a person's nude image or the dissemination of a home address, and no "process of education" can undo their damage. Such unanswerable speech can only be prohibited, not countered.

THE CORPORATE CONNECTION

While the myth of the marketplace is poorly suited to protect the general welfare or truth, it is remarkably well suited to serve corporate interests. The rise of marketplace mythology may help explain the astonishing shift in free speech claims from the marginalized to the powerful. As Morrison Torrey writes,

> Initially, free speech claims were brought by draft resisters, labor organizers, civil rights activists, pacifists, communists, and similar progressive or left groups with less than their share of power and all too easily silenced by a hostile majority. Today, free speech claims are increasingly likely to be brought by rich, powerful, commercial entities (including tobacco companies and pornographers), by racist speakers, or to challenge progressive campaign reform legislation.[40]

Lincoln Caplan similarly observed in 2015 that "the most fervent champions" of free speech today "are not standing up for mistrusted outliers . . . or for the dispossessed and powerless." Instead, they "do the bidding of insiders—the super-rich and the ultra-powerful, the airline, drug, petroleum, and tobacco industries, all the winners in America's winner-take-all society."[41] John Coates concludes that "corporations have increasingly displaced individuals as direct beneficiaries of First Amendment rights," finding that almost "half of First Amendment legal challenges now benefit business corporations and trade groups, rather than other kinds of organizations or individuals."[42]

The worship of corporations by antigovernment libertarians is confounding as an initial matter, given that corporations are not the product of natural forces or unfettered competition but are literally created of government. The establishment and protection of corporate rights requires extensive government regulation. As Batchis notes, "This is the paradox of decrying government suppression of what we now call corporate speech: There can be no such thing as corporate speech without government."[43]

What is more, corporations fundamentally disrupt the nature of human interaction and competition. The ability of any individual human being to engage in risky or harmful behavior is, in theory, limited by the potential of personal liability for negative outcomes. An entirely artificial entity, however, is able to sever risks from responsibilities. The structure of corporations creates a classic moral hazard: "[T]he nature of corporate action, where bureaucracy dictates that most of the actors are far removed from the actual harm that might occur as a result of their decisions, increases the likelihood of egregious conduct."[44] Being allowed to reap nearly limitless benefits from risky behavior without facing the costs of that behavior means that corporate liberty will always outstrip individual liberty. As Joel Bakan describes in *The Corporation: The Pathological Pursuit of Profit and Power,* "The corporation's legally defined mandate is to pursue, relentlessly and without exception, its own self-interest, regardless of the often harmful consequences it might cause to others."[45]

The Role of the Supreme Court: Citizens United

As evocatively expressed in the title of Adam Winkler's book *We the Corporations,* corporations have increasingly replaced people in the eyes of the law.[46] Beginning in 1886, when the Supreme Court held that corporations were "persons" entitled to due process and equal protection, corporations have acquired an ever-expanding number of rights previously thought to only belong to individuals. In the landmark Supreme Court case *Citizens United v. FEC,* decided in 2010, the First Amendment right to free speech was added to that list. The case dramatically demonstrated the fundamentalist shift in First Amendment focus from the downtrodden to the dominant and from the individual to the corporation.

In 2007, a conservative nonprofit organization called Citizens United produced a derogatory political documentary about Hillary Clinton, who was at the time a candidate for the Democratic presidential nomination. The organization attempted to sell the film through a video-on-demand service just before the 2008 Democratic primary, but was prohibited from doing so by the Bipartisan Campaign Reform Act (also known as the McCain–Feingold Act), a 2002 federal rule against "electioneering communications" by corporations or unions within thirty days of a primary election.

Among the parties lobbying hard for a ruling favorable to corporations were the multi-billionaire Koch brothers. Charles and David Koch are the owners of the second-largest private company in America, Koch Industries, which operates oil refineries in three states and "owns Brawny paper towels, Dixie cups, Georgia-Pacific lumber, Stainmaster carpet, and Lycra."[47] Several groups funded by the Kochs "filed a series of amicus briefs arguing that unlimited corporate money in politics is protected by the First Amendment," including the Cato Institute, which "called for 'unfettered' corporate 'speech,'" and the Institute for Justice, which argued that "campaign finance laws prohibiting unlimited corporate money 'trump the First Amendment.'"[48]

The Supreme Court, in a 5–4 decision that split along partisan lines, found that the prohibitions against corporations and unions from making independent expenditures and "electioneering communications" violated the First Amendment. The ruling effectively declared that corporations and unions have a constitutional right to spend unlimited amounts on political advertising to influence elections. The case has implications far beyond political speech. As Tamara Piety explains in *Brandishing the First Amendment*,

> *Citizens United*, by framing such corporations as citizens with distinct rights of expression, provides ammunition to collapse the distinction between commercial speech, which currently only has limited constitutional protection, and protected political or artistic expression, which enjoys heightened protection. Such a collapse would imperil existing consumer protection legislation and strangle in their infancy any efforts to assert greater regulatory supervision over critical industries like banking, pharmaceuticals, insurance, and many others.[49]

The ruling was effusively praised in many conservative quarters and vehemently denounced in many liberal ones. University of Chicago law professor M. Todd Henderson hailed the decision as "a victory for our democracy,"[50] while philosopher and constitutional law scholar Ronald Dworkin decried it as a "radical decision of the five conservative justices . . . not supported by any plausible First Amendment theory."[51]

But support for the right of corporate free speech was not limited to conservatives. Along with usual suspects such as the Cato Institute and the NRA, the ACLU filed a brief in support of the conservative corporation.

The ACLU's position on the case surprised and disappointed many, including many members of the ACLU itself, who condemned the organization's leadership for "endors[ing] a deeply contested and incorrect reading of the First Amendment as a rigid deregulatory straitjacket that threatens the integrity of American democracy."[52]

Corporate Civil Liberties

But the ACLU's defense of corporate interests in the name of free speech began long before *Citizens United*. Historian Leigh Ann Wheeler argues that the ACLU's First Amendment advocacy is defined by consumerism. Her book, *How Sex Became a Civil Liberty*, details how "ACLU leaders reinterpreted the First Amendment to protect not only the right to speak but also the right to consume speech." This is, in Wheeler's view,

> a stealthily executed innovation that expanded the amendment's potential beneficiaries to include not just orators, authors, publishers, and filmmakers, but *anyone* who might want to listen to a particular speech, read a particular book, subscribe to a particular magazine, or watch a particular movie.[53]

The consumerist interpretation of free speech had the virtue of serving the interests of multiple industries while encouraging average Americans to think of their right to free speech primarily in terms of purchasing power. The ACLU's commodification of the First Amendment "resonated with the individualistic ethos of a culture in which consumption has become a fundamental right" so successfully "that it has become almost an article of faith."[54]

The ACLU's consumerist interpretation of free speech endeared it to the pornography industry, which found ways to return the favor. The organization had found a longstanding and lucrative benefactor in the late Hugh Hefner, the founder of *Playboy* magazine. Hefner held elaborate fundraisers for the ACLU in his mansions in the 1960s and 70s, including a black tie event that raised $100,000 for the organization in 1971. After former ACLU attorney Burton Joseph became the executive director and special counsel to *Playboy* and Playboy Foundation, then-ACLU president Aryeh Neier appealed to him for funding by high-lighting the cases he thought would appeal to Hefner: "sexual civil liberties cases involving abortion, voluntary sterilization, birth control, and 'bralessness.'" The Playboy Foundation gave Neier $40,000 to start the ACLU's Women's Rights Project and provided printing services for the organization's pamphlets and abortion rights materials.[55] The October 1971 issue of *Playboy* included a seven-page article hailing the ACLU as "'the nation's chief defender of personal liberty' and urging readers to join or donate to it."[56]

The ACLU also enjoyed close ties with the tobacco industry. In the 1990s—as the tobacco industry was facing government regulation, lawsuits, and public outcry for deliberately concealing knowledge of tobacco's harmful effects—it found a powerful ally in the ACLU. The civil liberties organization provided testimony, press statements, and "Dear Senator" letters against restrictions on tobacco advertising, characterizing them as an infringement of First Amendment rights. The relationship was mutually beneficial: According to journalist Morton Mintz, the ACLU asked for and received $500,000 from leading cigarette manufacturer Philip Morris between 1987 and 1992. In his 1993 report "Allies: The ACLU and the Tobacco Industry," Mintz had initially concluded that the clandestine relationship between the ACLU and the tobacco industry, while surprising and in his view troubling, did not rise to the level of actual impropriety.

Mintz changed his mind in 1996, however, following the publication of a book by former ACLU employee John Fahs titled *Cigarette Confidential: The Unfiltered Truth About the Ultimate American Addiction*. The book contained numerous internal documents that demonstrated that the ACLU provided its support to the industry "in direct exchange for funding"—to the tune of nearly a million dollars—in "a quid pro quo arrangement in direct conflict with the institution's status as a government-subsidized, tax-exempt, nonprofit institution."[57] According to Fahs, the ACLU's National Task Force on Civil Liberties in the Workplace receives "more than 90 percent of its annual budget" from grants from Philip Morris and R. J. Reynolds Tobacco Company. The relationship between the tobacco industry and the ACLU prompted former ACLU legal director Melvin Wulf to issue a harsh critique of the organization:

The justification that the money is used to support workplace rights is a sham. There is no constitutional right to pollute the atmosphere and threaten the health of others. . . . [T]he ACLU's mission is being corrupted by the attraction of easy money from an industry whose ethical values are themselves notoriously corrupt and which is responsible for the death annually of 350,000 to 400,000 persons in the U.S. alone.[58]

Following the election of Donald Trump, the ACLU was flooded with donations. The organization received a record-breaking $24 million in donations in a single weekend in January 2017[59] and raised more than $80 million total between November 8, 2016, and March 2017.[60] In January 2017, it was announced that the ACLU would be partnering with the powerful Silicon Valley startup accelerator Y Combinator, a relationship that would include funding and mentoring from the startup. ACLU Executive Director Anthony Romero said in a statement that "[b]eyond financial contributions, the Silicon Valley community can help organizations like ours harness recent membership surges and spread the word about what the ACLU is doing to protect people's rights from violations by the Trump administration."[61] Some critics observed that one member of Trump's administration and major Trump donor, billionaire Peter Thiel, is a part-time partner in Y Combinator.[62]

The ACLU has also joined forces with corporate powers to advance more ostensibly progressive agendas. In 2011, several media outlets reported that the Koch brothers had donated $20 million to the ACLU to fight government surveillance, though this donation has not been confirmed.[63] What has been confirmed, however, is that Koch Industries joined the ACLU and other groups in 2015 to form the Coalition for Public Safety, which works for criminal justice reform.[64] The Koch brothers' involvement with the ACLU's criminal justice reform efforts have been praised as an example of principled bipartisanship, but skeptics warn that the billionaires' motives may have more to do with self-interest:

Charles Koch, the company's chairman and CEO, has said he became interested in criminal-justice reform after a grand jury's 1995 indictment of a Koch refinery in Texas for 97 felony violations of environmental law.

The company spent six years fighting the charges and eventually settled with the government for $10 million. Seen in this light, the criminal-justice pitch is just another attempt to manipulate the political process to advance the company's financial interests.[65]

This impression was reinforced in November 2015, when the House Judiciary Committee approved a mens rea reform measure supported by the Koch brothers that would make the prosecution of white-collar crime much more difficult—a measure that would benefit a minority of white, wealthy, and privileged individuals far more than the poor people of color disproportionately impacted by mass incarceration. The bill caused a rift in the coalition between the conservatives who favored the measure and the liberals who did not. Jeffery Robinson, the deputy legal director of the ACLU, criticized the bill but stated that the organization would not oppose it.[66]

Other criminal justice reform efforts funded by the Koch brothers have raised concerns, among them the Inmate Civics Education Enhancement Project (ICEEP). While ostensibly a program aimed at reducing recidivism and facilitating prisoner re-integration, ICEEP's curriculum and comments made by its director Marshall DeRosa suggest that "an additional goal may be to convert felons in prison, who are more likely to vote for Democrats, to conservatism and then re-enfranchise them."[67] In December 2015, the ACLU announced the opening of its Trone Center for Criminal Justice Reform, whose advisory board includes Mark Holden, general counsel and senior vice president of Koch Industries.[68]

FREE SPEECH AND REVENGE PORN

One illuminating example of the fundamentalist and corporatist approach to free speech is the ACLU's dogged opposition to legislative and policy reform on issues of technology-facilitated abuse. Online stalking, harassment, and "revenge porn" disproportionately affect women and minorities and are disproportionately perpetrated by white men. In response to these abuses, women and girls are forced to leave jobs, change schools, retreat from public discourse, and refrain from expressive activity generally. Technology-facilitated abuse drives women and girls out of public spaces, both online and offline, and removes their voices and their contributions from public discourse. This allows powerful groups to replicate and reinforce the status quo, shutting down possibilities for diversity and evolution.

Despite the devastating impact of these abuses on the speech and privacy rights of vulnerable groups, the ACLU has framed such abuses as exercises of free speech and efforts to combat them as censorship. The ACLU's fight to protect revenge porn in particular is reflective of a larger, disturbing tendency to treat women's constitutional and civil rights as secondary and subordinate to men's and has artificially constrained reflection and reform on these issues.[69]

Revenge porn, more accurately described as "nonconsensual pornography," refers to the disclosure of sexually explicit images and video without consent and for no legitimate purpose. The term encompasses footage obtained by hidden cameras, consensually exchanged images within a confidential relationship, stolen photos, and recordings of sexual assaults. Nonconsensual pornography often plays a role in intimate partner violence, with abusers using the threat of disclosure to keep their partners from leaving or reporting their abuse to law enforcement.[70] Traffickers and pimps also use nonconsensual pornography to trap unwilling individuals in the sex trade.[71] Rapists record their attacks not only to further humiliate their victims, but also to discourage them from reporting sexual assaults.[72] Nursing home workers have been caught posting nude photos of elderly and disabled patients to social media.[73]

Nonconsensual pornography can cause immediate, devastating, and in many cases, irreparable harm. With a click of a button, an ex-partner, hacker, or rapist can expose a victim's naked body to the entire world. In a matter of moments, that image can dominate the search engine results for the victim's name, reducing her digital reputation to a scroll of obscene links. The material can be transmitted through e-mail or social media to the victim's family, employers, coworkers, and peers.[74] Victims are frequently threatened with sexual assault, stalked, harassed,[75] fired from jobs,[76] and forced to change schools.[77] Some victims have committed suicide.[78] While nonconsensual pornography affects both male and female individuals, available evidence to date indicates that the majority of victims are women and girls, and that women and girls often face more serious consequences as a result of their victimization.[79]

Nonconsensual pornography creates social as well as individual harms. The practice normalizes nonconsensual sexual activity and sexual surveillance. It sends the message that sexual exploitation is an acceptable form of entertainment or punishment, or both, especially of women who act in ways men find unacceptable. It is not surprising that many female targets of nonconsensual pornography are successful women, from movie stars to politicians to law school students. The predominantly male perpetrators and predominantly male consumers of these images can be described as attempting to put powerful women "in their place." This abuse inhibits women's expression, movement, and participation in society, which leads to a loss of women's voices in workplaces, schools, and community.

Revenge porn existed before there was a term for it. Perhaps the first high-profile instance of nonconsensual pornography involved *Playboy*'s publication of nude photos of Marilyn Monroe without her consent in its inaugural issue. When Monroe was still a struggling actress named Norma Jeane Baker, she had posed for a photographer named Tom Kelley "out of desperation."[80] Monroe reportedly told Kelley, "You must promise to never tell anyone about my posing for you in the nude. I want you to promise me that you will take the pictures so that I wouldn't be recognisable in them." Monroe signed the release for the photographs with a false name, "hoping that they wouldn't come back to haunt her." After Monroe became famous, *Playboy* founder and ACLU benefactor Hugh Hefner paid $500 for the photos and published them on the cover of *Playboy* in 1953, making the magazine an overnight success.

In the 1980s, hard-core porn magazine *Hustler* began running a feature called "Beaver Hunt," which published reader-submitted sexually explicit photographs.[81] The women depicted in these photographs had often not consented to their submission or publication: Some photographs had been stolen, some were submitted by exes with malicious purposes, and some were simply published without consent.[82] The feature was controversial, resulting in numerous lawsuits against *Hustler*,[83] but it continues today.

As recording devices became smaller and cheaper, many online communities and websites began featuring "amateur porn" of uncertain provenance.[84] In many cases, it seems clear that the depicted individuals were unaware that they were being filmed or had not consented to the material being made public.[85] Yet the amateur porn industry flourishes largely without investigation or regulation, betraying a lack of social or political interest in ensuring that those featured in such intimate scenarios had consented to being seen in this way.[86]

Before 2003, no law in the United States clearly criminalized the unauthorized disclosure of sexually explicit images of another adult person.[87] The issue received little attention from the media or from lawmakers. That began to change in 2010, when Hunter Moore created a website featuring stolen or user-submitted sexually explicit imagery of people, mostly women, without their consent.[88] Moore's site also provided detailed personal, contact, and other identifying information about the people depicted on the site.[89] In 2011, Christopher Chaney was arrested for hacking the e-mail accounts of dozens of female celebrities to obtain suggestive or explicit images of the women.[90]

Despite high-profile cases like these and a rise in revenge porn sites, before 2013 only three states had criminal laws applicable to the conduct. Victims mostly suffered in silence for fear of greater exposure. Those who did attempt to seek help in law enforcement were often mocked. Even sympathetic police officers and lawyers told victims, not inaccurately, that what happened to them was "not against the law."[91]

In 2013, a victim of nonconsensual pornography named Holly Jacobs founded a nonprofit organization called the Cyber Civil Rights Initiative (CCRI) to advocate for legislative, technological, and social reform on the issue. CCRI[92] and other victim advocacy organizations helped transform the legal and social landscape on the issue in just a few years. In 2015, major tech companies including Google, Microsoft, Facebook, and Twitter announced that they were banning this abuse and implementing takedown procedures for victims.[93]

On July 14, 2016, Congresswoman Jackie Speier (D-Calif.) introduced the Intimate Privacy Protection Act,[94] a bipartisan federal bill addressing nonconsensual pornography reintroduced as the ENOUGH Act in November 2017. As of July 2018, forty states and the District of Columbia had passed laws criminalizing the nonconsensual distribution of private, sexually explicit images. In July 2018, the Uniform Law Commission (ULC) approved the Uniform Civil Remedies for the Unauthorized Distribution of Unauthorized Images Act.[95]

When the issue of nonconsensual pornography first began receiving extensive public attention, the ACLU took the position that *no* criminal law prohibiting the nonconsensual distribution of sexually explicit images was permissible within the bounds of the First Amendment.[96] The ACLU maintained, in effect, that revenge porn was free speech. For reasons that have never been made clear, the organization soon quietly backed away from this view[97] and attempted a different approach, which was to insist on an arbitrarily narrow definition of the crime. This definition required that perpetrators be current or former intimate partners and be motivated by the intent to harass their victims. Despite having no basis for claiming that either of these limitations is necessary to survive First Amendment challenge and, indeed, ignoring that both limitations *create* First Amendment vulnerabilities, the ACLU has succeeded in intimidating several state legislatures into watering down their laws according to the ACLU's specifications.

In May 2014, Arizona passed a law criminalizing nonconsensual pornography.[98] In September 2014, the ACLU initiated a lawsuit challenging the law on behalf of itself and a group of booksellers.[99] In a letter to Arizona lawmakers, the ACLU demanded that the state redefine the crime, asserting that any law criminalizing revenge porn must be limited to circumstances where

(1) a person who was or is in an intimate relationship with another person and who, (2) during and as a result of that relationship, obtained a recognizable image of such other person in a state of nudity, (3) where such other person had a reasonable expectation of privacy and an understanding that such image would remain private, (4) to display such image (5) without the consent of such other person, (6) with the intent to harass, humiliate, embarrass, or otherwise harm such other person, and (7) where there is no public or newsworthy purpose for the display.[100]

How exactly the ACLU arrived at this definition and what made the ACLU qualified to define this conduct have never been made clear. But the ACLU has reiterated this definition in statements to the media and in testimony in opposition to legislation against nonconsensual pornography in other states.[101]

To support its claim that the Arizona statute was overbroad, the ACLU listed a handful of scenarios it alleged were potentially prosecutable under Arizona's statute, including bookstores selling volumes that contained photographs from Abu Ghraib or parents sharing pictures of their babies taking baths.[102] Leaving aside for the moment the merits of any of these particular examples, the Supreme Court has clarified that constitutional overbreadth concerns "must not only be real, but substantial as well, judged in relation to the statute's plainly legitimate sweep."[103] Mere conjecture that a statute could be applied very broadly is not in itself sufficient grounds to invalidate it.[104] The ACLU was not able to point to a single actual case of overapplication, despite similar laws being on the books of some states for over a decade, including New Jersey's, passed in 2003,[105] and Alaska's, passed in 2006.[106]

Despite this, the government of Arizona agreed to amend the law. This left many Arizona revenge porn victims without a legal remedy and others in a state of confusion about where their case stood. On the ACLU's website, an ACLU staff attorney celebrated the outcome, asserting that "Arizona is a little bit freer today."[107] In 2016, Arizona passed a new version of its law that restricted the statute to offenders who act with "the intent to harm, harass, intimidate, threaten or coerce the depicted person."[108]

The most pernicious aspect of the ACLU's position is its attempt to reframe nonconsensual pornography as a form of emotional distress or harassment instead of an invasion of privacy. In addition to mischaracterizing the nature of the harm caused, as discussed above, this position ignores the fact that harassment laws already exist at both the state and federal level. If such laws were effective in addressing this conduct, there would be no current epidemic of nonconsensual pornography—an epidemic that currently affects more than one in eight adult social media users in the United States.[109] Making nonconsensual pornography laws into harassment laws does nothing more than duplicate existing, ineffective measures. What is more, prohibiting only disclosures of sexually explicit images when they are intended to cause distress, while allowing disclosures that are not, renders a law vulnerable to objections of underinclusiveness[110] and viewpoint discrimination.[111]

Rendering laws ineffective or susceptible to First Amendment challenge appears to be the ACLU's unstated goal. In addition to being unsupported by First Amendment doctrine, the ACLU's insistence upon intent-to-harass requirements is bizarre given the organization's own position that concepts such as harassment and emotional distress are unconstitutionally overbroad. In objecting to federal stalking provisions of the Violence Against Women Act in 2013,[112] the ACLU characterized intent to cause "substantial emotional distress" elements, as well as intent to "harass" or "intimidate" elements, as "unconstitutionally overbroad."[113] Thus, the ACLU paradoxically insists that in order for nonconsensual pornography laws to be constitutional, they must include the very element that, according to the ACLU, makes stalking laws unconstitutional.

Statutes written according to the ACLU's demands allow any person who discloses private, sexually explicit material for profit, reputation enhancement, entertainment, or any other non-harassing motive to act with impunity.[114] A 2015 case involving the Penn State chapter of the Kappa Delta Rho (KDR) fraternity illustrates the consequences of such a position. After it came to light that fraternity brothers were posting photos of naked, unconscious women to a members-only Facebook page, a KDR member defended the group's actions by claiming that "[i]t wasn't malicious whatsoever. It wasn't intended to hurt anyone. It wasn't intended to demean anyone."[115] Fortunately for these fraternity members—and unfortunately for the women they victimized—Pennsylvania's nonconsensual pornography law was precisely the kind of arbitrarily narrow law endorsed by the ACLU.[116] Enacted in 2014, that law is restricted to those who, "with intent to harass, annoy or alarm a current or former sexual or intimate partner . . . disseminate[] a visual depiction of the current or former sexual or intimate partner in a state of nudity or engaged in sexual conduct."[117] The sponsor of the legislation stated that she intended to close the "relationship loophole" in light of the KDR case;[118] she did not state whether she intended to address the "intent to harass" requirement as well.

The ACLU's position on nonconsensual pornography laws directly conflicts with its own advocacy on privacy rights. On its Technology and

Privacy Project web page, the ACLU proclaims, "The ACLU works to expand the right to privacy, increase the control individuals have over their personal information, and ensure civil liberties are enhanced rather than compromised by technological innovation."[119] The ACLU supports laws that protect many forms of private information, such as Social Security numbers, genetic information, biometric markers, and even geolocation data. The ACLU has urged the Federal Trade Commission to pursue data brokers who buy and sell information about consumers;[120] written a letter of support[121] for the Genetic Information Nondiscrimination Act as a means of protecting "extremely personal sensitive information"; and encouraged Congress to pass legislation that would require patient consent for the use of medical records for "secondary purposes."[122]

All of these measures emphasize the right of individuals not to have their private information disclosed without consent, without any reference to harm. None requires that perpetrators act with the intent to harass their victims, and certainly none requires that the perpetrator and victim be intimate partners. What they reflect is the century-old understanding that, in the words of Warren and Brandeis, "the absence of 'malice' in the publisher does not afford a defence" to privacy violations; "[p]ersonal ill-will is not an ingredient of the offence, any more than in an ordinary case of trespass to person or to property."[123]

The ACLU clearly believes in other contexts that the protection of private information does not violate the First Amendment. The ACLU has advocated for legislation that would make negligent disclosures of geolocation data a federal crime[124] and authored laws forbidding merchants from asking customers for Social Security numbers on pain of criminal penalty.[125] These reforms use the criminal law to suppress speech in order to protect privacy. And yet the ACLU fights measures that attempt to protect the privacy of information arguably far more intimate than geolocation data or Social Security numbers.

The ACLU's determined efforts to characterize revenge porn as protected free speech that can only be regulated when it takes the form of harassment distorts both First Amendment and privacy doctrine. It is difficult to avoid the conclusion that its motivation for doing so has to do with the gender dynamics of the abuse. The ACLU's position allows the primarily male perpetrators of revenge porn to ruin their primarily female victims' reputations, career opportunities, intimate relationships, and mental health in the name of free speech. Once again, men's freedom to express themselves is protected at the expense of women's ability to do the same.

THE COLLEGE SPEECH CRISIS THAT WASN'T

Another vivid illustration of the distorting effects of First Amendment fundamentalism can be found in the near-universal panic over free speech on college campuses. According to the prevailing narrative, since at least 2015 American campuses have been alternately terrorized and sanitized by leftist students demonstrating shocking intolerance against conservative speakers, faculty members, and policies that do not reflect their own narrow conceptions of acceptable academic discourse. The situation is apparently so dire that it eclipses all other higher education issues and demands steady critique and intervention from forces outside academia.

The reports of violent leftist suppression of conservative ideas, however, have been greatly exaggerated. While some disturbing campus incidents have occurred, there is no evidence that institutions of higher learning are in the midst of a widespread and systematic epidemic of intellectual intolerance. What is more, many of the most serious incidents have involved attacks *on* left-leaning individuals, not *by* them. The distorted narrative of intense campus unrest and conservative persecution is not merely a result of poorly sourced, sensationalist reporting, but a product of a deliberate and well-funded strategy by powerful conservative nonprofit organizations.

As Amy Binder, co-author with Kate Wood of the 2013 book *Becoming Right: How Campuses Shape Young Conservatives*, describes it, "For decades, a handful of organizations has been working in the trenches with conservative college students to stage events" that create the impression of leftist intolerance. "With their emphasis on conservative victimhood and liberal indoctrination, these organizations have fostered right-leaning student activism and suspicion about higher education, which have created fertile soil in which larger-scale political attacks on higher education germinate and grow."[126]

The game plan is roughly this: Force a public university to host, at great financial cost and commitment of institutional resources, a high-profile conservative speaker who will deliberately antagonize students and faculty. The more outrageous the speaker's views, the greater the likelihood that the event will generate publicity and protests. Frame the ensuing confusion and chaos as a violation of the speaker's free speech rights and as evidence of student intolerance. Use the media attention to push for harshly punitive "anti-heckling" bills that restrict students' rights of free speech in the name of protecting free speech. Fully exploit the outsized attention to campus protests so that other serious campus issues—such as sexual assault, white supremacist recruitment efforts, and school shootings—escape scrutiny.

Fueled by First Amendment fundamentalism, liberals have assisted conservatives in painting this highly misleading picture of campus censorship. The distorted narrative of campus speech puts many ills of First Amendment fundamentalism on display: the reduction of complex issues of gender and racial inequality to simplistic debates about free speech; the magnification of harm to the powerful and minimization of harm to the vulnerable; manipulation by powerful corporate interests; the framing of privileged forms of expression as free speech and underprivileged forms of expression as censorship; and, finally, the perpetuation of a free speech hierarchy that grants the greatest resources, attention, and protection to speech that serves the interests of white men.

Manufacturing the Crisis

Conservatives have a long history of criticizing "political correctness" on university campuses. Throughout the 90s, conservatives used the term to denounce what they characterized as an attack on higher education's humanistic tradition. They built on the success of books like Allan Bloom's *The Closing of the American Mind*, which railed against what Bloom saw as the liberal takeover of academia and the rise of anti-intellectual "cultural relativism."

A primary tactic of the well-funded, conservative movement against political correctness was to take thinly sourced, out-of-context anecdotes and present them as evidence of a sustained leftist campaign against free-dom of thought. As Moira Weigel observed in 2016,

> "Political correctness" became a term used to drum into the public imagination the idea that there was a deep divide between the "ordinary people" and the "liberal elite," who sought to control the speech and thoughts of regular folk. Opposition to political correctness also became a way to rebrand racism in ways that were politically acceptable in the post-civil-rights era.[127]

The political correctness wars faded in the 2000s but returned with a vengeance beginning in the last years of President Obama's second term. This time, the critique of political correctness is as likely to come from high-profile liberals as from conservatives. One of the most widely read popular-press articles decrying political correctness was written by Jonathan Chait in *New York Magazine* in 2015.[128] In it, Chait followed the playbook of 90s conservatives by citing a few scattered examples of liberal intolerance as proof of an all-out assault on freedom of thought and speech by hysterical leftists. An avalanche of popular press articles decrying the takeover of college campuses by the oversensitive and censo-rious left followed Chait's piece. While it is hardly surprising to observe far-right provocateurs like Milo Yiannopoulos and Ann Coulter energeti-cally denouncing leftist censorship, their complaints are now echoed by respected liberals.

The University of Chicago received effusive praise across the political spectrum in 2016 for a welcome letter from the dean of students that directly addressed campus speech controversies. The letter informed in-coming students that the university does "not support so-called trigger warnings, we do not cancel invited speakers because their topics might prove controversial and we do not condone the creation of intellectual safe spaces where individuals can retreat from ideas and perspectives at odds with their own."[129] In May 2016, Floyd Abrams, one of the most prominent First Amendment lawyers in the country and the author of the book *The Soul of the First Amendment*, stated that the single greatest threat facing free speech today "comes from a minority of students who strenuously and . . . contemptuously, disapprove of the views of speakers whose view of the world is different from theirs, and who seek to prevent those views from being heard."[130]

Some of the incidents that these critics cite are indeed alarming. Perhaps the most egregious such event occurred at Middlebury College in March 2017 during the speaking visit of Charles Murray. Murray is one of the authors of the 1994 book *The Bell Curve*, which has been widely criticized for making unfounded, racist claims about intelligence. Murray, who had been invited by a conservative group, was reportedly prevented from giving his speech by dozens of shouting students. Protesters pulled fire alarms in an attempt to disrupt his delivery of the speech in a different room. As Murray was leaving the building with Allison Stanger, his faculty interviewer, protesters became physically aggressive, leaving Professor Stanger with a concussion. After the two entered a vehicle to leave, protesters rocked the car back and forth and jumped on the hood.

Other violent protests occurred at the University of California–Berkeley in February 2017 in advance of a scheduled appearance by Milo Yiannopoulos, a then senior editor for the far-right publication Breitbart. Yiannopoulos, an enthusiastic Donald Trump supporter who calls himself a "cultural libertarian," is notorious for racist, misogynist, homophobic (despite being gay himself), and Islamophobic diatribes. Yiannopoulos enjoys a huge social media following and was permanently banned from Twitter following claims he helped facilitate an online harassment campaign against Leslie Jones, an African American actress who starred in the 2016 reboot of *Ghostbusters*. His previous speaking engagements at college campuses had been marked by controversy; during an appearance at the University of Wisconsin–Milwaukee prior to his scheduled Berkeley appearance, Yiannopoulos targeted a transgender student by name, ridiculing the student for filing a Title IX complaint about bathroom access. It had been rumored that Yiannopoulos was planning to name undocumented students during his Berkeley talk. The day the event was scheduled to take place, a large protest began outside the venue where Yiannopoulos was to speak. At some point, a group of demonstrators set fires, damaged property, set off fireworks, and threw rocks at police. Citing concerns about the danger to public safety, the university canceled the event. In a statement posted to Facebook, Yiannopoulos wrote, "The left is absolutely terrified of free speech and will do literally anything to shut it down."

Concerns about public safety also plagued a planned appearance at Berkeley by the conservative political commentator Ann Coulter in April 2017. It was widely reported that Berkeley had canceled Coulter's lecture due to threats of violence. Though Coulter had initially said that she would show up on the planned date anyway, she eventually stated that she would not go through with her appearance, calling the incident "a sad day for free speech."[131] As with the protests over Murray and Yiannopoulos, the furor over Coulter drew extensive criticism not only in rightwing circles, but across the political spectrum. Prominent liberal figures, including Senator and former presidential candidate Bernie Sanders and Senator Elizabeth Warren, publicly condemned the incident. Senator Sanders, while expressing distaste for Coulter's views, recommended that critics "[a]sk her the hard questions. Confront her intellectually. Booing people down, or intimidating people, or shutting down events, I don't think that that works in any way."[132] Senator Warren told CNN's Jake Tapper, "My view is, let her speak. . . . If you don't like it, don't show up."[133]

David Cole, the legal director of the ACLU, went even further, releasing a public statement on the Coulter controversy. "The unacceptable threats of violence that have led to the 'hecklers' veto' of Ann Coulter's speech at Berkeley are inconsistent with free speech principles that protect us all from government overreach," Cole wrote.[134] Acknowledging the intense reactions provoked by divisive figures like Coulter, Cole continued:

> Hateful speech has consequences, particularly for people of color, LGBTQ people, immigrants, and others who have been historically marginalized. But if the government gets to decide which speech counts as hate speech, the powers that be may later feel free to censor any speech they don't like.[135]

Cole concluded by pointing to the larger First Amendment implications of the incident:

For the future of our democracy, we must protect bigoted speech from government censorship. On college campuses, that means that the best way to combat hateful speech is through counter-speech, vigorous and creative protest, and debate, not threats of violence or censorship.[136]

A Closer Look

The intense attention and nearly universal condemnation these campus protests have received created the impression that there is an out-of-control, violent, and highly effective leftist student movement to silence conservative voices on university campuses. The reality, however, is quite different: Dramatic incidents like the ones described above are rare; there is little evidence that they are driven primarily by liberal students or even students at all; silencing efforts against liberal speakers are at least as common and effective as those against rightwing speakers; and there are no real indications that rightwing viewpoints are being suppressed either on college campuses or elsewhere. That the reality diverges so much from the perception can be attributed in large part to the strategic efforts of extremely well-funded conservative nonprofit organizations, though these efforts are greatly aided by liberal free speech fundamentalists strangely eager to embrace a narrative that validates prejudices against women, minorities, and fellow liberals.

One of the organizations that arranges college speaking tours for Ann Coulter and other conservative celebrities is the Young America's Foundation (YAF). The YAF listed nearly $60 million in assets and $23 million in expenditures in 2014. Its funding sources include the Koch brothers, the Lynde and Harry Bradley Foundation, and Betsy Devos. According to Amy Binder,

> YAF fuels a provocative style for what one of our interviewees called "Average Joe" college students. Enticed by slogans depicting faculty as "tree-hugging, gun-taking, wealth-hating, and leftist-loving," students are taught in "boot camps" to fight "persecution" on campus with an "activist mentality," confronting their liberal peers and professors head-to-head with "aggressive" tactics. Students take up the combative charge by staging showy events like "Affirmative Action Bake Sales" and "Catch

an Illegal Alien Day." This provocative style of right-wing activism is designed to poke fun at liberals, get them angry, protest their events and, when chaos ensues, attract media attention.[137]

Other well-funded, rightwing organizations sponsoring conservative campus events include the Leadership Institute, Turning Point USA, and the American Enterprise Institute. Several of these organizations are members of the State Policy Network (SPN), a network of rightwing, tax-exempt think tanks with close ties to the Koch brothers and global corporations including Microsoft, Verizon, and Comcast that advances "an extreme right-wing agenda that aims to privatize education, block healthcare reform, restrict workers' rights, roll back environmental protections, and create a tax system that benefits most those at the very top level of income."[138]

The Foundation for Individual Rights in Education (FIRE), a nonprofit organization whose stated mission is "to defend and sustain individual rights at America's colleges and universities," has been one of the loudest voices proclaiming a state of emergency for freedom of expression in higher education. While FIRE characterizes itself as a nonpartisan foundation, its "funding, board members, and closest associations are heavily right wing."[139] In 2015, the organization listed $7 million in revenue and $6 million in assets. It receives generous funding from rightwing nonprofits such as the Lynde and Harry Bradley Foundation and the Koch brothers' DonorsTrust.[140]

FIRE claimed in 2017 that "the climate for free speech on campus is in many ways more precarious than ever." FIRE has maintained a database of attempts to disinvite college speakers since 2000. Its methodology is, to put it mildly, informal: According to its website, FIRE "collect[s] data from a number of sources, including news accounts and case submissions to FIRE and other organizations." Based on this database, FIRE raised the alarm regarding what it describes as "a record number of attempts by students, faculty, and others to prevent those with whom they disagreed from speaking on campus in 2016." That record number of attempted disinvitations in 2016 was, according to FIRE's database, forty-two. Eleven of these were disinvitations of a single speaker, Milo Yiannopoulos. As of 2014, there were 4,724 degree-granting institutions of higher education in the United States.[141] Even if each of these institutions held only one speaker event a year, the percentage of attempted disinvitations would be less than one-tenth of a percent.

Violent protests in response to controversial speech are even more rare. In the unusual instances that made headlines, many in the media and the general public assumed that the individuals who shouted, heckled, and otherwise expressed nonviolent disagreement with the speakers were also responsible for the violence and property damage that occurred during these incidents. However, according to the Middlebury and Berkeley administrations, there is no evidence showing that their students were responsible for the unlawful behavior. There is, however, evidence indicating that outside agitators of far-right, far-left, and indeterminate ideological affiliation infiltrate high-profile protests for their own ends. For example, during a protest of Yiannopoulos's speech at the University of Washington, a Yiannopoulos supporter with no connection to the university shot a demonstrator in the stomach, critically wounding him. According to police, the shooter, Elizabeth Hokoana, and her husband had gone to the UW campus with the specific purpose of provoking altercations with protesters. Hokoana's husband had sent a message to a friend on Facebook the day before Yiannopoulos's talk that stated, "I can't wait for tomorrow. I'm going to the milo event and if the snowflakes get out off [sic] hand I'm going to wade through their ranks and start cracking skulls," and he noted that his wife would be armed.[142]

Given that the majority of protests on college campuses have been nonviolent, it is perplexing that they should be denounced as spectacles of intolerance instead of being praised as strategies of counter-speech. After all, that is supposedly the best way to handle bad speech, at least according to free speech fundamentalists.[143] Visitors to public institutions have First Amendment rights, but so do the institution's students and faculty. A speaker's rights do not trump those of his audience. The right to peaceful protest is an essential aspect of the right to free speech, and peaceful protest on college campuses is a long and respected tradition in America. While conservative antipathy toward student protests has a long history, the student protest movements of the 1960s and 70s were widely encouraged and embraced by liberals.[144]

It is doubtful that anyone would deny that students have the right to express their opinions about issues such as construction budgets or curricular reform; they surely have as much right to express their views about which speakers get to consume university resources and be given an institutional platform.[145] But the heated criticism surrounding student protests indicates that at least some people do not believe that there are any permissible ways to express objections to a speaker or event. Some self-styled champions of free speech are apparently committed to silencing protest.

Backlash Bills

The spate of bills that have been proposed to limit students' rights of protest in the wake of the incidents at Berkeley and Middlebury support this conclusion. The bills are based on model legislation drafted by the Goldwater Institute and the Ethics and Public Policy Center with the Orwellian title of "Campus Free Speech Act."[146] The two organizations have received millions of dollars in funding from the Koch brothers; the Ethics and Public Policy Center has also received funding from several wealthy conservative family foundations, including nearly $2 million from the Lynde and Harry Bradley Foundation. In March 2017 alone, bills were filed in eight different states.

Among the model bill's most troubling provisions are Section 1.4, which states that "protests and demonstrations that infringe upon the rights of others to engage in or listen to expressive activity shall not be permitted and shall be subject to sanction," with the exception of "professors or other instructors . . . maintaining order in the classroom"; Section 1.7, which states that "anyone under the jurisdiction of the institution who interferes with the free expression of others" will be subjected to "a range of disciplinary sanctions"; Section 1.9, which dictates that a "student who has twice been found responsible for infringing the expressive rights of others will be suspended for a minimum of one year, or expelled"; and Section 1.10, which states that the academic institution (1) "shall strive to remain neutral, as an institution, on the public policy controversies of the day," and (2) "may not take action, as an institution, on the public policy controversies of the day in such a way as to require students or faculty to publicly express a given view of social policy."

The policy does not make clear how "interfering with the free expression of others" or "infringing the expressive rights of others" should be defined. Would it include chanting quietly? Holding up large signs? Turning one's back to the speaker? Such ambiguity would normally prompt First Amendment advocates to express concerns about chilling effects, particularly given the harshness of the sanctions imposed for violations. The clause requiring institutions to "remain neutral on the public policy controversies of the day" is difficult to describe as anything other than naked censorship. As Ralph Wilson, co-founder of UnKoch My Campus, a campaign to keep corporate influence out of education, writes, the bills can be likened to the *Citizens United* ruling in that they "bend the definition of free speech to favor corporate funded speech (campus speakers sponsored by outside groups, or corporate funded student groups). Spontaneous protest will be pre-empted by sponsored speakers."[147]

In October 2017, the University of Wisconsin system approved a policy that closely tracked the Goldwater bill, including a provision that suspends students who have been "found to have twice engaged in violence or other disorderly conduct that disrupts others' free speech." The policy, like the Goldwater bill and a version of the bill that passed in the Wisconsin Assembly in June 2017, does not specify what disruptive conduct is. Sixteen of the board of regents' eighteen members were appointed by Republican Governor Scott Walker. Only one regent, Democrat Tony Evers, dissented, stating that "this policy will chill and suppress free speech on this campus and all campuses." The system president, Ray Cross, spoke without any apparent irony about the importance of "teach[ing] students how to engage and listen to those with whom they differ," leaving it unclear how suspending students for expressing disagreement would convey this lesson.[148]

Tennessee's anti-protest bill was referred to as "the Milo bill." A supporter speaking at the press conference for the bill read a statement from Yiannopoulos that included these words: "We are winning the war. And we will continue to win as long as students, and now defenders of free speech within the government, stand up to ivory tower intellectuals and left-wing administrators intent on shutting up any speech they don't find convenient."[149] According to Senator Joey Hensley, one of the sponsors of the bill, "Too many times we've seen classrooms where the professor doesn't want to hear both sides of an issue, we've heard stories from many students that, honestly, are on the conservative side that have those issues stifled in the classroom."[150] The statement seemed to suggest that the bill would give students authority over professors in the classroom, a sentiment that was echoed by another speaker at the press conference, Luke Elliot, the vice president of the University of Tennessee College Republicans: "Students are often intimidated by the academic elite in the classroom, Tennessee is a conservative state, we will not allow out of touch professors with no real world experience to intimidate eighteen-year-olds."[151]

John K. Wilson, editor of the Academe Blog, provided a detailed critique of the bill in February 2017, noting that its sponsors had previously cut $436,000 from the University of Tennessee–Knoxville's diversity and inclusion programs and attempted to prohibit funding for Sex Week programs, which aim to "foster a comprehensive and academically-informed conversation about sex, sexuality, and relationships." Wilson concluded that the bill

> is a disaster for everyone. It imposes bizarre and burdensome regulations that administrators will struggle to understand and implement. It takes away from professors the ability to control the classroom and threatens their academic freedom. And it subjects students and staff to repressive new rules that can easily be abused to punish campus protest and dissent. This proposed law isn't a defense of free speech, it's an attack on it.[152]

Less-Told Tales

Accurate and objective reporting of these politically charged, media-saturated conflicts can be hard to come by, especially in a culture long on outrage and short on attention span. The facts of the Berkeley–Coulter episode in particular were widely misrepresented in the media and by many of the high-profile figures who criticized it.[153]

Many news outlets reported that Berkeley had canceled Coulter's talk and suggested that it had done so out of a bias against conservative speakers. But in reality, Coulter was never officially scheduled to speak at Berkeley.[154] The organizations that had invited Coulter had asked for but not received confirmation of an available venue. Berkeley administrators reportedly only learned of the invitation by reading about it in the newspaper. After receiving what the university characterized as "very specific intelligence" regarding violent demonstrations, Berkeley officials announced that they would not be able to provide adequate security to host Coulter in the venue requested on April 27. Instead, they offered to host Coulter at a different venue on May 2. Coulter and the groups that invited her did not find this alternative acceptable, and Coulter claimed she would show up on April 27. Berkeley administrators reiterated that they could not provide a secure location on that date, but that they would arrange for police presence to attempt to maintain public safety if Coulter did show up. After the conservative organizations that invited Coulter stated that they could no longer support the event due to safety concerns, Coulter decided not to show up after all.[155]

Berkeley's attempt to accommodate Coulter suggests that the university tried in good faith to honor both her right to speak and its commitment to the safety of its students. Berkeley Chancellor Nicholas B. Dirks criticized the apparent lack of concern for student safety in a communication to students and faculty, stating "This is a university, not a battlefield. We must make every effort to hold events at a time and location that maximizes the chances that First Amendment rights can be successfully exercised and that community members can be protected."[156]

The Coulter controversy underscores that controversial speech imposes literal as well as symbolic costs. While Berkeley generally sets aside around $200,000 a year to pay for security at campus protests, it spent $1.5 million between February and September of 2017, not counting the million or so it anticipated having to spend for "Free Speech Week," a four-day rally organized by Milo Yiannopoulos.[157] The events also cause substantial disruption to class schedules, invited speaker events, and campus life generally.

Serious attempts to shut down discussion of controversial speech on campuses are rare and more complicated than the attention they receive would indicate. What is more, many of the most egregious cases of campus censorship involve attacks on liberal and left-leaning speakers, which goes unmentioned in the rush to confirm and condemn the caricature of liberal intolerance. One of the most appalling incidents of violent censorship on a college campus involved Anita Sarkeesian, a cultural critic best known for her critiques of sexism in video games. Sarkeesian's work has made her a target for violent, misogynist abuse since 2012, abuse that intensified during GamerGate, the 2014 high-profile harassment campaign against women in the gaming industry.

On October 14, 2014, the day before Sarkeesian was scheduled to give a talk at Utah State University, university administrators received an anonymous e-mail from a person who threatened to carry out "the deadliest school shooting in American history" if her talk was not canceled. The anonymous author referenced Marc Lépine, who, in the name of "fighting feminism," murdered fourteen women at the École Polytechnique in Montreal in 1989. The e-mail stated:

> I have at my disposal a semi-automatic rifle, multiple pistols, and a collection of pipe bombs. . . . You have 24 hours to cancel Sarkeesian's talk . . . Anita Sarkeesian is everything wrong with the feminist woman, and she is going to die screaming like the craven little whore that she is if you let her come to USU. I will write my manifesto in her spilled blood, and you will all bear witness to what feminist lies and poison have done to the men of America.[158]

Sarkeesian originally planned to proceed with her talk, in keeping with her stated commitment to refuse to be silenced by threats. Given the specific reference to firearms in the threat, however, she requested that the university implement metal detectors or pat-downs for the event. The university, however, refused on the grounds that Utah is an open-carry state. The administration stated, "in accordance with the State of Utah law regarding the carrying of firearms, if a person has a valid concealed firearm permit and is carrying a weapon, they are permitted to have it at the venue."[159] Sarkeesian asked if the audience could be screened for guns and allowed in if they had permits, but the university declined to undertake this measure. According to USU spokesman Tim Vitale, "campus law enforcement officers believed that would have been needlessly invasive for the audience."[160]

In the university's opinion, Sarkeesian had received violent threats before and "none of the threats had materialized into anything specific, that . . . led us to believe that the threat was not imminent or real."[161] In light of the university's refusal to screen for weapons, Sarkeesian canceled her talk, stating, "It's unacceptable that the school is unable or unwilling to screen for firearms at a lecture on their campus, especially when a specific terrorist threat had been made against the speaker."[162]

In this case, a high-profile speaker was targeted with specific threats of violence solely based on the perceived content of her speech, threats that extended to the student audience of the event. The university administration declined to take the threat seriously, which left Sarkeesian with the choice of speaking and risking death or injury to herself and her audience, or not speaking at all.

The similarities to the events surrounding Ann Coulter's talk at Berkeley are clear, and yet Sarkeesian's case did not generate anything close to the outrage and condemnation by prominent figures on either the right or the left. The attempt to violently suppress Sarkeesian's speech was not denounced in rightwing outlets so quick to drape themselves in the First Amendment when it comes to speakers like Yiannopoulos or Coulter, or used as an example of cowardly intolerance of uncomfortable ideas by Jonathan Chait or Floyd Abrams. The ACLU never issued a statement decrying the "heckler's veto" of Sarkeesian or used the incident to encourage those on college campuses to use "counter-speech, vigorous and creative protest, and debate, not threats of violence or censorship." The relative inattention paid to the silencing of Sarkeesian suggests that self-styled civil libertarians do not find speech advocating racial and gender equality as deserving of the same robust defense as speech that advocates sexism and racism.

Sarkeesian's story is only one of many rightwing attempts to silence liberal speakers that fails to generate the attention or outrage of incidents involving rightwing provocateurs. In June 2017, *Inside Higher Ed* published an article highlighting recent threats against academics. Five of the six incidents targeted liberal professors, and yet the only incident on the list that has received sustained condemnation was the single case involving a conservative professor, Bret Weinstein of Evergreen College.

The targets who received far less support include Princeton University Professor Keeanga-Yamahtta Taylor, who gave a commencement speech at Hampshire College in May 2017 in which she called Donald Trump "a racist, sexist megalomaniac" who had "fulfilled the campaign promises of a campaign organized and built upon racism, corporatism and militarism."[163] Shortly after Fox News reported on her speech, Taylor was targeted with threats of violence, including lynching and being shot. She canceled planned speeches in Seattle and the University of California–San Diego over concerns for her safety. In another case, Johnny Eric Williams, an associate professor of sociology at Trinity College, was subjected to physical threats after he shared an article that suggested black people should not come to the aid of bigots. Trinity College shut down for a day over the threats and placed Williams on leave. In another incident, a classics professor at the University of Iowa was threatened and harassed simply for noting that many ancient Western statues were not originally white.[164]

Rod Dreher, the senior editor of *The American Conservative*, sparked one notable incident of faculty harassment. Dreher writes frequently about student "social-justice warriors" whose "petty outrages" are poisoning college campuses. In 2017, he was sent an anonymous tip that "a black professor at Texas A&M was saying racist things about white people, and the university was letting it happen."[165] The professor in question was Tommy Curry, a professor of philosophy at Texas A&M University. In 2012, Curry had frequently appeared on a radio show to discuss race and politics. Dreher discovered one episode in which Curry discussed the Tarantino film *Django Unchained* and black violence. In the episode, Curry says,

> [T]he fact that we've had no one address, like, how relevant and how solidified this kind of tradition is, for black people saying, "Look, in order to be equal, in order to be liberated, some white people may have to die." I've just been immensely disappointed, because what we look at, week after week, is national catastrophe after catastrophe where black people, black children, are still dying. . . . [W]hen we turn the conversation back and say, "Does the black community ever need to own guns? Does the black community have a need to protect itself? Does the black individual have a need to protect himself from police officers?", we don't have that conversation at all.[166]

Because Dreher thought that Curry "sounded like a bully," he wrote a blog post about Curry that included a link to the radio show titled "When Is It OK to Kill White People?" Within two days, the blog post had made it onto the far-right conspiracy theorist website Infowars and the neo-Nazi website Stormfront. Conservatives who claimed to be committed to free speech condemned Curry's words: "Certainly, no one should be stopped for sharing and debating ideas; the country has seen too many prohibitions of speech in past years," wrote Ron Meyer, editor of Red Alert Politics, a Washington-based blog. "However, paying a professor to share radical ideas on behalf of a university has nothing to do with free speech." Curry began receiving death threats and left town.[167]

Calls for Curry to be fired began to circulate on an A&M community site, and donors began making angry calls. Instead of defending Curry, Texas A&M president Michael Young distributed a statement to the university community that called Curry's views "reprehensible" and conflicted with the university's values. Though Curry had just received tenure—becoming the first black full professor in the philosophy department—the university has offered him no plan for protection or granted him leave.[168]

Compare Curry's experience with that of Glenn Reynolds, a law professor at the University of Tennessee– Knoxville who is also known as the far-right blogger Instapundit. On September 21, 2016, protests in Charlotte, North Carolina, following the fatal police shooting of Keith Lamont Scott, prompted a local news station to issue an advisory on Twitter: "LIVE NOW: Protesters on I-277 stopping traffic and surrounding vehicles. AVOID." Reynolds, who tweets under the handle @Instapundit, responded to the tweet with the message "Run them down."

After investigating the matter, University of Tennessee Law Dean Melanie D. Wilson announced that no disciplinary action would be taken against Reynolds. Wilson concluded that Reynolds's tweet was "an exercise of his First Amendment rights" despite the fact that it "offended many members of our community and beyond, and I understand the hurt and frustration they feel."[169]

A white professor advocates driving a vehicle into a crowd of African American protesters mourning the death of another man at the hands of police, and it barely causes a stir; a black professor references a fictional film to discuss the history of black self-defense, and he is targeted with death threats. The difference speaks volumes about the state of academic free speech.

Several professors who have been harassed and threatened have been featured on the rightwing website Professor Watchlist, whose stated purpose is to identify faculty who "discriminate against conservative students and advance leftist propaganda in the classroom." The site provides the professors' institutional affiliations and faculty photos as well as a summary of their alleged infractions. The websites Campus Reform and College Fix feature similar stories. According to the American Association of University Professors, "Individual faculty members who have been included on such lists or singled out elsewhere have been subject to threats of physical violence, including sexual assault, through hundreds of e-mails, calls, and social media postings."[170]

These professors are facing violent, targeted threats that have directly affected their sense of physical safety and their livelihood. Nearly all of them were targeted simply because their critics found their ideas—their views on racism, sexism, or white male supremacy—offensive. If concerns about freedom of expression in academia are sincere, then these incidents should receive at least the same amount of attention and generate at least as much outrage as those involving rightwing celebrities. Indeed, anyone truly concerned about intellectual freedom on college campuses should find direct threats to professors' livelihoods far more troubling than protests over famous media personalities with multiple outlets for expressing themselves. Professors engage in intellectual discourse for a living: When they are silenced at their own institutions, they have few alternative means in which to express their ideas.

Intellectual intolerance on college campuses is indeed disturbing and should be taken seriously. But the caricature of beleaguered conservatives struggling to be heard over the din of rioting liberal reactionaries is a grotesque distortion of reality. True instances of violent, intolerant suppression of ideas on college campuses are rare; those specifically targeting conservative ideas are even rarer.

While it is not particularly surprising that the right wing exaggerates censorship of conservative speech while ignoring the censorship of progressive speech, it is disheartening to see so many prominent liberal figures follow suit. What is even more regrettable is that the outsized focus on isolated, headline-grabbing incidents takes attention away from many pressing issues facing college campuses. Those who raise the alarm about universities' growing intolerance for uncomfortable ideas and students' alleged demands for "safe spaces" are silent, for example, about the passage of "campus carry" laws, which allow fearful students to intimidate and silence their peers by carrying firearms, as well as putting them in physical danger. Self-proclaimed campus free speech defenders like FIRE and the ACLU say little when legislators threaten to revoke institutional funding if students are allowed to write affirmatively about abortion, when high school teachers are fired for making comparisons between Trump's policies and fascism, when university administrators impose gag rules on campus rape victims, or when southern state school textbooks engage in blatant historical revision of the Civil War.

They also have very little to say, for that matter, about rampant rape and sexual assault in college communities, widespread sexual harassment of female students by male faculty members, or racialized threats—including nooses, references to lynching, and bomb threats specifically targeting minority students. It is nothing short of extraordinary that anyone, especially eminent constitutional scholars, can claim that the single greatest threat facing free speech today is student protests of controversial campus speakers. Any one of the issues listed above imposes a greater risk of chilling effects and censorship on college campuses, and they are not even the tip of the iceberg when it comes to the endangerment of freedom of speech in society at large.

THE HIGH COST OF FREE SPEECH:
"IT BEGAN WITH WORDS"

In striking down the Skokie ordinance that prohibited the public display of the swastika, the Illinois Supreme Court drew heavily from the 1971 Supreme Court case *Cohen v. California*. In that case, the Court reversed the conviction of Robert Cohen, who had been charged with disturbing the peace for wearing a jacket displaying the words "Fuck the Draft" inside a courthouse. Justice Harlan, writing for the majority, rejected the argument that the phrase was a "fighting word" unprotected by the First Amendment. Fighting words, according to Harlan, are "personally abusive epithets which, when addressed to the ordinary citizen, are, as a matter of common knowledge, inherently likely to provoke violent reaction." While some people might find the phrase on Cohen's jacket offensive, the words were not personally directed at anyone, and there was no evidence that Cohen either intended to inspire a hostile reaction or that any such reaction did in fact transpire.[171]

Thus, the Court concluded that the government did not have the power to eject an idea from the marketplace simply because some might find it offensive. After all, Justice Harlan observed, "one man's vulgarity is another's lyric." To inhibit freedom of speech merely on the basis that the content of the speech might be offensive to some hearers would be to allow a "heckler's veto" inconsistent with the principles of the First Amendment.[172]

The Illinois Supreme Court likened the city's attempt to prohibit the display of swastikas in public demonstrations to the attempt to punish Cohen for the profane phrase on his jacket. The court asked,

> How is one to distinguish [the swastika] from any other offensive word (emblem)? . . . [W]hile the particular four-letter word (emblem) being litigated here is perhaps more distasteful than most others of its genre, it is nevertheless often true that one man's vulgarity is another's lyric. Indeed, we think it is largely because governmental officials cannot make principled distinctions in this area that the Constitution leaves matters of taste and style so largely to the individual.[173]

In the Illinois court's view, the swastika and the words "Fuck the Draft" were equivalent: Both are forms of "offensive speech" that are ultimately matters of "taste and style."

But this is a false equivalence. The phrase "Fuck the Draft" expresses a political view, however crudely phrased. It was directed at no particular audience and conveyed no animus toward any person. The swastika, by contrast, does not convey a political view, at least not one consistent with the values of a democratic society. It is not a random "four-letter word" that could be used to signify anything or nothing. It is a symbol—arguably *the* symbol—of the genocidal slaughter of millions of people. Its meaning is not ambiguous, at least not when displayed by a group calling itself the National Socialist Party of America, which openly praises genocide and white supremacy. To characterize its impact on viewers in general—to say nothing of Jewish people in particular, especially Holocaust survivors and their relatives—as merely "offensive" or a matter of "taste and style" is grotesque. The Supreme Court's belief that a man wearing a jacket with the words "Fuck the Draft" inside a courthouse is not "inherently likely to provoke violent reaction" is plausible; the Illinois Supreme Court's contention that the same is true of a swastika displayed by neo-Nazis marching through a town of Holocaust survivors is not.

Indeed, the court had clear evidence that the swastika would provoke a violent reaction. News of the neo-Nazis' planned march had inspired aggressive responses among Jewish organizations in Skokie and beyond. As many as 12,000 to 15,000 counter-demonstrators were expected to appear at the event, including roughly 1,000 Jewish Defense League (JDL) members who announced their intentions to "'use whatever kind of violence' is necessary 'to stop the march, if it means taking a baseball bat.'"[174] But instead of concluding that the swastika constituted unprotected fighting words, the Illinois court held that its "display on uniforms or banners by those engaged in peaceful demonstrations cannot be totally precluded solely because that display may provoke a violent reaction by those who view it." This assertion effectively rejects the category of fighting words altogether.

What is more, the fighting words designation was not originally restricted to speech that inspires a violent reaction. In *Chaplinsky v. New Hampshire*, the Supreme Court defined fighting words as words that "by their very utterance, inflict injury *or* tend to incite an immediate breach of the peace."[175] Fighting words are not just those that lead to immediate violence, but words that impose harm in themselves. Though the idea of inherently injurious speech has fallen out of constitutional vogue, it tracks the longstanding common law distinction between assault and battery. The injury of assault is the fear of suffering physical harm whereas the injury of battery is the physical harm itself.

According to the court testimony of David Guttman, a professor of psychiatry, the psychological impact of the proposed march in Skokie was exactly this type of injury:

> Jews are aware that the attitudes and words of even polite anti-Semitism can—all too easily—become the preludes and accompaniments of murder. Accordingly, the Jew is not being paranoid when he takes anti-Semitic epithets very seriously, and views them with great apprehension, as intrinsic parts of a larger scenario that can include persecution and mass murder. What would be paranoia for others is sober realism for Jews. . . . [T]he words of any Nazi to any Jew have, by definition, lost the usual intent and limitation of words: they are symbolic continuations of the Holocaust, literal perpetuations of the climate of the Holocaust, and preparations for a new Holocaust. No matter what words their placards bear, when Nazis march in Skokie, their presence and their regalia says to Jews: "You thought you escaped. You did not. We know where you are. When our strength is sufficient and when the time is ripe, we will come and get you."[176]

The swastika is thus a "fighting word" in both senses expressed in *Chaplinsky*. It inflicts actual injury on Holocaust survivors, and it provokes them to violent response. It is not the case that "their sensibilities are being offended," but rather that "[t]hey are being forced to protect themselves from the infliction of real harm."[177]

Regardless of what one makes of the fighting words designation, the failure to distinguish between merely offensive speech and speech that inflicts injury is disingenuous and dangerous. This fuzziness feeds into false persecution narratives, allowing bigots to claim that they are harmed by messages of racial or gender equality. But personal discomfort is not the same thing as injury. The message that "Jews are inferior" may be merely offensive. The message that "Jews should be exterminated" is not. The same is true of other speech about race, religion, gender, sexual orientation, and the like. Censoring the expression of preferences for certain races or beliefs in the superiority of particular religions on the basis that it causes personal offense would indeed be counterproductive and open to abuse.

But statements advocating discrimination or violence toward individuals or groups on the basis of race, religion, gender, and the like are not merely offensive: They inflict actual injury and undermine democratic values, a reality on which the entire body of antidiscrimination law rests.

Less than two weeks after the election of Donald Trump as president of the United States, white nationalists gathered a few blocks from the White House in a federal building named for Ronald Reagan. In front of a crowd of mostly young men, the group's leader, Richard Spencer, celebrated the election of Trump and waxed poetic about the superiority of the white race.

> He railed against Jews and, with a smile, quoted Nazi propaganda in the original German. America, he said, belonged to white people, whom he called the "children of the sun," a race of conquerors and creators who had been marginalized but now, in the era of President-elect Donald J. Trump, were "awakening to their own identity."

> As he finished, several audience members had their arms outstretched in a Nazi salute. Mr. Spencer called out: "Hail Trump! Hail our people!" and then, "Hail victory!"—the English translation of the Nazi exhortation "Sieg Heil!" The room shouted back.[178]

The U.S. Holocaust Museum in Washington, DC, issued a statement expressing its alarm at the event, which included the somber reminder that "The Holocaust did not begin with killing; it began with words."

Racist and misogynist speech is in no danger of suppression, on college campuses or anywhere else. There has perhaps never been a safer time in America to express virulently misogynist, racist, and xenophobic speech. Donald Trump ran an entire campaign fueled by such speech and was elected president of the United States. His cabinet and advisors are overwhelmingly white, male, radical conservatives. Many of them have personal histories of violence against women and open prejudices against racial minorities, the LGBT community, immigrants, and Muslims. Republicans control every branch of the federal government and the majority of state governments. They operate enormous media enterprises that produce a steady stream of rightwing propaganda in television, radio, and the Internet outlets. Multibillionaire "philanthropists" like the Koch brothers use their vast wealth to shape politics and educational institutions toward conservative ends. When isolated instances of intolerance against conservative views do occur, they are roundly denounced by both conservatives and liberals.

From Skokie to Charlottesville, the message has remained the same: "Free Speech for the White Man." But white men do not need more First Amendment protection. White men have used their unlimited speech privileges to threaten and incite violence over any sign that the world is not perfectly shaped to their interests: the removal of Confederate statues, gun control, Starbucks cups, women's birth control, diversity training, black men kneeling, black men standing, a black man as president, a female candidate for president, a black woman giving witness. When white men's speech is given so much breathing room, it leaves no air for anyone else.

CHAPTER 4

THE CULT
OF THE INTERNET

SECTION 230, COMMUNICATIONS DECENCY ACT

No provider or user of an interactive computer service shall be treated as the publisher or speaker of any information provided by another information content provider.

"A website is speech. It is not a bomb."

–Matthew Prince, Co-Founder of Cloudflare

Jane Doe No. 1 ran away from home when she was 15 years old. She soon fell into the hands of sex traffickers, who advertised her on an online classifieds site known as Backpage. Jane Doe No. 1's photo appeared in over 300 ads on the site between June 2013 and September 2013. Each ad featuring Jane Doe No. 1 was listed as an offer of "escort" services and "included known signifiers for child prostitution such as "young," "girl," "fresh," "tiny," "roses," and "party."[1] Jane Doe No. 1 was forced to engage in ten to twelve sexual transactions with adult males over the course of eighteen months; in total, she was raped over 1,000 times.

Jane Doe No. 1 and two other teenaged girls who had been trafficked on Backpage brought suit against the site, arguing that Backpage benefited from child sex trafficking by knowingly featuring ads that offered illegal services. Their case was dismissed on the grounds that to hold Backpage responsible for the actions of advertisers on its site, even when it benefited financially from those actions, would violate Section 230 of the Communications Decency Act.[2] In the conclusion of his ruling, the judge stated:

> To avoid any misunderstanding, let me make it clear that the court is not unsympathetic to the tragic plight described by Jane Doe No. 1, Jane Doe No. 2, and Jane Doe No. 3. Nor does it regard the sexual trafficking of children as anything other than an abhorrent evil. Finally, the court is not naïve—I am fully aware that sex traffickers and other purveyors of illegal wares ranging from drugs to pornography exploit the vulnerabilities of the Internet as a marketing tool. Whether one agrees with its stated policy or not . . . Congress has made the determination that the balance between suppression of trafficking and freedom of expression should be struck in favor of the latter in so far as the Internet is concerned.[3]

FOUNDING THE CULT OF THE INTERNET

John Perry Barlow, who founded the Electronic Frontier Foundation (EFF) with John Gilmore and Mitch Kapor in 1990, outlined his vision of the Internet in a 1996 document modestly titled "Declaration of the Independence of Cyberspace." Borrowing heavily from the rhetoric of the Declaration of the Independence and the Constitution, Barlow wrote, "I declare the global social space we are building to be naturally independent of the tyrannies you seek to impose on us. . . . Governments derive their just powers from the consent of the governed. You have neither solicited nor received ours." Invoking "the dreams of Jefferson, Washington, Mill, Madison, De Tocqueville, and Brandeis," Barlow proclaimed,

> We are creating a world that all may enter without privilege or prejudice accorded by race, economic power, military force, or station of birth. We are creating a world where anyone, anywhere may express his or her beliefs, no matter how singular, without fear of being coerced into silence or conformity.[4]

The declaration was clearly meant to situate Barlow and his fellow cyberspace pioneers firmly within the American revolutionary tradition and to invoke the principles of the founding era. Barlow decried the "increasingly hostile and colonial measures" of Internet regulation, which "place us in the same position as those previous lovers of freedom and self-determination who had to reject the authorities of distant, uninformed powers."

The analogy was more apt than Barlow likely intended. Like the founders, Barlow, Gilmore, and Kapor were white men who felt entitled themselves to speak for the collective "we." Barlow's high-minded rejection of "privileges and prejudices accorded by race, economic power, military force, or station of birth" (note the lack of any reference to gender), like the founders' professions of equality in the Declaration of Independence, appears less noble in light of these men's membership in a race and class that tended to enjoy privilege without suffering prejudice.

And yet a keen sense of persecution pervades Barlow's declaration. The litany of abuses supposedly suffered by the citizens of cyberspace are, notably, both vague and speculative: Barlow accuses governments of "invad[ing] our precincts" to solve problems "that don't exist"; "trying to ward off the virus of liberty by erecting guard posts at the frontiers of Cyberspace"; and "proposing laws, in America and elsewhere, that claim to own speech itself throughout the world." Barlow provides no specific details of actual oppression, and his manifesto indicates that whatever sinister threats the "colonizers" have planned have yet to actually materialize.

Barlow's vision, established not only through the declaration but through the work of the enormously influential organization he co-founded, has had a profound influence on the development of the Internet. His vision of cyberspace as a utopia, "a civilization of the Mind" that promises to be "more humane and fair than the world your governments have made before" as long as it keeps the dark forces of government intervention at bay, was enshrined in the federal law that would come to be known as the most important law of cyberspace, Section 230 of the Communications Decency Act.

If Barlow's manifesto can be thought of as the Internet's Declaration of Independence, Section 230 of the Communications Decency Act can be likened to its Constitution. Drafted in 1996 by two white male members of Congress, Section 230 has been called the Magna Carta of the Internet and the "cornerstone of Internet freedom." Section 230 was a tiny part of the law that Barlow identified in his Declaration as a threat to the Internet: the 1996 U.S. Telecommunications Reform Act. The act included a provision to regulate obscenity and indecency on the Internet, known as the Communications Decency Act (CDA). Several members of Congress, both Republican and Democrat, shared Barlow's concerns about the effect of the CDA on the future of the Internet. Two of these congressmen, Republican Christopher Cox and Democrat Ron Wyden, authored an amendment to the CDA that offered a much softer approach to regulation. The amendment was Section 230, and its most influential provision, (c)(1), has been broadly interpreted as immunizing interactive computer service providers from facing liability for harm caused by their users.[5]

The findings section of Section 230 echoes Barlow's idealized vision of the Internet: "The Internet and other interactive computer services offer a forum for a true diversity of political discourse, unique opportunities for cultural development, and myriad avenues for intellectual activity." Because the Internet has "flourished, to the benefit of all Americans, with a minimum of government regulation," one of the stated goals of Section 230 is "to preserve the vibrant and competitive free market that presently exists for the Internet and other interactive computer services, unfettered by Federal or State regulation."

Between Barlow's declaration and Section 230, one could get the impression that the Internet in 1996 was a Lockean state of nature,

> wherein all the power and jurisdiction is reciprocal, no one having more than another; there being nothing more evident than that creatures of the same species and rank, promiscuously born to all the same advantages of nature and the use of the same faculties, should also be equal one amongst another without subordination or subjection.[6]

In such a state, the Internet requires no centralized authority to impose laws, delegate the boundaries of conduct, or mete out punishment. The Internet is Paradise before the Fall: No laws are needed because no sins have been committed.[7] The only real harm in cyberspace is the harm of government interference.

But there was already abundant evidence in 1996 that the Internet was not the utopia that enthusiasts made it out to be. When Barlow's declaration and Section 230 were written, the Internet had existed for more than two decades, though not in a form that would be easily recognizable to users today. Created in 1969 in the form of four linked sites, the Internet in its first twenty years was primarily focused on military and academic research. Access was largely restricted to an exclusive group of government officials and scholars, and commercial activity and spam were forbidden. When the World Wide Web was invented in 1989, it was completely text-based. The ban on commercial activity was lifted in 1992; in 1993, web browsers began to display images. That same year, universities began providing students with e-mail accounts and Internet access.

Almost as soon as the potential to use the Internet to engage in mass communication became apparent, it was used to promote prejudice and violence against women and nonwhite men. The year before Barlow's declaration, in one of the first instances of content going viral, an e-mail by four male Cornell students with the subject line, "75 Reasons Why Women (Bitches) Should Not Have Freedom of Speech" was rapidly redistributed and posted across the web.[8] This list included "15. The 2nd and 19th amendments," "24. God forbid, a woman president," and "39. Of course, if she can't speak, she can't say no."[9] That same year, a University of Michigan student named Jake Baker was arrested by the FBI after he posted a story to an online discussion board that fantasized about raping, torturing, and murdering one of his female classmates.[10]

In 1985, a story appeared in the *New York Times* about the Aryan Liberty Net, a neo-Nazi organization that had "established a computer-based network to link rightist groups and to disseminate a list of those who it says 'have betrayed their race.'"[11] One list, titled "Know Your Enemy," included "the addresses and telephone numbers of regional offices of the Anti-Defamation League of B'nai B'rith and the offices of the Communist Party U.S.A. It also includes names and addresses of 'race traitors' and 'informers.'" The group described itself as "a pro-American, pro-White, anti-Communist network of true believers who serve the one and only God—Jesus, the Christ," restricted to "Aryan patriots only." Messages on the network praised the recent murder of an FBI informer against the KKK ("He was blown to pieces on a recent morning, when he opened his mailbox to remove his newspaper. Oh, glorious day!") and celebrated the new "young lions" of the movement, who "are the armed party which is being born out of the inability of white male youths to be heard." A message titled "At Last, Unity" reads: "Finally, we are all going to be linked together at one point in time. Imagine, if you will, all the great minds of the patriotic Christian movement linked together and joined into one computer."[12]

Neither Barlow's declaration nor Section 230 noted the violent misogyny and racism that had already taken hold in cyberspace by 1996. Neither document acknowledged that some of the first uses of this powerful mass communication tool involved advocating for the censorship of women and promoting white supremacist violence. Early Internet enthusiasts were apparently also untroubled by the Internet gender gap: The Internet's infrastructure and design was overwhelmingly controlled by white men, despite women's key contributions in creating the computer codes that laid the foundation for the Internet, and men outnumbered women online by about four to one in 1994 and by more than two to one in 1996.[13]

In an echo of the Constitutional Convention, the soaring, universalist rhetoric of the founders and architects of the Internet simply ignored the abuses suffered by women and nonwhite men and their lack of equal representation. The founding fathers of the Internet, like the founding fathers of America before them, recognized only one threat: government interference with the rights of people like them.

The cult of the Internet does more than repeat the gestures of the founding fathers. It also aggregates and intensifies fundamentalist tendencies across the political spectrum, in particular the tendency toward free speech extremism. In the words of Danielle Keats Citron, "the Internet's very essence is to aggregate expressions so as to convert them into actions."[14]

Far from being a utopia, the Internet, now firmly in the hands of powerful corporations, has worsened existing inequalities and forms of exploitation. As the Internet blurs distinctions between speech and conduct, it encourages impulsive and irrational habits and facilitates new forms of discrimination, abuse, and violence. First Amendment fundamentalists have succeeded in framing the Internet as a realm of pure speech, obscuring the physical and material reality of the harms it produces. This framework has made it virtually impossible to prevent the Internet from being used to engage in destructive harassment, disseminate harmful misinformation, and to radicalize and mobilize violent extremism if all kinds.

THAT OBSCURE OBJECT OF REGULATION: SECTION 230

The civil libertarianism so pervasive in fundamentalist attitudes toward gun and speech rights dominates Internet theory and practice. Techno-libertarianism is if anything even more staunchly antiregulatory than traditional civil libertarianism. In this it suffers, like all libertarianism, from a fundamental paradox. The Internet would not exist if it were not for the interventions of the "Governments of the Industrial World" that Barlow so contemptuously dismisses in his declaration. Contrary to his startling claim that cyberspace "is an act of nature," the U.S. government in particular was essential to the creation of the Internet.[15] The U.S. government began developing the Internet in the 1960s for military purposes, with the Department of Defense, Department of Energy, the National Science Foundation, and the National Aeronautics and Space Administration all playing significant roles.[16]

As Cass Sunstein writes,

> Those who complain most bitterly about *proposed* regulation are often those who most profit, often financially, from *current* regulation. . . . What they are complaining about is not regulation as such—they need it—but a regulatory regime from which they would benefit less than they do under the present one.[17]

The Internet is, contrary to the libertarian mythology, intensely regulated by government, corporate, and individual forces. Techno-libertarians, like all libertarians, only characterize interventions that conflict with their self-interest as regulations; interventions that serve their self-interest are viewed as "freedoms" or "liberties" or "neutrality." As Larry Lessig wrote in 2000,

> Our choice is not between "regulation" and "no regulation." The code regulates. It implements values, or not. It enables freedoms, or disables them. It protects privacy, or promotes monitoring. People choose how the code does these things. People write the code.[18]

The techno-libertarian's professed antipathy to laws and regulations, expressed by Barlow's statement that "legal concepts of property, expression, identity, movement, and context do not apply" in cyberspace, is equally nonsensical. Barlow's EFF, which describes itself as "the leading nonprofit organization defending civil liberties in the digital world," bases its entire legislative and policy platform on the First Amendment and on Section 230. Both the First Amendment and Section 230 are "legal concepts" of "expression"—American legal concepts, to be precise. Section 230 is a government regulation, part of the very Telecommunications Reform Act that Barlow explicitly denounced in his declaration.

MORAL HAZARDS AND GOOD SAMARITANS

Internet fundamentalists often describe Section 230 as the cornerstone of the Internet. Without it, they claim, the Internet would collapse. But Section 230 has been interpreted to remove incentives for powerful online intermediaries to take responsibility for the harms facilitated by the users of their platforms, even when those intermediaries directly benefit from the harmful behavior. In economics, the lack of incentive to guard against risk because one is protected from its negative consequences is known as a moral hazard. Section 230 creates a moral hazard, compounding the multiple difficulties that people facing online abuse face in attempting to protect themselves.

One of these difficulties is anonymity: The ease with which harassers and other malicious users can hide their identity online makes it difficult if not impossible for their victims to engage in self-help or legal remedies. Burner e-mail accounts and anonymizing software such as Tor can prevent a victim from discovering a user's true IP address or other identifying information. Another challenge victims face is asymmetry of power: Harassers often have far more resources and time to engage in harassment than the victim does to fight it. Another is scale: Online mobs can easily overwhelm a single victim. All of these factors stack the deck against individual victims of abuse.

But perhaps the greatest obstacle to justice for victims of online abuse is the lack of incentive for those with power to intervene. Section 230 has been interpreted to immunize online intermediaries from liability for the unlawful conduct of their users, even when those intermediaries directly benefit from that conduct. Such morally hazardous immunity is unique to the Internet.

In the offline world, tort, criminal, and civil rights law all allow liability to be imposed not only on those who directly engage in unlawful behavior but also on those who facilitate or assist such behavior in certain circumstances. The publisher of a defamatory book can be sued in addition to the book's author, as can the distributor of the book if she had knowledge of the book's unlawful content. The owner of a hotel can be criminally prosecuted for the illegal activity he allows another person to conduct in one of his rooms. An employer can be penalized for failing to respond appropriately to sexually harassing behavior by one of its employees.

Extending liability beyond direct actors can be justified on both fairness and public policy grounds. First, it is only fair that people who benefit from the illicit actions of others should be held partly accountable for the harm they cause. Second, third-party liability creates incentives for powerful intermediaries to engage in proactive steps to discourage unlawful conduct before it happens, and to respond quickly and effectively when it does.

Conversely, eliminating third-party liability not only removes incentives for intermediaries to prevent unlawful conduct, but creates incentives for them to allow such conduct if they can benefit from it: a clear moral hazard. That is precisely what courts have largely interpreted Section 230 to do.

The most influential and controversial parts of Section 230 are two provisions in section (c), which is titled "Protection for 'Good Samaritan' blocking and screening of offensive material." Provision (c)(1) states that "No provider or user of an interactive computer service shall be treated as the publisher or speaker of any information provided by another information content provider."[19] Provision (c)(2) shields providers and users of an interactive computer service from civil liability with regard to any action that is "voluntarily taken in good faith to restrict access to or availability of material that the provider or user considers to be obscene, lewd, lascivious, filthy, excessively violent, harassing, or otherwise objectionable" or "taken to enable or make available to information content providers or others the technical means to restrict access" to such material.

Given the title of this section, it seems clear that Section 230 is meant to provide "Good Samaritan" immunity in much the same sense as other "Good Samaritan" laws. Such laws do not, as the name might suggest, create a duty to aid, but instead provide immunity to people who attempt to aid others in distress. Such laws are intended to remove disincentives for offering such aid. Without Good Samaritan laws, people may be deterred from offering assistance out of fear that they will be held liable if such assistance inadvertently causes harm.

Two cases help explain the problem that Section 230 was seemingly intended to address and why it uses the terms "speakers" and "publishers," which come from defamation law. In 1991, an online communications service called CompuServe was sued for defamatory posts that appeared on one of the service's 150 or so discussion forums, on the theory that CompuServe was a publisher of the content. Under defamation law, the publishers of libelous speech can be sued as well as the creators of the libelous speech under the theory that they have knowledge of its unlawful content. The court found that because CompuServe did not review the content it hosted—and therefore it could not have knowledge of its unlawful nature—it could not be treated as a publisher of the defamatory speech in question.[20]

In 1995, "wolf of Wall Street" Jordan Belfort sued the web services company Prodigy over allegedly libelous remarks that appeared on one of the online bulletin boards hosted by Prodigy. In contrast to CompuServe, Prodigy was found liable for the defamatory content. The key difference between Prodigy and CompuServe in the view of the court was that Prodigy had attempted to moderate some of the thousands of posts made to its boards, whereas CompuServe had made no effort to do so. Prodigy's partial attempt to filter some content on its site made it liable for all the content on its site.[21]

The decision effectively punished Prodigy for attempting to keep harmful content off its site and created a disincentive for any online intermediary to engage in such moderation. Section 230's "Good Samaritan" provision was a direct response to this ruling, clearly intending to encourage content moderation by offering immunity from liability to those who engage in it.

The text of Section 230 seems to provide that intermediaries are immunized from civil liability when they act like publishers, that is, when they act voluntarily and in good faith to remove or restrict objectionable material. "On its face, section 230's entire focus is on immunizing good faith publishing functions."[22]

The statute's primary purpose seems to be to encourage interactive service providers to voluntarily remove or restrict offensive content. One way to incentivize online intermediaries to act responsibly and to take an active role in voluntarily filtering out unlawful or harmful content is to eliminate the potential negative consequences of doing so. Exempting intermediaries from publisher liability when they exercise good faith editorial control is justified on the grounds that it will encourage more intermediaries to engage in socially beneficial self-regulation.

Whose Speech?

But courts have interpreted Section 230 much more broadly than this. In addition to protecting online intermediaries from liability when they actively remove content in good faith for socially beneficial purposes, courts have read Section 230 as protecting online intermediaries from liability when they make no attempt to remove content and regardless of whether they act in good faith. What this means is that an online intermediary can get the benefit of immunity not only when it engages in a good faith attempt to prevent or remove harmful content (the straightforward meaning of Section 230), but also when it *fails* to prevent or remove harmful content, even if it is *fully aware* of its harmful nature. The last form of immunity is beyond anything available in the offline context. In the offline world, distributors can face liability when they know, or should know, the unlawful nature of content.

Using Facebook as an example, the very broad interpretation of Section 230 means: (1) if Facebook deletes a post it believes is unlawful, it will be immune from liability; (2) if Facebook fails to delete a post not knowing whether it is unlawful, it will be immune from liability; and (3) if Facebook fails to delete a post knowing that it is unlawful, Facebook will be immune from liability.

The first outcome in our Facebook example is expressly indicated by the text of Section 230, including three of the policy goals outlined in section (b) of the law: "to encourage the development of technologies which maximize user control over what information is received by individuals, families, and schools who use the Internet and other interactive computer services"; "to remove disincentives for the development and utilization of blocking and filtering technologies that empower parents to restrict their children's access to objectionable or inappropriate online material"; and "to ensure vigorous enforcement of Federal criminal laws to deter and punish trafficking in obscenity, stalking, and harassment by means of computer." Imposing liability on Facebook for removing a post would treat Facebook like a publisher, which Section 230 expressly and reasonably forbids.

The second outcome is also easy to justify based on the history and text of Section 230. Two other policy goals enumerated in Section 230(b) are "to promote the continued development of the Internet and other interactive computer services and other interactive media" and "to preserve the vibrant and competitive free market that presently exists for the Internet and other interactive computer services, unfettered by Federal or State regulation." Section 230 was intended to avoid outcomes like the 1995 Prodigy case, which forced online intermediaries who wished to engage in *some* moderation to be responsible for *all* moderation. The costs of presumptive screening of all hosted content could be prohibitively high, especially for intermediaries that deal with massive amounts of content, such as search engines or popular social media applications. The likely result would be that intermediaries would err on the side of caution and remove any content that might be questionable, to the detriment of the free exchange of ideas. Holding Facebook liable for not removing a post when it was not aware of its unlawful nature would be another version of treating Facebook like a publisher, which is expressly and justifiably forbidden by Section 230.

The third outcome, however, is difficult to justify based on either the text or policy of Section 230. To allow an intermediary to enjoy immunity from liability even when it is aware of and fails to remove unlawful content does not serve the policy goals of encouraging innovative self-regulation for socially beneficial purposes, nor is it necessary to promote further development of the Internet or to preserve the status quo. Imposing liability on Facebook for *not* removing a post when it *is* aware of its unlawful content would not be treating Facebook as a speaker or a publisher; it would be treating Facebook as a distributor, which is not forbidden by the text of Section 230.

Given that many online intermediaries profit from the speech of others, it is justifiable to hold them responsible for this speech in some cases. To grant them blanket immunity not only removes incentives for intermediaries to monitor content, but *creates* incentives not to do so. The business model of many online intermediaries is to generate revenue through advertising. The more content users voluntarily provide (posts, shares, likes, etc.), the more users interact on the platform, and the more companies like Facebook can target users with increasingly personalized advertising. If harmful content provided by a user generates a high level of engagement from a large number of other users, then the advertising benefit of that post goes up, which means more money in Facebook's pocket. By not treating Facebook as a speaker or even as a publisher in such cases, Section 230 allows Facebook and similar intermediaries to take the risk of making potentially harmful content available to the public without absorbing the negative consequences of that risk.

To the extent that the moral hazard created by Section 230 can be justified, it must be on the basis that there is a greater overall good to be gained by allowing tech companies to act this way. Immunizing online intermediaries from publisher liability makes it possible for platforms like Facebook to exist at all, which they likely could not if they had the obligation to review all content before making it available to the public. Social media platforms in particular, which allow near-instantaneous posting and sharing of information by users in real time, could not exist if intermediaries had an affirmative obligation to screen the content of their users.

However, it is not necessary or beneficial to immunize Facebook and similar social media platforms from *distributor* liability for the posts, likes, shares, and so on of third-party content, as the term is understood in defamation law. A distributor makes content available to the public without exerting editorial control over this content. Libraries and bookstores are offline examples. Accordingly, distributor liability for unlawful content is limited to situations in which the distributor knows or should have known of the unlawfulness of that content: "where certain parties, such as news vendors or interactive computer services, will be held to have 'published' material provided by third parties because they fail to take reasonable steps to prevent the dissemination of that defamatory information."[23]

Treating online intermediaries as distributors strikes a good balance between making online intermediaries bear too much of the costs of harmful speech and not making them bear any at all. This is especially true considering that so many intermediaries directly profit from the speech that they make available to the public, regardless of its harmful content. The alternative is for an online intermediary to share in the benefits, but none of the costs, of harmful third-party content, which creates a moral hazard that is not outweighed by the greater social good. This is especially true given that harmful content can often be more profitable than benign content. The moral hazard of facing zero liability for such content creates perverse incentives for intermediaries to actively favor harmful content over non-harmful content. Treating online intermediaries as distributors would also not violate the text of 230(c)(1), which only forbids treating an interactive computer service as "the publisher or speaker" of content. Unfortunately, an early and influential Section 230 case slammed the door on this possibility.

Section 230 as Shield and Sword: The Case of *Zeran v. AOL*

Less than a week after the 1995 Oklahoma City bombing that left 168 people dead, Kenneth Zeran began receiving threatening phone calls. Unbeknownst to Zeran, an anonymous hoaxer had posted a message on an America Online (AOL) bulletin board advertising T-shirts and other paraphernalia glorifying the attack and encouraging interested buyers to call Zeran's home phone number. Zeran had no idea who the hoaxer was or why the hoaxer was attempting to associate him with pro-terrorism sentiments. Although AOL complied with Zeran's request to remove the message from the board, new messages with similar content continued to be posted to the site, leading to a deluge of threatening phone calls to Zeran. After an Oklahoma City radio host who believed the hoax urged his listeners to call Zeran, the phone calls became so threatening that Zeran's house was placed under protective surveillance.

Zeran sued AOL for negligence, arguing that the company had failed to respond appropriately after being made aware of the nature of the posts. The case made its way to the Fourth Circuit, which held that Section 230 preempted Zeran's claim.[24] In reaching its decision, the court stated, "Congress' clear objective in passing § 230 of the CDA was to encourage the development of technologies, procedures and techniques by which objectionable material could be blocked or deleted" and that holding AOL liable as a distributor for offensive content would conflict with this objective. The court reasoned that the possibility of distributor liability, which, as described above, applies when a distributor is made aware of the unlawful nature of the content and fails to act, would prompt intermediaries like AOL to refrain from monitoring content at all.

The Fourth Circuit's reasoning is bizarre: Imposing liability on entities such as AOL for being nonresponsive to unlawful content would encourage them to be *more* nonresponsive to unlawful content. The court provided no evidence for this counterintuitive conclusion and simply failed to acknowledge that taking distributor liability for interactive computer services off the table would have "the effect of discouraging self-policing of content," contrary to the goal the court itself accurately identified.[25] As one commentator describes it, after *Zeran*, interactive service providers "know that no matter how inflammatory third-party postings are, complaints from aggrieved parties will be to no avail, even after notice to the website or ISP."[26]

By completely immunizing AOL from liability, even when the company was made aware of the unlawful content and given ample opportunity to mitigate the harm, the court effectively eliminated incentives for intermediaries to address harmful and destructive uses of their services.

This ruling made AOL, like Facebook, Google, and the other corporate entities that now dominate the market of online intermediaries, doubly morally hazardous. The way corporations are structured in itself creates moral hazard:

> Unlike other business models, the corporation not only allowed individuals to pool large amounts of money for a venture, it also allowed them to do so without the risk of any personal loss beyond the amount of their investment. . . . [T]he nature of corporate action, where bureaucracy dictates that most of the actors are far removed from the actual harm that might occur as a result of their decisions, increases the likelihood of egregious conduct.[27]

Corporations are able to derive tremendous profits from their enterprises because they have the power to shift negative consequences of these
activities onto third parties. Section 230, as interpreted in *Zeran* and
most cases since then, provides interactive service providers with the same
power. It is no surprise, then, that corporations that are also interactive
service providers now dominate not only the Internet but the economy
generally.

In 2017, Amazon, Apple, Facebook, Google, and Microsoft were the
five largest firms in the world based on market value, and they exert enormous influence on Internet communication and commerce. The corporations that enjoy near-monopoly control of the Internet, reaping massive
benefits, are doubly protected from the costs of their risky ventures. Given
that the dominant business model of social media services is based on advertising revenue, they have no natural incentive to discourage abusive or
harmful conduct: "[A]busive posts still bring in considerable ad revenue
and . . . the more content that is posted, good or bad, the more ad money
goes into their coffers."[28]

As Astra Taylor writes in *The People's Platform*, social media platforms
and search engines are "commercial enterprises designed to maximize
revenue, not defend political expression, preserve our collective heritage,
or facilitate creativity."[29] Their control over the Internet—and the control of the Internet over society—widens social, economic, and political
inequality. Jonathan Taplin writes that such

> inequality is not the inevitable by-product of technology and globaliza-
> tion or even the lopsided distribution of genius. It is a direct result of
> the fact that since the rise of the Internet, policy makers have acted as if
> the rules that apply to the rest of the economy do not apply to Internet
> monopolies. Taxes, antitrust regulation, intellectual property law—all are
> ignored in regulating the Internet industries.[30]

Section 230 is one of the most powerful tools of this destructive Internet
exceptionalism. By allowing online intermediaries to reap endless profits
from harmful activity while removing virtually all incentives to regulate it,
Section 230 creates a supercharged moral hazard. Between the rapacious

nature of corporate activity and Section 230 immunity, there is virtually no way to hold these increasingly powerful entities accountable for the harm they cause both online and off.

Double Standards: The Case of Backpage

Section 230 takes free speech fundamentalism to an entirely new level. The First Amendment on its own has been used to allow powerful groups, particularly white men, to enjoy the benefits of free speech without absorbing any of its costs. Section 230 goes even farther, allowing intermediaries to benefit from not only their own but *other people's* speech while being shielded from the costs of that speech. At the same time, online intermediaries have been able to use Section 230 to directly silence the speech of others.

The underlying premise of Section 230 immunity as it is currently interpreted is that it is unfair to hold online intermediaries responsible for the speech of other people, even when those intermediaries benefit from that speech. In effect, Section 230 allows intermediaries to say, "The speech I facilitate is not my speech." The responsibility for unlawful speech, in this view, should lie solely with the actual speaker, not with the intermediary. In light of Section 230's powerful immunity, regulatory and law enforcement agencies have increasingly shifted their focus from online intermediaries to those directly involved in unlawful behavior. This is a shift that online intermediaries should welcome, given the logic of Section 230. However, some online intermediaries have aggressively countered the attempt to more directly regulate bad actors, which undermines the entire basis for their immunity under Section 230.

To understand the significance of what these intermediaries have been able to accomplish, it is necessary to briefly discuss "standing." Standing is the capacity for a particular party to bring a legal claim. To bring claims in federal court, private parties must demonstrate that they have suffered actual injury, that the injury can reasonably be traced to the actions of the defendant, and that the injury is likely to be rectified by a ruling in their favor. When courts allow intermediaries to challenge statutes and other regulatory efforts against the third parties whose content they facilitate, they are allowing these intermediaries to claim that they are injured when the third party is injured. When these challenges are made on First

Amendment grounds, courts are allowing online intermediaries to claim a free speech right in the content they facilitate. In other words, online intermediaries get to have it both ways: They are granted immunity from other people's speech under Section 230, but they enjoy rights to other people's speech under the First Amendment.

One corporation that has made particularly effective use of this double standard is Backpage.com, LLC. Backpage is a website that has been offering classified advertisements for various products and services since 2004. Until 2017, Backpage included an adult section that listed a variety of sexually themed products and services. In 2011, the company came under scrutiny after allegations that its adult section was being used to facilitate sex trafficking, prostitution, and sexual assault, including of minors. Backpage produces almost two-thirds of all U.S. online prostitution advertisements and earns more than $22 million a year from these ads. Between 2009 and 2015, the Cook County Sheriff's Police Department made more than 800 arrests related to adult service ads on Backpage, 50 of which were for sex trafficking, involuntary servitude, or promoting prostitution.[31]

Backpage directly and materially profits from the unlawful content on its platform. In an offline context, Backpage could potentially face criminal accomplice liability or joint tort liability on various theories. But online, because of Section 230, it is shielded from such liability except with regard to violations of federal criminal law. To date, Backpage has successfully used Section 230 and the First Amendment to prevail as a defendant against almost every lawsuit brought against it. But it has also prevailed as a plaintiff in almost every case it has brought seeking to invalidate criminal laws prohibiting online sex advertising on First Amendment grounds. Not only has Backpage succeeded in defending itself against liability for the illegal activity of third parties, but it has succeeded in striking down attempts to hold those third parties responsible.

The use of Section 230 to protect intermediaries who indirectly facilitate criminal activity has frustrated law enforcement's efforts to combat sex trafficking. In 2009, Sheriff Tom Dart of Cook County, Illinois, attempted to shut down the adult services section of Craigslist, a site that had been similarly implicated in sex trafficking, only to be rebuffed by that site's invocation of Section 230 immunity. In 2015, Sheriff Dart tried a tactic that did not involve targeting either Backpage or the advertisers of sex trafficking themselves. He sent a letter to the Visa and Mastercard credit card companies that urged them to cease processing payments for Backpage ads. "As the Sheriff of Cook County," read the letter,

> a father and a caring citizen, I write to request that your institution immediately cease and desist from allowing your credit cards to be used to place ads on websites like Backpage.com. . . . Your cards have and will continue to be used to buy ads that sell children for sex on sites like Backpage.com.[32]

Within days, Visa and Mastercard stopped processing payments for Backpage ads, and Backpage experienced considerable financial impact as a result.

Backpage sued in federal court, asking for a temporary restraining order and a preliminary injunction against Dart. The grounds for the suit were not, as might be expected, that Dart's actions interfered with Backpage's right to do business. Instead, Backpage argued that Dart's actions violated Section 230 as well as Backpage's First Amendment rights. The lawsuit claimed that the sheriff's letter constituted an informal prior restraint on Backpage's right to free speech. The district court denied the injunction, but a three-judge panel of the Seventh Circuit reversed. In a decision widely praised by tech industry and civil liberties groups, Judge Richard Posner ruled in favor of Backpage.

The court's opinion focused primarily on the question of whether Sheriff Dart's letter constituted a prior restraint on Backpage's First Amendment rights. At first glance, this is an odd claim. Dart did not communicate with Backpage at all, or even with Backpage's advertisers. He communicated with the payment processors of Backpage's advertisers. In that communication, Dart did not threaten the credit companies, but rather implied that legal sanctions were possible if the advertisements in question were found to violate the law.

The indirect nature of Dart's actions seems to have troubled Judge Posner the most. The Supreme Court dealt with a somewhat similar set of facts in *Bantam Books, Inc. v. Sullivan* (1963),[33] and Judge Posner relied heavily on this case to reach the conclusion that Dart's letter did in fact constitute a prior restraint.

At issue in *Bantam Books* was Rhode Island's creation of a commission to suppress the distribution of books considered "objectionable." As described by the Court,

> The Commission's practice has been to notify a distributor on official Commission stationery that certain designated books or magazines distributed by him had been reviewed by the Commission and had been declared by a majority of its members to be objectionable for sale, distribution or display to youths under 18 years of age. . . . The typical notice to Silverstein [a book distributor] either solicited or thanked Silverstein, in advance, for his "cooperation" with the Commission, usually reminding Silverstein of the Commission's duty to recommend to the Attorney General prosecution of purveyors of obscenity. Copies of the lists of "objectionable" publications were circulated to local police departments, and Silverstein was so informed in the notices.[34]

In response to these communications, Silverstein, a book distributor, took steps to prevent the further circulation of books named by the commission, including sending back unsold copies of the books and refusing to fill new book orders, out of fear of potential prosecution. The Court rejected Rhode Island's characterization of the commission's activities as "simply exhort[ing] booksellers and advis[ing] them of their legal rights."[35] According to the Court, "[i]t would be naive to credit the State's assertion that these blacklists are in the nature of mere legal advice, when they plainly serve as instruments of regulation independent of the laws against obscenity."[36]

Judge Posner and many of the commentators on the case maintained that *Backpage v. Dart* was directly analogous to *Bantam Books v. Sullivan*. In this analogy, Dart's letter to the credit card companies processing payments for Backpage was like the commission's communications with book distributors: It constituted an informal sanction that was no less effective for being informal. As with *Bantam Books*, it is of no import that the sanction did not target Backpage directly. In the words of Judge Posner, the "distributor of the plaintiffs' books" in *Bantam Books* "correspond[s] to the credit card companies in this case."

Setting aside whether the Seventh Circuit's characterization of Dart's letter as a thinly veiled threat of prosecution is convincing, the analogy between the two cases does not hold up under closer examination. The credit card companies are not analogous to the book distributors in *Bantam Books*. Unlike book distributors, Visa and Mastercard are not engaged in the publication or distribution of speech. They are engaged in a purely commercial transaction of processing credit card payments. While threatening future legal action against the distributors of books, newspapers, films, periodicals, and other forms of speech and expression may be an impermissible prior restraint of speech, threatening future legal action against credit card processors who may be aiding and abetting criminal activity is not. To the extent that Sheriff Dart's actions caused the credit card companies injury, it was not an injury to a constitutionally protected right. Whatever collateral injury Backpage may have suffered, then, it is not an injury to a First Amendment right.

What is more, even if Visa and Mastercard could be said to have First Amendment interests in payment processing, the analogy between *Bantam Books* and Backpage would still fail. Unlike the book distributor in *Bantam Books*, the credit card companies never suggested that they took action in response to the threat of official sanction. While Judge Posner asserts that this was the case, neither Visa nor Mastercard made such a claim; Visa stated in an affidavit that it made the choice to stop processing payments for Backpage independently of Sheriff Dart's letter. While Backpage may have experienced financial injury when the credit card companies stopped processing payments for those ads, the cause of this injury was the companies' actions, not Dart's.

And even if Sheriff Dart could be considered the cause of Backpage's injury, his actions at most would constitute an injury to the website's ability to conduct business. This might give rise to a tortious interference with contract or similar claim, but it is not clear how it gives rise to a First Amendment claim. Judge Posner appears to explain this by referring to "at least some of the speech in the ads on Backpage's website" as "'constitutionally protected.'" This is likely true, but this only proves that the creators of that speech-and, perhaps, the potential audiences for that speech—have First Amendment rights in the ads.

But according to Section 230, Backpage is not the creator of this speech. It is, as it incessantly reminds the courts, an interactive computer service provider that cannot, under Section 230, be treated as "a publisher or speaker" nor, after *Zeran*, as a distributor for content provided by other information content providers. And yet the Seventh Circuit, as well as several pro-Section 230 civil liberties groups who filed amicus briefs on Backpage's behalf, casually referred to Backpage as a distributor and directly analogized it to book distributors for the purpose of granting it rights—though not responsibilities—under the First Amendment.

Backpage v. Dart is thus the most vivid illustration to date of how Section 230 functions as not only a shield, but as a sword. Backpage is allowed to simultaneously defend itself against liability for unlawful content on the basis that it *is not* a distributor of that content while asserting its First Amendment rights on the basis that it *is* a distributor of that content. The result is richly rewarding to online intermediaries: They get to avoid being speakers for the purposes of paying costs, but are allowed to be speakers for the purposes of reaping benefits.

Among those benefits is the ability to chill the speech of others. In *Backpage v. Dart*, the Seventh Circuit imposed an injunction against Sheriff Dart that forbade him, as well as "his office, and all employees, agents, or others who are acting or have acted for or on behalf of him," from taking any "actions, formal or informal, to coerce or threaten credit card companies, processors, financial institutions, or other third parties with sanctions intended to ban credit card or other financial services from being provided to Backpage.com."[37] The court interpreted Section 230 and the First Amendment to grant a corporation the right to prevent a law enforcement officer from interfering with its ability to profit from sex trafficking.

Super-Immunity

Far from encouraging the innovation and development of measures to fight online abuse and harassment, Section 230 removes incentives for online intermediaries to deter or address harmful practices no matter how easily they could do so. What Section 230 does for the tech industry is similar to what the Protection of Lawful Commerce in Arms Act (PLCAA), discussed in Chapter 2, does for the firearms industry: It provides a kind of super-immunity for powerful corporations, allowing them to engage in reckless conduct in pursuit of profit without fear of liability.

The PLCAA eliminates incentives for manufacturers to develop safer guns or secure storage products, and the gun lobby actively discourages them from doing anything that might undercut profits. Section 230 similarly eliminates incentives for Internet corporations to design safer platforms or more secure products, and the tech lobby actively discourages the adoption of any measures that would reduce profitability. A system that allows interactive service providers, especially giant corporations, to generate both revenue and First Amendment protection through every click or engagement—while leaving users to absorb the negative consequences—produces an entirely predictable result: an Internet rife with abuse, threats, revenge porn, conspiracy theories, sex trafficking, and live-streamed crimes.

The protections of Section 230 are, in the view of the courts and the public, coextensive with free speech. As the previous chapter described, First Amendment fundamentalism has transformed the right to free speech from a minimalist, negative protection from government punishment into a super-right that allows the most powerful groups in society to demand affirmative accommodation for an increasingly expansive conception of speech, regardless of the costs to other rights or other groups. Section 230 dramatically ramps up this morally hazardous conception of the First Amendment—allowing giant corporations to risk the safety, security, and wellbeing of billions of people in the pursuit of profit—in the name of free speech.

CENSORSHIP, CENSORSHIP EVERYWHERE

First Amendment fundamentalists are fond of invoking the founding fathers to justify an ever-expanding conception of free speech, but much of what is considered speech today would no doubt be a shock to the drafters of the First Amendment: flag burning, exotic dancing, Nazi salutes, virtual child pornography, violent video games, corporate donations, credit card surcharges, just to name a few. Much would have surprised even Americans of only a few generations ago. Internet fundamentalists view virtually everything on the Internet as speech, whether it is revenge porn, bomb-making instructions, terrorist recruitment videos, conspiracy theories, hacked medical records, upskirt photos, even spam and computer viruses. Some have even argued that three-dimensional wireless printing, capable of creating everything from bikinis to firearms, should be considered speech for First Amendment purposes.

As speech becomes a broader category, so does censorship. In the past, the term "censorship" was most often used to refer to official government action to restrict speech. Private regulation of speech was largely considered neutral, even positive, in the libertarian mindset: "Letting the market handle it" was urged as the best solution to bad speech. Autonomous individuals freely interacting in the marketplace of ideas were the ones we should trust to develop solutions.

But private companies and actors making belated attempts to address online inequality and abuse are now being denounced as censors as well. Today, it not only visible government regulation of the Internet—no matter how narrow, minimally burdensome, or socially beneficial—that is labeled censorship. So too are a wide swath of activities undertaken by private actors to exert control, express preferences, or improve quality in their online interactions. The charge of censorship has been hurled against stalking laws, revenge porn statutes, anti-harassment training, diversity initiatives, blocking users on Twitter, criticizing sexism in video games, pointing out racism, closing comments sections, speaking out against sexual harassment, shutting down neo-Nazi websites, reporting racial epithets, campaigning against conspiracy theories, flagging misleading content, and removing defamatory information from search engines.

These kneejerk responses have hobbled attempts to build a truly diverse and robust online free speech culture. Techno-libertarians refuse to acknowledge that there is not now nor has there ever been any such thing as a neutral platform or free market. The Internet is not some organically developing phenomenon, but the product of powerful political and corporate forces. Naturalizing these forces, or treating them as divinely inspired, makes them harder to critique and resist. The selective denunciation of regulation that does try to resist these forces stifles innovation and perpetuates status quo inequality.

The Myth of the Neutral Platform

"The wide-scale spread of jihadist ideology, especially on the Internet, and the tremendous number of young people who frequent the Jihadist Web sites [are] a major achievement for jihad," wrote Osama bin Laden in a May 2010 letter. One of the first terrorist groups to use the social media platform Twitter for propaganda and organization purposes was an al-Qaeda-affiliated organization called al-Shabab. In September 2013, the group used Twitter to broadcast its terror attack on the Westgate shopping mall in Nairobi in real time. The attack killed 60 people and wounded nearly 200. Twitter removed al-Shabab's accounts the same day, but the organization simply created new Twitter accounts under different names.

According to Mark Wallace, head of the nonprofit Counter Extremism Project, "Twitter is providing a communication device, a loudspeaker for ISIS. . . . If you are promoting violence and a call to violence, you are providing material support. Twitter should be part of the solution. If not, they are part of the problem."[38] Speaking at a Constitution Project dinner honoring Twitter for "its leadership on First Amendment issues," Twitter's head of global public policy, Colin Crowell, conceded that Twitter had been used to promote violence and terrorism. But it is also "a place where people can find . . . information, conversation and where empathy can be shared." Crowell insisted, "The platform of any debate is neutral. The platform doesn't take sides."

The tech industry's use of the word "platform" is impressively obfuscating. It echoes Second Amendment fundamentalists' insistence that firearms are mere tools, innocent implements that cause no harm by themselves. The word "platform" evokes neutrality, objectivity, and passivity. It suggests that if there is prejudice, inequality, or violence on the platform, it is not the fault or the responsibility of the platform, which merely offers a space for people to do as they will. Like the First Amendment itself, the platform is content-neutral and value-free. Much as the gun lobby insists that "guns don't kill people, people kill people," the tech lobby insists that it is people, not tech platforms, who incite violence, disseminate propaganda, or invade privacy. At the same time, just as the gun lobby lauds "good guys with guns" for stopping violence, the tech lobby is happy to take credit for positive uses of its products, from Twitter's role in Arab Spring to Facebook's role in highlighting police brutality.

Neutral terms such as "platform" and "intermediary" and "content" help the tech industry present itself as merely a mirror held up to the world, passively reflecting the existing order. When called upon to address inequality or violence, industry players often demur on the grounds that intervention on their part would be censorship. This is doubly disingenuous.

First, private companies have no First Amendment obligations. They can "censor" anyone and anything they choose with virtually no legal repercussions. Implying that their passivity is anything other than a free choice is fundamentally dishonest.

Fredrick Brennan is a case in point. Brennan is the founder of 8chan, the notorious image board website that is home to a trove of misogynist, racist, and pornographic material and whose users have engaged in extensive harassment campaigns against female gamers and game critics. Brennan maintains that his fidelity to the First Amendment demands that he not remove any content from 8chan, no matter how objectionable. As he puts it, "his only responsibility is to free speech and the laws that govern the United States, where his website is hosted."[39] But, as the journalist Patrick Howell O'Neill wrote after interviewing Brennan,

> the site is not bound by the U.S. Constitution. Brennan has no obligation to the First Amendment. The rules that govern his website are strictly his own decision. As such, there's one person who is ultimately responsible for what is allowed on 8chan: Brennan himself.[40]

Second, platforms engage in censorship all the time. Every tech platform or product is designed to promote some content and discourage others, to favor some speakers and disfavor others, to manipulate users' experience in a way that serves the platform's bottom line—which is, in almost every case, "user engagement" or profit. Twitter "censors" any post longer than 280 (previously 140) characters; Facebook for years only allowed users to express their reaction to posts by "liking" them; Google structures search engine results according to algorithms that boost its own products.

Virtually every tech platform and product also has extensive terms, conditions, and rules that are enforced in ways largely hidden from the user. This is true even of platforms that boast of their absolutist commitment to free speech, including sites like Reddit, 4chan, Voat, and Gab. Reddit's content policy forbids spam, vote manipulation, and impersonation, among a host of other behaviors. 4chan's seventeen "Global Rules" include an age limit (18), a prohibition against advertising, a ban on doxing (posting other people's personal information), as well as Rule 8: "Complaining about 4chan (its policies, moderation, etc.) on the imageboards may result in post deletion and a ban."[41]

Voat automatically checks visitors' browsers to "make sure they are not offensive to our servers" before allowing access to the site and forbids, among other behavior, the posting of "any graphics, text, photographs, images, video, audio or other material that we deem to be junk or spam." Gab's lengthy community guidelines include the requirement to tag pornographic content with the hashtag #NSFW or risk having it removed. The site notes that "Gab follows the Stewart Standard *Jacobellis v. Ohio*, 378 U.S. 184 (1964) on what constitutes pornography and obscene content," a reference to Justice Stewart's infamous comment that "I know it when I see it."

Internal Facebook documents leaked in 2017 revealed some surprising and disturbing details about the way the company interprets its hundreds of rules governing conduct on the platform. According to a ProPublica report,

> [T]he documents suggest that, at least in some instances, the company's hate-speech rules tend to favor elites and governments over grassroots activists and racial minorities. In so doing, they serve the business interests of the global company, which relies on national governments not to block its service to their citizens.[42]

The documents included slides explaining how to apply Facebook's hate speech policy. The question posted on one slide asked which of three groups—female drivers, black children, and white men—was protected from hate speech. The correct answer was white men. Facebook removes attacks directed at "protected categories": race, sex, gender identity, religious affiliation, national origin, ethnicity, sexual orientation, and serious disability/disease. "Subsets" of protected categories are less protected. As ProPublica explained, "White men are considered a group because both traits are protected, while female drivers and black children, like radicalized Muslims, are subsets, because one of their characteristics is not protected."[43]

Danielle Citron, a law professor and author of the book *Hate Crimes in Cyberspace*, observed that Facebook's approach will "protect the people who least need it and take it away from those who really need it."[44] This concern seems particularly justified in light of Facebook's apparent willingness to bend the rules for powerful individuals: Even though Donald Trump's Facebook posts about banning Muslims violated the company's rules against "calls for exclusion" of a protected group, Facebook founder and CEO Mark Zuckerberg refused to remove them.[45]

Facebook and other tech giants increasingly rely on algorithms to sort and review content. They also increasingly invoke these algorithms to defend themselves against accusations of bias. In response to accusations that Facebook's "trending topics" section was biased against rightwing news outlets, Facebook stated that the stories were sorted by a neutral algorithm. But as Zeynep Tufekci writes, "'surfaced by an algorithm' is not a defense of neutrality, because algorithms aren't neutral."[46] While algorithms are built on data, they also "'optimize' output to parameters the company chooses, crucially, under conditions also shaped by the company."[47] On Facebook, these include user engagement, comments, and sharing, which privileges

> content designed to generate either a sense of oversize delight or righteous outrage and go viral, hoaxes and conspiracies as well as baby pictures, happy announcements (that can be liked) and important news and discussions.[48]

Algorithms, in other words, are human choices all the way down.[49]

"The first step forward," writes Tufekci, is for tech companies "to drop the pretense that they are neutral."[50] The techno-libertarian focus on the government as the source of censorship perpetuates the false impression that nongovernment entities pose no threat to free speech. Corporate giants like Facebook and Google are in many ways more powerful than governments, and their means of regulating, censoring, and filtering the marketplace of ideas are much harder to detect and resist.

Legal Intervention

Libertarian orthodoxy—whether about guns, free speech, or the Internet—insists that government interference with the market reduces freedom. As noted above, this "free market" fundamentalism ignores that there is no such thing as an unregulated market and that the government plays an essential role in establishing and protecting all freedoms.

The market is regulated not only by the government but by corporate power and private action. Government, however imperfect, is one of the only powerful forces shaping society that can theoretically be held accountable for its actions. We may have good reason to mistrust the government, but we have good reason to mistrust corporations and private entities as well—and far less effective ways of holding them in check. In theory, at least, we elect officials to represent our interests; if they fail to do so they can be removed through free and fair elections. The premise of our democracy is that the government belongs to "we the people." Generalized contempt for the government is at bottom contempt for democracy and the people.

Two years before Barlow wrote his "Declaration of the Independence of Cyberspace," President Bill Clinton signed into law the 1994 Violence Against Women Act (VAWA). The law was controversial from its inception and has continued to generate controversy as it has been amended and reauthorized over the years. In 2006, VAWA was amended to address what is colloquially referred to as "cyberstalking," setting out a somewhat unwieldy definition of the prohibited conduct. The language of this provision was revised in 2013 to read, in relevant part, that any person

> with the intent to kill, injure, harass, intimidate, or place under surveillance with intent to kill, injure, harass, or intimidate another person, uses the mail, any interactive computer service or electronic communication service or electronic communication system of interstate commerce, or any

other facility of interstate or foreign commerce to engage in a course of conduct that places that person in reasonable fear of the death of or serious bodily injury . . . or . . . causes, attempts to cause, or would be reasonably expected to cause substantial emotional distress to a person . . . shall be punished.

The cyberstalking amendment was met with negative responses from two of the most influential civil liberties organizations in America: the Electronic Frontier Foundation and the American Civil Liberties Union. According to the EFF, the cyberstalking provision "strayed the statute from what is permissible under the First Amendment." By allowing criminal liability for causing "substantial emotional distress," the law was "dangerously vague as it hinged on a person's subjective state of mind rather than an objective threat to do harm." The ACLU similarly criticized the law for allowing "prosecution when the defendant acts with the intent to 'harass' and/or 'intimidate,'" which are, according to the ACLU, "unconstitutionally overbroad" terms. As they would do with many other laws prohibiting harassment, and invasions of privacy decades later, these organizations warned that the cyberstalking provision would chill speech.

As discussed in the previous chapter, actual evidence of chilling effects caused by anti-harassment and anti-stalking laws is hard to come by, while evidence abounds of the chilling effects of harassment and other forms of abuse. Previous studies have shown that harassment discourages women's participation in online spaces and drives many women offline altogether. A 2017 study found that rather than chilling online speech, laws criminalizing online harassment and stalking "may actually facilitate and encourage more speech, expression, and sharing by those who are most often the targets of online harassment: women."[51] The author of the study surmises that when women "feel less likely to be attacked or harassed," they become more "willing to share, speak, and engage online." Knowing that there are laws in place prohibiting harassment "may actually lead to more speech, expression, and sharing online among adult women online, not less."[52]

Not only is there no reason to believe that government regulation inevitably chills speech, there is compelling evidence to believe that government regulation, done carefully and well, can enhance speech and encourage more people to freely engage in speech—a result that free speech advocates should support.

Private Intervention

Private companies have tremendous power to regulate online harassment and abuse. For many years, however, they did not make much effort to do so. In the last decade, tech industry leaders have finally begun to take some of these issues seriously. Tech companies have developed tools and policies to address revenge porn, racist message boards, mugshot sites, fake news, and terrorist propaganda.

As detailed in the previous chapter, following months of collaboration with several nonprofit victim advocacy groups, in particular the Cyber Civil Rights Initiative (CCRI), nearly every major tech company banned revenge porn, more accurately known as nonconsensual pornography, from their platforms and implemented reporting procedures to investigate complaints in 2015.

Reddit was the first major company to take action against the content. Its February 24, 2015, announcement that it was banning images of nonconsensual pornography came as a surprise to many.[53] Only months before, Reddit had served as one of the primary publication outlets for the hacked nude photos of female celebrities.[54] The images were featured on one of the site's 9,000 popular subreddits, crudely referred to as r/TheFappening.[55] After lawyers for the celebrities began publicly demanding that the material be removed, the subreddit was banned.[56]

This was an unusual move for the site, which had, since its inception, prided itself on its "anything goes" ethos, an ethos that spawned popular subreddits such as r/beatingwomen2 and r/rapingwomen. The CEO of Reddit at the time of the hack, Yishan Wong, issued a bizarre statement that purported to explain not why the celebrity hack subreddit was banned, but why most subreddits with questionable content would not be banned: Reddit, he wrote, was "not just a company running a website . . . but the government of a new type of community. The role and responsibility of a government differs from that of a private corporation, in that it exercises restraint in the usage of its powers."[57] Two months later, in November

2014, Wong resigned as CEO. Ellen Pao, the site's chief operating officer, stepped in as interim CEO, and the site's co-founder, Alexis Ohanian, returned to the company to serve as its chairman.[58] Shortly after that, the site announced the ban.[59] Reddit later referred to the celebrity hack as a missed chance "to be a leader" and stated that it was "so proud to be leading the way among our peers when it comes to your digital privacy and consider this to be one more step in the right direction."[60]

Two weeks after Reddit's announcement, Twitter announced that it too was banning nonconsensual pornography.[61] Specifically, Twitter added a clause to its existing policy against publishing "private information." Previously, the policy only referred to "credit card numbers, street address or Social Security/National Identity numbers"; it now also states that users "may not post or share intimate photos or videos of someone that were produced or distributed without their consent."[62] Twitter also implemented a specific reporting process for such material.[63] Facebook announced an express ban against nonconsensual pornography in March 2015.[64]

On June 19, 2015, the senior vice president of Google Search announced that the search engine would "honor requests from people to remove nude or sexually explicit images shared without their consent from Google Search results."[65] The policy change seemed to acknowledge that Google search results are essentially the resume of the digital age and that revenge porn results can wreak havoc on a victim's employment, educational, and personal potential. The company, well known for its reluctance to openly regulate search results on the basis of content, acknowledged that search engines play a role in maximizing the destructive impact of nonconsensual pornography.[66]

In April 2017, Facebook announced that it would begin using photo hashing technology in nonconsensual pornography cases, making it the first major company to publicly adopt this strategy.[67] Microsoft developed photo hashing technology, PhotoDNA, to screen for and remove child pornography.[68] PhotoDNA uses "'robust hashing,' which calculates the particular characteristics of a given digital image—its digital fingerprint or 'hash value'—to match it to other copies of that same image."[69] Companies such as Google, Facebook, and Yahoo use PhotoDNA to scan images and videos uploaded to or transmitted through their platforms.[70] The developer of PhotoDNA, Hany Farid, is heading up a project to apply this technology to extremist content, "proposing a system that proactively flags extremist photos, videos, and audio clips as they're being posted online."[71]

While the decision of tech companies to fight nonconsensual pornography on their platforms was praised by victims and advocacy groups, civil liberties groups expressed reservations:

> Civil libertarians are also monitoring the situation, concerned that the anti-revenge-porn rule might be so broad that it ends up censoring lewd speech that doesn't pose a serious privacy violation. "Creating a take-down regime is often fraught, for reasons unrelated to the content," says Lee Rowland, a staff attorney with the ACLU's Speech, Privacy, and Technology Project. . . . Protecting user privacy is "a laudable goal," Rowland says, and Reddit is within its rights to make decisions about the types of content it hosts on its platform. Still, "anytime a company creates the potential for censorship, it should be very clear about the ground rules in order to avoid making its users frustrated and confused."[72]

In the many months that the ACLU spent criticizing the criminalization of nonconsensual pornography, the organization cautioned against government regulation of speech. But as soon as private companies began to voluntarily regulate the content itself—the "free market" at work—the ACLU criticized this as well. While paying lip service to Reddit's freedom as a private company to regulate as it sees fit, the ACLU nonetheless invoked the specter of "censorship."

Around the same time it announced its ban on revenge porn, Reddit also banned two notorious subreddits: r/fatpeoplehate and r/CoonTown. The decision caused considerable controversy. Critics argued that Reddit's "censorship" would backfire—that the hateful speech from those subreddits would simply migrate to other subreddits. But a 2017 study that examined the effects of the bans concluded that this did not happen. As the authors of the study explain,

> [T]he ban *worked for Reddit*. It succeeded at both a user level and a community level. Through the banning of subreddits which engaged in

racism and fat-shaming, Reddit was able to reduce the prevalence of such behavior on the site. The amount of hate speech generated across Reddit by treatment users went down drastically following the ban. By shutting down these echo chambers of hate, Reddit caused the people participating to either leave the site or dramatically change their linguistic behavior (as measured via our hate lexicons).

At a community-level, the ban also worked. The subreddits that inherited the activity of former r/fatpeoplehate and r/CoonTown users did not inherit their previous behavior.[73]

Banning hateful communities decreased hateful speech on Reddit. This is not simply because many of the members of these communities left, though some did, but because the ones who stayed reduced their use of hateful speech.

Like the ACLU, the EFF invoked the specter of censorship with regard to Reddit's actions. According to Jillian York of the EFF, Reddit "has for years proclaimed itself a place for free speech, which is one of my criteria for when a platform is 'too big to censor.'"[74] York's view was that since Reddit had previously left the regulation of subreddits to individual moderators, it should continue to do so. Why regulation by an individual moderator is necessarily superior to the site as a whole for making decisions is not clear, nor is it clear why Reddit or any other successful site should not be allowed to regulate content on its own site simply because it had held itself out as a "place for free speech." Reddit, like virtually every platform, had always engaged in extensive regulation of content through its structure and its site policies without acknowledging it.

In a 2017 interview about the twenty-year anniversary of Section 230, ACLU lawyer Chris Hansen expressed similar concerns about private regulation. In his view,

[T]he greater censorship dangers today involve attempts by nongovernmental entities—such as Facebook, Twitter, Google, and other internet companies—to decide what speech is appropriate online, and those efforts largely are directed at hate speech. Facebook and other internet companies aren't bound by the First Amendment, which only applies to the government. As the government increasingly pressures companies to remove online content, we're creating a censorship system that applies to an enormous amount of communications that don't enjoy constitutional protections.[75]

Tech innovations to curb abuse on their platforms have not only reduced harassment and hateful speech, but have fostered more speech by more diverse groups. Their efforts do not implicate the First Amendment or involve any powers of the state. Techno-libertarians should be thrilled: These innovations are the market correcting itself. Yet Internet fundamentalists are not only not thrilled, but they are actively critical of these efforts. If the government is not an acceptable arbiter of expression, and private companies are also not an acceptable arbiter, who is?

THE NIHILISM OF INTERNET FUNDAMENTALISM: CLOUDFLARE AND THE NAZIS

Cloudflare is a tech security company that protects websites against various cyberthreats, including distributed denial-of-service (DDoS), where attackers flood a website with requests in the hopes of overwhelming its systems and taking it offline. In 2013, a journalist named James Cook sent Cloudflare's CEO, Matthew Prince, a series of questions about one of the company's clients, the Kavkaz Center. According to Cook, the Kavkaz Center belongs to a terror group associated with al-Qaeda, and it uses its website to plan terrorist bombings and to share graphic photos of the attacks. Prince published Cook's questions, along with his responses, in a blog post. Prince wrote,

> A website is speech. It is not a bomb. There is no imminent danger it creates and no provider has an affirmative obligation to monitor and make determinations about the theoretically harmful nature of speech a site may contain.[76]

Cloudflare reiterated its stance repeatedly as it was criticized for providing services to a number of other controversial sites, including Andrew

Anglin's white supremacist site the Daily Stormer. Cloudflare was specifically criticized when it came to light that it handed over the names and e-mail addresses of people who had made complaints about sites like the Daily Stormer to the owners of those sites, leading them to receive threats and harassment.[77] Prince insisted that Cloudflare "will continue to abide by the law, serve all customers, and hold consistently to a belief that our proper role is not that of Internet censor."[78]

In the wake of Heather Heyer's murder by a white supremacist during the "Unite the Right" rally in Charlottesville, Virginia, GoDaddy stopped managing the Daily Stormer website's domain registration. The site attempted to move its domain registration to Google, which refused it. On August 16, 2017, Cloudflare terminated the Daily Stormer's account.[79]

In a blog post explaining the decision, Prince wrote,

> Our terms of service reserve the right for us to terminate users of our network at our sole discretion. The tipping point for us making this decision was that the team behind Daily Stormer made the claim that we were secretly supporters of their ideology. . . . We could not remain neutral after these claims of secret support by Cloudflare.[80]

Prince then called his own actions "dangerous." Prince explained that there are not that many services like Cloudflare, and they are sometimes the only line of defense for controversial sites. That gives the few companies that provide security a lot of power. As Prince put it in an internal e-mail to his staff, "I woke up in a bad mood and decided someone shouldn't be allowed on the Internet. No one should have that power."[81]

Prince concluded his post by suggesting that while online access is most often associated with free speech, "the more important principle is Due Process." While America's free speech protections are not shared globally,

> the concept of Due Process is close to universal. At its most basic, Due Process means that you should be able to know the rules a system will follow if you participate in that system. Due Process requires that decisions be public and not arbitrary.[82]

In a passionate statement posted on August 17, 2017, the EFF harshly criticized the actions of Cloudflare and the other companies that broke off ties with the Daily Stormer. Immediately after claiming to "defend the right of anyone to choose what speech they provide online," the authors stated that "what GoDaddy, Google, and Cloudflare did here was dangerous."[83] The authors of the EFF statement claimed that "any tactic used now to silence neo-Nazis will soon be used against others, including people whose opinions we agree with. Those on the left face calls to characterize the Black Lives Matter movement as a hate group."

As explored in the previous chapter, the shopworn idea that it is necessary to protect the speech we hate in order to protect the speech we like does not hold up to scrutiny. The reason to prohibit neo-Nazi speech is not because it is unpleasant, but because it causes harm. Similarly, the reason to protect the speech of Black Lives Matter or pro–civil rights groups is not because they are, as the EFF would have it, "causes we love." It is because they comport with our country's stated commitment to racial and gender equality. The law is equipped to handle such distinctions even if the EFF is not, and private companies are entitled to make decisions as they see fit.

The EFF warned that "every time a company throws a vile neo-Nazi site off the Net, thousands of less visible decisions are made by companies with little oversight or transparency."[84] But why was one neo-Nazi site going dark the occasion to sound the alarm about those "thousands of less visible decisions"? It is true that private companies are engaged in obscure and subtle manipulations of us all. But that is a problem that exists independently of one company's decision to finally sever ties with a group advancing a murderous ideology.

One of the many ironies of the EFF's statement is that it violates the principles espoused by its own founder, John Perry Barlow, and the original goal of Section 230. "Where there are real conflicts, where there are wrongs, we will identify them and address them by our means,"[85] Barlow wrote in 1996. Section 230's entire original purpose was to remove disincentives for online intermediaries to remove harmful content. GoDaddy, Google, and Cloudflare exercised their own First Amendment and Section 230 rights by cutting ties with the Daily Stormer. If the EFF does not approve of this exercise, it should recall its own free speech fundamentalist logic that it is the speech we do not like that warrants the strongest First Amendment protection.

Internet fundamentalism is, at bottom, mindlessly absolutist: "[N]o one—not the government and not private commercial enterprises—should decide who gets to speak and who doesn't."[86] The techno-libertarian position is that the government should not be allowed to regulate speech; private companies should not be allowed to regulate speech; no one should ever regulate anyone's speech. This view of free speech, of the Internet, of the world, is fundamentally nihilistic.

INTERNET FUNDAMENTALISM AND DEMOCRACY

The consequences of Internet fundamentalism are even more serious today than they were in 1996. Far from equalizing power relations or radically democratizing culture, the Internet has exacerbated existing gender, racial, and class inequality. Misinformation campaigns, conspiracy theories, and propaganda have poisoned public discourse and promoted scientific, political, and cultural illiteracy. Popular social media platforms are rife with violent bigotry and sexual hostility, thousands of sites are dedicated to radicalizing young men and fostering foreign and domestic terrorism, and invisible databases are silently being built out of intricate profiles containing individuals' detailed private information. Abundant empirical evidence demonstrates that women, racial minorities, and sexual minorities experience a very different Internet than straight white men do. The Internet has been used to chill the intimate, artistic, and professional expression of vulnerable groups in unprecedented ways.

The impact of Internet fundamentalism on women has been particularly severe. As detailed in previous chapters, women have throughout history been silenced and subordinated through domestic assault, sexual violence, private discrimination, and the official denial of basic rights. They have been threatened, stalked, harassed, beaten, sexually assaulted, and even killed for entering spaces traditionally considered the exclusive provinces of men—from voting booths to marathons to the military. The hostility directed at women in public spaces, workplaces, and schools has delivered a clear message: Shut up or get out.

The Internet has not liberated women from this state of affairs.[87] While the Internet has multiplied the possibilities of expression, it has also multiplied the possibilities of repression. As the Internet has provided new avenues of communication, it has given tremendous power and voice to a regressive and censorious attitude toward women. The Internet lowers the costs of engaging in abuse by providing abusers with anonymity and social validation, while providing new ways to increase the range and impact of that abuse. The online stalking and harassment of women compromises their ability to participate in the Internet on equal terms with men and amplifies the sexual stereotyping and discrimination women experience in the offline world.

The Internet has never been a place where a woman a can "express . . . her beliefs, no matter how singular, without fear of being coerced into silence or conformity."[88] Women who publicly express opinions on any subject, from sports to video games to politics, are routinely subjected to a barrage of sexualized and violent threats online. Sexual harassment of women in schools and workplaces has migrated from in-person communication to social media, where it can be both more pernicious and harder to regulate.[89] Victims of stalking and domestic violence face a new array of sophisticated and invasive surveillance technologies that place them and their loved ones in increased danger.[90] Revenge porn, as discussed in the previous chapter, destroys women's careers, family relationships, educational opportunities, and psychological health.[91] The ubiquitous presence of undetectable recording devices (and the ability to transmit footage to the world at large within seconds) has produced a cottage industry of sexual humiliation, from upskirt photos to video footage of sexual assaults.

The cumulative effect of misogynist online abuse is the silencing of women. Women are encouraged to be docile, submissive, sexless, conventional, and devoid of opinions—or else face devastating injury to their privacy, their careers, their safety, their families.

Internet fundamentalism encourages online intermediaries to be increasingly reckless with regard to abusive and unlawful content on their platforms. Today, the Internet is awash in violent white supremacy, threats, harassment, defamation, revenge porn, propaganda, misinformation, and conspiracy theories. These abuses cause material harm to vulnerable groups, while the corporations that facilitate this abuse reap enormous profits.

As with politics, the economy, education, entertainment, and the media, white men enjoy a virtual monopoly on the Internet. In contrast to women and racial, sexual, and religious minorities, white men as a group are able to access the tremendous benefits of the Internet while being shielded from its harms. This is, as the saying goes, not a bug but a feature of the Internet, an intentional product of legislative and policy design. And yet the Internet is convulsed by the culture of white male complaint: pathological fury over "ethics in gaming journalism"; petulance over being suspended from Twitter; revolt at the banning of a handful of racist and sexist message boards; self-righteousness over protecting neo-Nazis and sex traffickers; and endless claims of being persecuted by feminists, "social justice warriors," and political correctness. The voice of white men dominates virtually every online and offline space, crying out ceaselessly of censorship.

UNTIL WE
ALL ARE FREE

AMENDMENT XIV, SECTION I

. . . No state shall make or enforce any law which shall abridge the privileges
or immunities of citizens of the United States; nor shall any state deprive any
person of life, liberty, or property, without due process of law; nor deny to any
person within its jurisdiction the equal protection of the laws.

"[H]ow easily men satisfy themselves that the Constitution is
exactly what they wish it to be."
                    –Justice Joseph Story, Letter to Simon Greenleaf (1845)

Robert Jay Lifton writes that people are drawn to cults by "the ever-
present human quest for the omnipotent guide—for the supernatural force,
political party, philosophical ideas, great leader, or precise science—that
will bring ultimate solidarity to all men and eliminate the terror of death
and nothingness."[1] When cults fail, as they inevitably do, to fulfill these
impossible promises, their followers turn to hostility and violence. The
cult mindset encourages

> a retreat into doctrinal and organizational exclusiveness, and into all-or-
> nothing emotional patterns more characteristic . . . of the child than of
> the individuated adult.

. . . This combination of personal closure, self-destructiveness, and hostility toward outsiders leads to the dangerous group excesses so characteristic of ideological totalism in any form. It also mobilizes extremist tendencies in those outsiders under attack, thus creating a vicious circle of totalism.[2]

In 2016, Cody Wilson, a "3D gun" designer, argued that the First Amendment protects his right to publish a software blueprint that would allow people to print untraceable and nearly undetectable three-dimensional guns at home. According to Wilson's lawyer, "I know people make it about guns, but it's about free speech."[3] In July 2018, the Trump administration entered an agreement with the designer that would allow him to proceed with his plans to make his blueprint available online. Hours before the plans were due to be posted on the Internet, a federal judge issued a restraining order that blocked their publication. The designer's lawyer condemned the order "as a massive prior restraint of free speech."[4] Despite the order, which extended in August 2018, some of the plans found their way online and were downloaded by more than a thousand people.[5]

Guns, speech, and the Internet: These are the colliding forces within the cult of the Constitution as white men struggle to maintain their monopoly on power. What does this mean for those of us who reject white male supremacy but wish to remain faithful the Constitution?

Standing before the crowd at the 1854 Fourth of July picnic in Framingham, Massachusetts, the abolitionist William Lloyd Garrison held up a copy of the U.S. Constitution and set it on fire. "So perish all compromises with tyranny!" he cried.[6] The explanation for this dramatic gesture was that, in Garrison's view, a document that permitted "the holding of human beings in bondage" could never be considered a "sacred compact." To Garrison, the Constitution defied both the laws of nature and the laws of God. Its authors "had no lawful power to bind themselves, or their posterity, for one hour—for one moment—by such an unholy alliance. It was not valid then—it is not valid now."[7]

If the Constitution is fatally compromised, as Garrison believed it to be—if white male supremacy truly is the heart of the Constitution— then constitutional fundamentalists are doing no more than taking the document at its word. It is of little import that they read the Constitution selectively and self-interestedly; the document in its entirety is worthy of little more. There is little point in criticizing fundamentalist approaches to the Constitution and advocating for different interpretations if this is the case. Those who believe this and desire equality must do as Garrison did: repudiate the Constitution in its entirety. If the Constitution stands for white male supremacy, it should be set on fire and burned down to ash.

Some legal scholars have advocated doing just that.[8] If constitutional reverence prevents us from achieving the values essential to a just and democratic society, then we should terminate our sentimental attachment to the document. Let the constitutional fetishists fight amongst themselves over the true meaning of the mysterious parchment while we work on more effective, modern ways to deal with deep political and legal divides and to advance equality.

This approach has much appeal. There are many potential benefits of "de-constitutionalization." Not every conflict needs to be invested with constitutional meaning; extra-constitutional measures can be more effective and more intelligible than the perpetual resort to ambiguous constitutional principles.

This approach, however, has obvious practical limitations. The Constitution is, for now, the nation's binding document, and it is unlikely that it will be set on fire, or even significantly amended, any time soon. Constitutional claims will probably always retain powerful rhetorical appeal, and those who criticize the Constitution will probably always be attacked as unpatriotic, perhaps even treasonous. The assertion that "the Constitution is not all that matters" will never be as compelling as the claim that "this is what the Constitution means," whether in a courtroom, a classroom, or a boardroom. The Constitution is the only political text that garners widespread recognition and respect in our society, and it is our best hope for improving our collective interests. There is little to be gained and much to be lost by ceding the constitutional field, even if it were true that the Constitution is not worth defending.

But the Constitution is worth defending. This is not because the document is divinely inspired, or because the founding fathers deserve our uncritical veneration, or because a text written more than two hundred years ago by self-interested elites is the best possible authority on complex contemporary conflicts. Such fundamentalist beliefs are the enemy of equality, liberty, and ultimately the Constitution itself.

What makes the Constitution worth defending is precisely that it is neither divine, nor fixed, nor infallible. The greatest virtue of the Constitution is that it can be changed. The greatest gift the framers bequeathed to us is this flash of humility, which they embedded in Article V's provisions for amending the Constitution. Reflecting on the Constitution's imperfections in 1787, George Washington wrote to his nephew that the remedy for these imperfections will come from future generations, who "will have the advantage of experience on their Side. . . . I do not think we are more inspired, have more wisdom, or possess more virtue, than those who will come after us."[9]

Those who came after the founders had enough wisdom to "reconstruct" the Constitution after the Civil War, attempting to reckon, belatedly, with America's original sins. Among those sins is the false claim of equality. To speak of "we the people" but really mean white men naturalizes the monopoly of white men over politics, culture, and the economy and hides the exploitation of women and nonwhite men. Disguising white male supremacy as equality makes it far more difficult to detect and to fight.

The Fourteenth Amendment treats equality as a proposition to be demonstrated, not a reality to be assumed. The command of equal protection is inherently anti-fundamentalist, as it necessitates the consideration of all rights and all people. It cannot be stripped out of context as a stand-alone superright with the power to elevate the interests of some over others. It is a rule as well as a right, a test that must be universally applied to all laws, including other constitutional rights. The Fourteenth Amendment tells us that if white men's rights to free speech or self-defense are protected more than women and nonwhite men's, the Constitution has been violated. If white men's rights to free speech or self-defense infringe upon those same rights of women or nonwhite men, the Constitution has been violated. Because of the Fourteenth Amendment, one can only honor the Constitution by honoring equality.

The Fourteenth Amendment thus commits the constitutional faithful to a position incompatible with supremacy or hierarchy of any kind. Like the Golden Rule and Immanuel Kant's categorical imperative, the equal protection imperative provides us with the means of distinguishing prejudice from principle. The Golden Rule states that we must treat others as we would wish to be treated; in Kantian terms, "It is always wrong to act in one way while wishing that everyone else would act otherwise."[10] However we interpret our constitutional rights, we must ask if we would wish for every person to have the same right in the same measure. Liberty must be a general principle: "the clear right of all the subjects within the realm," as Burke wrote, "or of none."[11]

Constitutional fundamentalism has for far too long allowed white men to enjoy the benefits of constitutional rights while forcing women and nonwhite men to shoulder the costs. This had led to an overly deferential approach to white men's rights that diminishes the rights of women and minorities. The kinds of constitutional claims that currently receive the most social attention, legitimatization, and formal protection are those that serve white men's interests. This distorted focus on the interests of white men has also fostered a groundless and volatile resentment that all too often erupts into physical violence.

To counter constitutional fundamentalism, it is necessary to engage in honest constitutional accounting. We must confront the fact that constitutional rights and resources have overwhelmingly been allocated to the interests of white men, and that the white male monopoly on constitutional power is neither natural nor benevolent.

If we want to build a robust, anti-fundamentalist constitutional culture, we must focus on the experiences of those who have suffered the most severe constitutional deprivations. As Kimberlé Crenshaw writes, when we address "the needs and problems of those who are most disadvantaged . . . then others who are singularly disadvantaged would also benefit."[12] Building constitutional defenses around the experiences of the most vulnerable improves the outcomes for everyone: "When they enter, we all enter."[13]

What does this good faith constitutionalism look like in practice? It looks like the rejection of selective fidelity to constitutional rights. It looks like denying attention to those who claim to honor the right to bear arms but look the other way when black men are shot dead for exercising them. It looks like demanding that those who defend the right of free speech respond to the silencing of women. It looks like the NRA members who canceled their memberships when the organization remained silent on the murder of Philando Castile, and the ACLU members who broke with the national leadership following the deadly events in Charlottesville, and the tech companies who refuse to allow bigots to use their platforms to advance their destructive agendas.

An anti-fundamentalist approach to the Constitution focuses on the groups who suffer the greatest deprivations of constitutional rights—devoting attention and resources to highlighting their experiences, advocating for their protection, and identifying hypocrisy and elitism in self-proclaimed civil libertarians. Because, contrary to the claims of constitutional fundamentalists, "our" constitutional rights are not under attack. White men have enjoyed more than two centuries of constitutional affirmative action; their rights are not only secure but dominant. To achieve the unfinished project of equality, we must reorient our constitutional attention to those whose rights have been excluded, ignored, and subordinated. In the words of Emma Lazarus, author of the poem "The New Colossus" engraved on the Statue of Liberty, "Until we are all free, we are none of us free."

ACKNOWLEDGMENTS

The task of writing acknowledgments causes me considerable anxiety, as I fear any list will inadvertently omit some of the colleagues, friends, family, and students who contributed to the realization of this project. With that caveat in mind, I would like to express particular gratitude to Claire Amador, Jean-Jacques Amat, Danielle Citron, Harold Flegelman, Dolores Franks, Carrie Goldberg, Patrick Gudridge, Holly Jacobs, Osamudia James, Erica Johnstone, Tamara Lave, Jonathan Metzl, Tamara Piety, Arden Rowell, Scott Sundby, and Jason Walta, as well as appreciation for my excellent research assistants, Stephen Byrnes and Justin Stern. I am also grateful to Dean Patricia White of the University of Miami School of Law for granting me a sabbatical to work on this book and to all of the wonderful individuals at Stanford University Press who helped bring this project to fruition, in particular Michelle Lipinski and Jennifer Gordon.

NOTES

INTRODUCTION

1. While a few women were also present, the demonstration was dominated by men.

2. Frances Robles, "Two Men Arrested in Connection with Charlottesville Violence," *New York Times* (Aug. 26, 2017), https://www.nytimes.com/2017/08/26/us/charlottesville-arrests.html?mcubz=0

3. David A. Graham, "Could Police Have Prevented Bloodshed in Charlottesville?" *The Atlantic* (Aug. 14, 2017), https://www.theatlantic.com/politics/archive/2017/08/could-the-police-have-prevented-bloodshed-in-charlottesville/536775/

4. Steven H. Shiffrin, *What Is Wrong with the First Amendment?* (Cambridge 2016).

5. *Morning Edition*, "Incident in Charlottesville Will Make Us Stronger, Gov. McAuliffe Says," *National Public Radio* (Aug. 14, 2017), http://www.npr.org/2017/08/14/543358169/incident-in-charlottesville-will-make-us-stronger-gov-mcauliffe-says

6. Dara Lind, "Why the ACLU Is Adjusting Its Approach to 'Free Speech' After Charlottesville," *Vox* (Aug. 21, 2017), https://www.vox.com/2017/8/20/16167870/aclu-hate-speech-nazis-charlottesville

7. "ACLU of California Statement: White Supremacist Violence Is Not Free Speech" *ACLU of Northern California* (Aug. 16, 2017), https://www.aclunc.org/news/aclu-california-statement-white-supremacist-violence-not-free-speech

8. Joe Palazzolo, "ACLU Will No Longer Defend Hate Groups Protesting with Firearms," *Wall Street Journal* (Aug. 17, 2017), https://www.wsj.com/articles/aclu-changes-policy-on-defending-hate-groups-protesting-with-firearms-1503010167

9. David French, "After Charlottesville, the First and Second Amendments Are Under Fire," *National Review* (Aug. 18, 2017), http://www.nationalreview.com/article/450615/aclus-second-amendment-troubles-after-charlottesville

10. Eugene Volokh, "Odd Statement from the ACLU: 'White Supremacist Violence Is Not Free Speech,'" *Washington Post* (Aug. 16, 2017), https://www.washingtonpost

.com/news/volokh-conspiracy/wp/2017/08/16/odd-statement-from-the-aclu-of-california
-white-supremacist-violence-is-not-free-speech/?utm_term=.6d372d365a78

11. *AirTalk*, "After Statement Saying White Supremacist Violence Isn't Free Speech, Are
CA ACLU Branches Breaking Rank?" *SCPR* (Aug. 17, 2017), https://www.scpr.org/programs
/airtalk/2017/08/17/58638/after-statement-saying-white-supremacist-violence/

12. Dahlia Lithwick and Mark Joseph Stern, "The Guns Won," *Slate* (Aug. 14, 2017),
http://www.slate.com/articles/news_and_politics/jurisprudence/2017/08/the_first_and_second
_amendments_clashed_in_charlottesville_the_guns_won.html

13. David Z. Morris, "Leaked Chats Show Charlottesville Marchers Were Planning
for Violence," *Fortune* (Aug. 26, 2017), http://fortune.com/2017/08/26/charlottesville
-violence-leaked-chats/

14. Madison Malone Kircher, "Was Neo-Nazi Website Daily Stormer Hacked by Anonymous After a Post About the Charlottesville Victim?" *New York Magazine* (Aug. 14, 2017),
http://nymag.com/selectall/2017/08/daily-stormer-not-hacked-by-anonymous-loses-godaddy
-domain.html

15. Katie Mettler and Avie Selk, "GoDaddy—then Google—Ban Neo-Nazi Site Daily
Stormer for Disparaging Charlottesville Victim," *Washington Post* (Aug. 14, 2017), https://www
.washingtonpost.com/news/morning-mix/wp/2017/08/14/godaddy-bans-neo-nazi
-site-daily-stormer-for-disparaging-woman-killed-at-charlottesville-rally/?utm_term
=.deacc66f436e

16. Tony Romm and Kurt Wagner, "Twitter Is Joining Its Fellow Tech Companies in Clamp-
ing Down on the Daily Stormer, a Neo-Nazi Website," *Recode* (Aug. 16, 2017), https://www.re-
code.net/2017/8/16/16158292/twitter-facebook-cloudflare-google-godaddy-daily-stormer-alt
-right-nazi-charlottesville.

17. Jeremy Malcolm, Cindy Cohn, and Danny O'Brien, "Fighting Neo-Nazis and the
Future of Free Expression," *Electronic Frontier Foundation* (Aug. 17, 2017), https://www
.eff.org/deeplinks/2017/08/fighting-neo-nazis-future-free-expression.

18. Michael D. Shear and Maggie Haberman, "Trump Defends Initial Remarks on
Charlottesville; Again Blames 'Both Sides,'" *New York Times* (Aug. 15, 2017), https://www
.nytimes.com/2017/08/15/us/politics/trump-press-conference-charlottesville.html?mcubz=3

19. The term is admittedly not fully comprehensive, as it does not highlight prejudice
based on class, sexual orientation, religion or lack thereof, gender identity, disability, or
immigration status, all of which are part of the story of American inequality. This book
focuses on the inequalities of gender and race that are literally foundational to American
constitutional culture.

20. Derrick Bell described a similar phenomenon in the context of racial remediation,
suggesting that whites will tolerate efforts to address racial inequality only so long as such
efforts do not negatively impact their own interests:

> Racial remedies may . . . be the outward manifestations of unspoken and perhaps sub-
> conscious judicial conclusions that the remedies, if granted, will secure, advance, or at
> least not harm societal interests deemed important by middle and upper class whites.

See Derrick A. Bell, Jr., "*Brown v. Board of Education* and the Interest-Convergence
Dilemma," *Harvard Law Review*, 93 (1980), 523.

21. Sanford Levinson, *Constitutional Faith* (Princeton University Press 1988), 14.

22. Michael Kammen, *A Machine That Would Go of Itself: The Constitution in American Culture* (Alfred A. Knopf 1986), 3.

23. Sharon C. Fitzgerald, "Survey: U.S. Admires, but Hasn't Read, Constitution," *Daily Progress* (Sept. 17, 2010), https://www.dailyprogress.com/news/survey-u-s-admires-but-hasn-t-read -constitution/article_a4d58bd4-3e2d-50e3-859b-fcede87ec145.html

24. "Kaine Statement on White Nationalist Demonstrations & Violence in Charlottesville" (Aug. 12, 2017),

https://www.kaine.senate.gov/press-releases/kaine-statement-on-white-nationalist -demonstrations-and-violence-in-charlottesville

25. Sally Yates, *Twitter* (Aug. 12, 2017), https://twitter.com/SallyQYates/status/896559844 085420032

26. Austin Wright, "McConnell: 'There Are No Good Neo-Nazis,'" *Politico* (Aug. 16, 2017), http://www.politico.com/story/2017/08/16/mitch-mcconnell-neo-nazi-trump-charlottesville -comments-241696

27. Ibid.

28. Tara Golshan, "GOP Senators React to Trump's Charlottesville Comments: 'Mr. President—We Must Call Evil by Its Name,'" *Vox* (Aug. 12, 2017), https://www.vox .com/2017/8/12/16139144/gop-senators-react-trump-charlottesville

29. Sandy Fitzgerald, "Va. Rep. Garrett Condemns White Supremacists: 'Not Who We Are as Americans,'" *NewsMax* (Aug. 12, 2017), https://www.newsmax.com/Headline /charlottesville-virginia-va-supremacists-garrett/2017/08/12/id/807318/

30. Ibid.

31. Matthew Kazin, "Charlottesville Tragedy: 'I'm Afraid for Our Future,' Says Virginia Rep. Garrett," *Fox Business* (Aug. 13, 2017), http://www.foxbusiness.com/features /2017/08/13/charlottesville-tragedy-m-afraid-for-our-future-says-virginia-rep-garrett .html

32. Examples include the Posse Comitatus, the Oath Keepers, the Three Percenters, the Constitutional Sheriffs and Peace Officers Association, and the Sovereign Citizens. See Daniel Levitas, *The Terrorist Next Door: The Militia Movement and the Radical Right* (St. Martin's Griffin 2004).

33. Rosamond C. Rodman, "Scripturalizing and the Second Amendment," in *The Bible and Feminism: Remapping the Field* (Yvonne Sherwood, ed.) (Oxford University Press 2017), 634.

34. See Christopher W. Schmidt, "The Civil Rights–Civil Liberties Divide," *Stanford Journal of Civil Rights and Civil Liberties,* 12 (2016), 1–41.

35. Ibid., 35.

36. Mary Ann Glendon, *Rights Talk: The Impoverishment of Political Discourse* (Free Press 1991), x.

37. See Mark A. Graber, *Transforming Free Speech: The Ambiguous Legacy of Civil Libertarianism* (University of California Press 1992).

38. See also Safiya Umoja Noble, *Algorithms of Oppression: How Search Engines Reinforce Racism* (NYU Press 2018); Virginia Eubanks, *Automating Inequality: How High-Tech Tools Profile, Police, and Punish the Poor* (St. Martin's Press 2017).

39. Jason Kessler, "Yes, Virginia (Dare), There Is Such a Thing as White Genocide," *VDARE* (June 19, 2017), http://www.vdare.com/articles/yes-virginia-dare-there-is-such-a-thing -as-white-genocide

40. Matt Pearce, "Tweet from the Account of Charlottesville Rally Organizer Insults Slain Protester Heather Heyer," *Los Angeles Times* (Aug. 19, 2017), http://www.latimes.com/nation/la-na-charlottesville-organizer-20170818-story.html

41. Kircher, "Was Neo-Nazi Website Daily Stormer Hacked by Anonymous After a Post About the Charlottesville Victim?"

CHAPTER ONE

1. Catherine Drinker Bowen, *Miracle at Philadelphia: The Story of the Constitutional Convention May to September 1787* (Little, Brown, and Co. 1966).

2. Rhode Island did not send a delegate.

3. Michael Medved, *The American Miracle: Divine Providence in the Rise of the Republic* (Crown Publishing Group 2016), 120.

4. *Federalist* No. 37.

5. Bowen, *Miracle at Philadelphia*, xvii.

6. Thomas C. Grey, "The Constitution as Scripture," *Stanford Law Review*, 37 (1984), 3.

7. Bowen, Miracle at Philadelphia, xiv.

8. Ibid.

9. Emphasis added.

10. Margaret A. Hogan and C. James Taylor, eds., *My Dearest Friend: Letters of Abigail and John Adams* (Belknap Press of Harvard University Press 2007), 47–48.

11. Thomas Day, *Fragment of an Original Letter on the Slavery of the Negroes, Written in the Year 1776* (Printed for John Stockdale 1784).

12. Jeff Forret, *Slavery in the United States* (Infobase Learning 2012), 38.

13. Thurgood Marshall, "Reflections on the Bicentennial of the United States Constitution," *Harvard Law Review,* 101 (1) (1987), 5.

14. Charles Austin Beard, *An Economic Interpretation of the Constitution of the United States* (Macmillan 1921), 324.

15. Sally G. McMillen, *Seneca Falls and the Origins of the Women's Rights Movement* (Oxford University Press 2008), 13.

16. Ibid.

17. Carol Berkin, *Revolutionary Mothers: Women in the Struggle for America's Independence* (Vintage Books 2005).

18. Ibid.

19. Ibid., 149.

20. Hogan and Taylor, *My Dearest Friend,* 110.

21. William Blackstone, *Commentaries on the Laws of England*, Vol. 1 (1765), 442–445.

22. In this sense, the founders resemble the sons in Sigmund Freud's "primal father" illustration of the social contract. In the state of nature, a single powerful male (the primal father) dominates the horde, enjoying exclusive access to power and sexual access to women. After the sons rise up against the father and kill him, they agree to share access to power and women among themselves. Sigmund Freud, *Moses and Monotheism* (Vintage Books 2001), 81–82.

23. Hogan and Taylor, *My Dearest Friend,* 116.

24. Carole Pateman, *The Sexual Contract* (Stanford University Press 1988), 102–110.

25. Hogan and Taylor, *My Dearest Friend,* 110.

26. Ibid., 112.

27. Berkin, *Revolutionary Mothers*, 158.

28. Tung Yin, "Tom and Jerry (and Spike): A Metaphor for *Hamdan v. Rumsfeld*, the President, the Court, and Congress in the War on Terrorism," *Tulsa Law Review*, 42 (2007), 527.

29. Alice S. Rossi, ed., *The Feminist Papers: From Adams to de Beauvoir* (Northeastern University Press 1973), 13.

30. Ibid., 15.

31. Edward Alexander Westermarck, *Christianity and Morals* (Routledge 2013), 70.

32. Immanuel Kant, *Grounding for the Metaphysics of Morals* (1993 [1785]).

33. Edmund Burke, "Letter to John Farr and John Harris, Esqrs., Sheriffs of the City of Bristol, on the Affairs of America" (1777).

34. Ibid.

35. Richard Jasnow, *A Late Period Hieratic Wisdom Text* (P. Brooklyn 47.218.135) (University of Chicago Press 1992), 95.

36. Roger K. Talley, *But That's Not What It Says! A Skeptic's Guide to the Bible* (Popea Press 2014), 50.

37. Talmud *Shabbat* 31a.

38. See McMillen, *Seneca Falls and the Origins of the Women's Rights Movement*, 12, and Marshall, "Reflections on the Bicentennial of the United States Constitution," 2:

> "We the People" included, in the words of the framers, "the whole Number of free Persons." On a matter so basic as the right to vote, for example, Negro slaves were excluded, although they were counted for representational purposes—at three-fifths each. Women did not gain the right to vote for over a hundred and thirty years.

39. Linda R. Monk, *The Words We Live By: Your Annotated Guide to the Constitution* (Hyperion 2003), 17.

40. Ibid.

41. Blaise Pascal, *Pensées* (W. F. Trotter, trans.) (Christian Classics 1910 [1660]), 100.

42. Mary Anne Franks, "Where the Law Lies: Constitutional Fictions and Their Discontents," in *Law and Lies: Deception and Truth-Telling in the American Legal System* (Austin Sarat, ed.) (Cambridge University Press 2015).

43. *Federalist* No. 10. See also Deseriee A. Kennedy, "Judicial Review and Diversity," *Tennessee Law Review*, 71 (2004), 290. Kennedy writes, "Distrust of the masses is reiterated in a number of the *Federalist Papers*." She cites Howard Zinn in her explanation:

> "In Federalist Paper #10, James Madison argued that representative government was needed to . . . control the factional struggles that came from inequalities in wealth. Minority factions could be controlled, he said, by the principle that decisions would be by vote of the majority." Thus, early democratic pronouncements were "not simply the work of wise men trying to establish a decent and orderly society, but the work of certain groups trying to maintain their privileges, while giving just enough rights and liberties to enough of the people to ensure popular support." (interior citations omitted)

44. Max Lerner, "Constitution and Court as Symbols," *Yale Law Journal*, 46 (1937), 1292.

45. Louis Althusser, "Theory, Theoretical Practice and Theoretical Formation: Ideology and Ideological Struggle," in *Philosophy and the Spontaneous Philosophy of the Scientists & Other Essays* [Part 1] (Gregory Elliot, ed.) (Verso 1990), 29.

46. Lerner, "Constitution and Court as Symbols," 1294.

47. Robert Jay Lifton, *Thought Reform and the Psychology of Totalism: A Study of "Brainwashing" in China* (Norton 1963), 419.

48. Robert Jay Lifton, "Cult Formation," *Harvard Mental Health Letter*, 7 (8) (February 1981), http://www.csj.org/studyindex/studycult/study_lifton2.htm

49. Sanford Levinson, *Constitutional Faith* (Princeton University Press 1988), 11.

50. A Pew Research study showed that Americans were more divided ideologically in 2014 than they had been in the previous two decades. Pew Research Center, "Political Polarization in the American Public" (June 12, 2014), http://www.people-press.org/2014/06/12/political -polarization-in-the-american-public/

51. It is hard to pinpoint when the popular conception of constitutional rights became so expansive, though Mary Ann Glendon's *Rights Talk* suggests that it was in force at least in the years leading up to that book's publication in 1991. Mary Ann Glendon, *Rights Talk: The Impoverishment of Political Discourse* (Free Press 1991).

52. David Cole, *Engines of Liberty: The Power of Citizen Activists to Make Constitutional Law* (Basic Books 2016), 10.

53. Michael Kammen, *A Machine That Would Go of Itself: The Constitution in American Culture* (Alfred A. Knopf 1986).

54. Sharon C. Fitzgerald, "Survey: U.S. Admires, but Hasn't Read, Constitution," *Daily Progress* (Sept. 17, 2010), https://www.dailyprogress.com/news/survey-u-s-admires-but-hasn-t-read -constitution/article_a4d58bd4-3e2d-50e3-859b-fcede87ec145.html

55. Annenberg Public Policy Center, "Americans Are Poorly Informed About Basic Constitutional Provisions" (Sept. 12, 2017), https://www.annenbergpublicpolicycenter.org/americans -are-poorly-informed-about-basic-constitutional-provisions/

56. Newseum Institute, "The 2015 State of the First Amendment," http://www .newseuminstitute.org/wp-content/uploads/2015/07/FAC_SOFA15_report.pdf

57. Annenberg Public Policy Center, "2015 Constitution Day/Civics Study" (Aug. 31, 2015), https://cdn.annenbergpublicpolicycenter.org/wp-content/uploads/Civics_Survey_2015_Trends .pdf

58. Jill Lepore, "The Commandments: The Constitution and Its Worshippers," *New Yorker* (Jan. 17, 2011), https://www.newyorker.com/magazine/2011/01/17/the -commandments

59. Annenberg Public Policy Center, "2015 Constitution Day/Civics Study."

60. Pew Research Center, "Division, Uncertainty over Court's Health Care Ruling" (July 2, 2012), http://www.people-press.org/2012/07/02/division-uncertainty-over-courts-health -care-ruling/

61. Meredith Dost, "Dim Public Awareness of Supreme Court as Major Rulings Loom," *Pew Research Center* (May 14, 2015), http://www.pewresearch.org/fact-tank/2015/05/14/dim-public -awareness-of-supreme-court-as-major-rulings-loom/

62. Adam Liptak, "Trump vs. the Constitution," *New York Times* (Nov. 29, 2016), https://www.nytimes.com/interactive/2016/11/29/us/politics/trump-constitution.html?_r=0

63. Charlie Savage, "Trump Calls for Revoking Flag Burners' Citizenship. Court Rulings Forbid It," *New York Times* (Nov. 29, 2016), https://www.nytimes.com/2016/11/29/us /politics/trump-flag-burners-citizenship-first-amendment.html

64. Jennifer Steinhauer, "Constitution Has Its Day (More or Less) in House," *New York Times* (Jan. 6, 2011), http://www.nytimes.com/2011/01/07/us/politics/07constitution.html

65. Fox News, "Purpose Behind Congressional Reading of Constitution Questioned After Amendments Are Omitted" (Jan. 6, 2011), http://www.foxnews.com/politics/2011/01/06 /constitutional-reading-sparks-debate-omitted-parts.html

66. David A. Fahrenthold, "Notable Passages of Constitution Left Out of Reading in the House," *Washington Post* (Jan. 6, 2011), http://www.washingtonpost.com/wp-dyn /content/article/2011/01/06/AR2011010603759.html?sid=ST2011010603624&tid=a_inl

67. Philip Rucker and David A. Fahrenthold, "After Wrangling, Constitution Is Read on House Floor, Minus Passages on Slavery," *Washington Post* (Feb. 25, 2011), https://www .washingtonpost.com/national-politics/after-wrangling-constitution-is-read-on-house -floor-minus-passages-on-slavery/2011/01/06/ABLmphD_story.html?utm_term=.f40c507 f2372

68. Fox News, "Purpose Behind Congressional Reading of Constitution Questioned After Amendments Are Omitted."

69. Ibid.

70. Rucker and Fahrenthold, "After Wrangling, Constitution Is Read on House Floor, Minus Passages on Slavery."

71. Juli Weiner, "Republicans to Spend $1.1 Million Reciting Constitution on House Floor," *Vanity Fair* (Jan. 4, 2011), http://www.vanityfair.com/news/2011/01/how-much-will-it -cost-republicans-to-recite-the-constitution-on-the-house-floor

72. Ezra Klein, "Goodbye and Good Riddance, 112th Congress," *Washington Post* (Jan. 4, 2013), https://www.washingtonpost.com/news/wonk/wp/2013/01/04/goodbye -and-good-riddance-112th-congress/?utm_term=.3cb9120282cb

73. Ezra Klein, "14 Reasons Why This Is the Worst Congress Ever," *Washington Post* (July 13, 2012), https://www.washingtonpost.com/news/wonk/wp/2012/07/13/13–reasons-why -this-is-the-worst-congress-ever/?utm_term=.b7aa7b9ea3e0

74. Henry Waxman, "New Report on the Anti-Women Voting Record of the 112th Congress Identifies 55 Anti-Women Votes by House Republicans," *Vote Smart* (Sept. 5, 2012), https:// votesmart.org/public-statement/739853/new-report-on-the-anti-women-voting-record-of -the-112th-congress-identifies-55-anti-women-votes-by-house-republicans

75. Annie-Rose Strasser and Aviva Shen, "The Worst Moments of the 112th Congress," *Think Progress* (Jan. 3, 2013), https://thinkprogress.org/the-worst-moments-of-the -112th-congress-25ba009d9ab5

76. CNN Wire Staff, "House Members Read the Constitution," *CNN* (Jan. 6, 2011), http://www.cnn.com/2011/POLITICS/01/06/house.constitution/index.html (emphasis added).

77. Louis Michael Seidman, *On Constitutional Disobedience* (Oxford University Press 2012), 7.

78. Seidman (2012, p. 141) explains,

When arguments are put in constitutional terms, they become absolutist and exclusionary. People can have good faith and friendly disagreements about ordinary issues and can agree to disagree, but not if one's stance on an issue places one outside the bounds of our community. When zealots claim their opponents are destroying the Constitution, they are making just this claim. They are effectively accusing their opponents of treason.

79. Morton J. Horwitz, "The Meaning of the Bork Nomination in American Constitutional History," *University of Pittsburgh Law Review,* 50 (1988–1989), 663.

80. Peter J. Smith and Robert W. Tuttle, "Biblical Literalism and Constitutional Originalism," *Notre Dame Law Review,* 86 (2) (2011), 709–710.

81. Ibid., 716–720.

82. Gary Lawson, "On Reading Recipes . . . and Constitutions," *Georgetown Law Journal,* 85 (1997), 1834.

83. Lepore, "The Commandments."

84. Ben Guarino, "Appeals Court Strikes Down Florida 'Docs v. Glocks' Law That Barred Physicians from Asking About Gun Ownership," *Washington Post* (Feb. 17, 2017), https:// www.washingtonpost.com/news/morning-mix/wp/2017/02/17/appeals-court-strikes-down -fla-docs-v-glocks-law-that-barred-physicians-from-asking-about-gun-ownership/?utm _term=.8675ea9f8293

85. Janie Campbell, "Florida Moves to Restrict Media Access to Stand Your Ground Case Records," *Huffington Post* (March 24, 2014), https://www.huffingtonpost.com/2014/03 /24/stand-your-ground-records_n_5007847.html

86. See Shaundra K. Lewis, "Crossfire on Compulsory Campus Carry Laws: When the First and Second Amendments Collide," *Iowa Law Review,* 102 (2017), https://ilr.law .uiowa.edu/print/volume-102-issue-5/crossfire-on-compulsory-campus-carry-laws-when -the-first-and-second-amendments-collide/

87. Dahlia Lithwick and Mark Joseph Stern, "The Guns Won," *Slate* (Aug. 14, 2017), http://www.slate.com/articles/news_and_politics/jurisprudence/2017/08/the_first_and_second _amendments_clashed_in_charlottesville_the_guns_won.html

88. Jeff Stein, "Bernie Sanders: It Is Not Good Enough for Someone to Say, 'I'm a woman! Vote for me!'" *Vox* (Nov. 21, 2016), https://www.vox.com/policy-and-politics/2016/11/21 /13699956/sanders-clinton-democratic-party

89. Lindy West, "Of Course Abortion Should Be a Litmus Test for Democrats," *New York Times* (Aug. 2, 2017), https://www.nytimes.com/2017/08/02/opinion/trump-democrats-abortion -litmus-test.html

90. Mark Lilla, "The End of Identity Liberalism," *New York Times* (Nov. 18, 2016), https://www.nytimes.com/2016/11/20/opinion/sunday/the-end-of-identity-liberalism.html ?_r=1

91. Katherine Franke, "Making White Supremacy Respectable. Again," *Los Angeles Review of Books* (Nov. 21, 2016), http://blog.lareviewofbooks.org/essays/making-white -supremacy-respectable/

[[notes 84-89 in original ch 1 moved to end of file]]

92. See Glendon, *Rights Talk,* 60, using the term "superright" to describe a right that is treated as unique among rights, "a trump."

93. Lifton, "Cult Formation."

94. Ibid.

95. Ibid.

96. McMillen, *Seneca Falls and the Origins of the Women's Rights Movement*, 67.

97. Ibid., 67–68.

98. Michael Kent Curtis, "The 1837 Killing of Elijah Lovejoy by an Anti-Abolition Mob: Free Speech, Mobs, Republican Government, and the Privileges of American Citizens," *UCLA Law Review*, 44 (1996–1997), 1168–1171.

CHAPTER TWO

1. Garry Wills, "Our Moloch," *New York Review of Books* (Dec. 15, 2012), http://www.nybooks.com/daily/2012/12/15/our-moloch/

2. *Paradise Lost* 1.392–396.

3. Wills, "Our Moloch."

4. Jugal K. Patel, "After Sandy Hook, More Than 400 People Have Been Shot in Over 200 School Shootings," *New York Times* (Feb. 15, 2018), https://www.nytimes.com/interactive /2018/02/15/us/school-shootings-sandy-hook-parkland.html

5. Philip Bump, "2018 Has Been Deadlier for Schoolchildren Than Service Members," *Washington Post* (May 18, 2018), https://www.washingtonpost.com/news/politics /wp/2018/05/18/2018–has-been-deadlier-for-schoolchildren-than-service-members/?utm _term=.610537E34108

6. Wills, "Our Moloch."

7. Robert E. Levy, "Joe the Plumber Said 'Your Dead Kids Don't Trump My Constitutional Rights.' Could He Be Right?" *Washington Post* (June 13, 2014), https://www .washingtonpost.com/posteverything/wp/2014/06/13/joe-the-plumber-said-your-dead -kids-dont-trump-my-constitutional-rights-could-he-be-right/?utm_term=.228ce01d6be5

8. Scott Eric Kaufman, "Ben Carson's Compassion: 'No Body with Bullet Holes Is More Devastating Than Taking the Right to Arm Ourselves Away," *Salon* (Oct. 7, 2015), https:// www.salon.com/2015/10/07/ben_carson_no_body_with_bullet_holes_is_more_devastating _than_taking_the_right_to_arm_ourselves_away/

9. Bill O'Reilly, "Mass Murder in Las Vegas," *billoreilly.com* (Oct. 2, 2017), https://www .billoreilly.com/b/Mass-Murder-in-Las-Vegas/851098107399788721.html

10. Sam Levin, "New Photos of Oregon Wildlife Refuge Reveal Damage Done by Bundy Standoff," *The Guardian* (March 24, 2016), https://www.theguardian.com/us-news/2016/mar /24/oregon-wildlife-refuge-damage-photos-militia-standoff

11. Kevin Sullivan and Juliet Eilperin, "In the Nevada Desert, Bundy Family Warns of Another Standoff," *Washington Post* (Nov. 1, 2016), https://www.washingtonpost.com/national /2016/11/01/c45bdf4e-a04c-11e6-a44d-cc2898cfab06_story.html?utm_term=.3e477d5438ae

12. Betsy Gaines Quammen, "The War for the West Rages On," *New York Times* (Jan. 29, 2016), http://www.nytimes.com/2016/01/30/opinion/the-war-for-the-west-rages-on.html

13. Nigel Duara, "Oregon Armed Protesters Invoke the Constitution—Annotated by a Conspiracy Theorist," *Los Angeles Times* (Jan. 21, 2016), http://www.latimes.com/nation/la-na -ff-oregon-standoff-constitution-20160121–story.html

14. Quammen, "The War for the West Rages On."

15. Chris Zinda, "The 50-Year Leap: Of Theo-Constitutionalists and Theme Parks," *Utah Independent* (April 18, 2016), https://web.archive.org/web/20170227084311/http:// suindependent.com/theo-constitutional/

16. Naomi LaChance, "Ultra-Right Annotated Edition of Pocket Constitution Tops Amazon Charts After Khizr Khan's DNC Speech," *The Intercept* (Aug. 1, 2016), https://theintercept.com/2016/08/01/ultra-right-annotated-edition-of-pocket-constitution-tops-amazon-charts-after-khizr-khans-dnc-speech/

17. Alexander Zaitchik, "Meet the Man Who Changed Glenn Beck's Life," *Salon* (Sept. 16, 2009), http://www.salon.com/2009/09/16/beck_skousen/

18. Jeffrey Rosen, "Radical Constitutionalism," *New York Times* (Nov. 26, 2010), https://www.nytimes.com/2010/11/28/magazine/28FOB-idealab-t.html

19. Arthur Goldwag, *The New Hate: A History of Fear and Loathing on the Populist Right* (Pantheon Books 2012), 35–43.

20. Jill Lepore, *The Story of America: Essays on Origins* (Princeton University Press 2012), 80.

21. Janell Ross, "Obama Revives His 'Cling to Guns or Religion' Analysis—for Donald Trump Supporters," *Washington Post* (Dec. 21, 2015), https://www.washingtonpost.com/news/the-fix/wp/2015/12/21/obama-dusts-off-his-cling-to-guns-or-religion-idea-for-donald-trump/?utm_term=.c060cc9135d4

22. Max Strasser, "For Militiamen the Fight for Cliven Bundy's Ranch Is Far from Over," *Newsweek* (April 23, 2014), https://www.newsweek.com/2014/05/02/militiamen-fight-over-cliven-bundys-ranch-far-over-248354.html

23. Adam Nagourney, "A Defiant Rancher Savors the Audience That Rallied to His Side," *New York Times* (April 23, 2014), https://www.nytimes.com/2014/04/24/us/politics/rancher-proudly-breaks-the-law-becoming-a-hero-in-the-west.html

24. Olivia Nuzzi, "What Cliven Bundy's Famous Backers Said, Before and After," *Daily Beast* (April 24, 2014), http://www.thedailybeast.com/what-cliven-bundys-famous-backers-said-before-and-after

25. Ibid.

26. Jason Sattler, "Trump Could Blow Lid Off GOP's Well-Mannered White Supremacy," *USA Today* (Aug. 29, 2017), https://www.usatoday.com/story/opinion/2017/08/29/trump-blow-lid-off-polite-gop-white-supremacy-jason-sattler-column/607732001/

27. See, for example, Ian Haney López, *Dog Whistle Politics: How Coded Racial Appeals Have Reinvented Racism and Wrecked the Middle Class* (Oxford University Press 2015).

28. Sattler, "Trump Could Blow Lid Off GOP's Well-Mannered White Supremacy."

29. Knights of the K.K.K., *Constitution and Laws of the Knights of the Ku Klux Klan* (Imperial Palace 1921).

30. Ibid.

31. Republican Senator Ted Cruz claimed in February 2017 that the Democrats "are the party of the Ku Klux Klan." Kristine Phillips, "Ted Cruz: 'The Democrats Are the Party of the Ku Klux Klan,'" *Washington Post* (Feb. 8, 2017), *https://www.washingtonpost.com/news/the-fix/wp/2017/02/08/ted-cruz-the-democrats-are-the-party-of-the-ku-klux-klan/?utm_term=.f5165aa56c49*. This is a profoundly disingenuous claim, as the political platforms of Democrats and Republicans essentially switched in the 1960s following the passage of the Civil Rights Act. That is, the modern-day Democratic Party bears strongest similarity to the Reconstruction-era Republican Party, and the modern-day Republican Party most strongly resembles the Reconstruction-era Democratic Party. See Sean Gorman,

"State Sen. Stephen Martin Says Democratic Party Created the Ku Klux Klan," *PolitiFact* (June 10, 2013), https://www.politifact.com/virginia/statements/2013/jun/10/stephen-martin/ state-sen-stephen-martin-says-democratic-party-cre/, quoting historian Carol Emberton:

> "Although the names stayed the same, the platforms of the two parties reversed each other in the mid-20th century, due in large part to white 'Dixiecrats' flight out of the Democratic Party and into the Republican Party after the passage of the Civil Rights Act of 1964. By then, the Democratic Party had become the party of 'reform,' supporting a variety of 'liberal' causes, including civil rights, women's rights, etc. whereas this had been the banner of the Republican Party in the nineteenth century."

32. Stuart Wexler, *America's Secret Jihad: The Hidden History of Religious Terrorism in the United States* (Counterpoint 2015) (quoting Patsy Sims, *The Klan*).

33. Daniel Levitas, *The Terrorist Next Door: The Militia Movement and the Radical Right* (St. Martin's Griffin 2004), 1.

34. Ibid., 2.

35. Ibid., 8.

36. Josh Horwitz, "20 Years After OKC Bombing, NRA Has Mainstreamed McVeigh's Insurrectionist Idea in Conservative Movement," *Huffington Post* (April 23, 2015), https://www.huffingtonpost.com/josh-horwitz/20-years-after-okc-bombin_b_7127440.html

37. Ibid.

38. Timothy McVeigh letter to a friend, Steve Hodge, in Barry J. Balleck, *Allegiance to Liberty: The Changing Face of Patriots, Militias, and Political Violence in America* (ABC-CLIO 2014), 176.

39. David A. Graham, "Matt Bevin's Apocalyptic Warnings of Bloodshed," *The Atlantic* (Sept. 13, 2016), https://www.theatlantic.com/politics/archive/2016/09/matt-bevin -clinton-blood/499754/

40. Greg Sargent, "Sharron Angle Floated Possibility of Armed Insurrection," *Washington Post* (June 15, 2010), http://voices.washingtonpost.com/plum-line/2010/06/sharron_angle _floated_possibil.html

41. Louis Jacobson, "In Context: Donald Trump's 'Second Amendment People' Comment," *PolitiFact* (Aug. 9, 2016), http://www.politifact.com/truth-o-meter/article/2016/aug/09/context -donald-trumps-second-amendment-people-comm/

42. Mary Ann Glendon, *Rights Talk: The Impoverishment of Political Discourse* (Free Press 1991), xi.

43. Joseph Blocher, "Gun Rights Talk," *Boston University Law Review,* 94 (2014), 815.

44. Michael Waldman, *The Second Amendment: A Biography* (Simon & Schuster 2014).

45. Wayne LaPierre, *Guns, Freedom, and Terrorism* (WND Books 2003), 45.

46. Ibid., 31.

47. Waldman, *The Second Amendment,* 52–53.

48. LaPierre, *Guns, Freedom, and Terrorism,* 30.

49. Adam Winkler, *Gun Fight: The Battle over the Right to Bear Arms in America* (Norton 2011), 12, 113–116.

50. Waldman, *The Second Amendment,* 55–56.

51. Winkler, *Gun Fight,* 253.

52. Ibid., 255.

53. Ibid., 67.

54. Reva B. Siegel, "Dead or Alive: Originalism as Popular Constitutionalism in *Heller*," *Harvard Law Review*, 122 (2008), 231.

55. Ibid., 232–233.

56. Ibid., 231.

57. Siegel 233–235. The Charlton Heston speeches excerpted in the chapter are from Siegel's article.

58. Scott Melzer, *Gun Crusaders: The NRA's Culture War* (NYU Press 2009), 59.

59. Deborah Homsher, "Response to Bernard E. Harcourt's 'On Gun Registration, the NRA, Adolf Hitler, and Nazi Gun Laws: Exploding the Gun Culture Wars (A Call to Historians),'" *Fordham Law Review*, 73 (2004), 718.

60. Michael C. Dorf, "Identity Politics and the Second Amendment," *Fordham Law Review*, 73 (2004), 568–569.

61. David C. Williams, "Constitutional Tales of Violence: Populists, Outgroups, and the Multicultural Landscape of the Second Amendment," *Tulane Law Review*, 74 (1999), 492.

62. Ben Popken, "America's Gun Business, by the Numbers," *NBC News* (Dec. 3, 2015), https://www.nbcnews.com/storyline/san-bernardino-shooting/americas-gun-business-numbers -n437566

63. Maggie McGrath, "Gun Stocks Surge as Obama Issues Executive Orders on Gun Safety," *Forbes* (Jan. 5, 2016), https://www.forbes.com/sites/maggiemcgrath/2016/01/05/gun-stocks -surge-as-obama-issues-executive-orders-on-gun-safety/#38e35b647681

64. Paul R. La Monica, "Gun Investors Love Obama," *CNN* (Jan. 5, 2016), http://money.cnn .com/2016/01/05/investing/gun-stocks-president-obama/index.html

65. Evan Osnos, "Making a Killing: The Business and Politics of Selling Guns," *New Yorker* (June 27, 2016), http://www.newyorker.com/magazine/2016/06/27/after-orlando -examining-the-gun-business

66. Violence Policy Center, "Blood Money II: How Gun Industry Dollars Fund the NRA" (Sept. 2013), http://www.vpc.org/studies/bloodmoney2.pdf

67. Sarah Ellison, "The Civil War That Could Doom the N.R.A.," *Vanity Fair* (June 27, 2016), http://www.vanityfair.com/news/2016/06/the-civil-war-that-could-doom-the-nra

68. Ibid.

69. Katie Zezima, "NRA Chief Executive Received Nearly $4 Million Retirement Payout in 2015," *Washington Post* (Feb. 9, 2017), https://www.washingtonpost.com/news/post-nation/wp /2017/02/09/nra-chief-executive-received-nearly-4-million-retirement-payout-in-2015/?utm _term=.bf078cb561e2

70. Linda Greenhouse, "How the GOP Outsourced the Judicial Nomination Process," *New York Times* (July 21, 2016), http://www.nytimes.com/2016/07/21/opinion/how-the-gop -outsourced-the-judicial-nomination-process.html. Greenhouse writes, "Over the past seven years, Senate Republicans have outsourced the confirmation process to the gun lobby. This is not hyperbole, but fact."

71. Mike Spies, "In Florida, the NRA Demands Total Obedience. These War Stories Show Why Orlando Won't Change That," *The Trace* (June 23, 2016), https://www.thetrace.org/2016 /06/nra-florida-no-tighter-gun-laws-orlando-shooting/

72. Richard Feldman, *Ricochet, Confessions of a Gun Lobbyist* (John Wiley & Sons 2008), 53.

73. Aaron Williams, "Have Your Representatives in Congress Received Donations from the NRA?" *Washington Post* (Feb. 15, 2018), https://www.washingtonpost.com/graphics/national/nra-donations/?utm_term=.481fe5bbf1a6

74. Ian Millhiser, "McConnell: No New Supreme Court Justice Until the NRA Approves of the Nominee," *Think Progress* (March 20, 2016), https://thinkprogress.org/mcconnell-no-new-supreme-court-justice-until-the-nra-approves-of-the-nominee-76aeof40e064/

75. Mike Spies and Ashley Balcerzak, "The NRA Placed Big Bets on the 2016 Election, and Won Almost All of Them," *Open Secrets* (Nov. 9, 2016), https://www.opensecrets.org/news/2016/11/the-nra-placed-big-bets-on-the-2016-election-and-won-almost-all-of-them/

76. John Wagner and Elise Viebeck, "'I Am Going to Come Through for You,' Trump Vows to NRA," *Washington Post* (April 28, 2017), https://www.washingtonpost.com/politics/i-am-going-to-come-through-for-you-trump-vows-to-nra/2017/04/28/3258b3e6-2c20-11e7-a616-d7c8a68c1a66_story.html?utm_term=.c9e333fa5ff6

77. Joe Palazzolo, "Trump to Address NRA, Breaking Decadeslong Presidential Precedent," *Wall Street Journal* (April 27, 2017), https://www.wsj.com/articles/trump-to-address-nra-breaking-decadeslong-presidential-precedent-1493332053

78. Michael Waldman, "How the NRA Rewrote the Second Amendment," *Politico* (May 19, 2014), https://www.politico.com/magazine/story/2014/05/nra-guns-second-amendment-106856?o=2

79. Winkler, *Gun Fight*, 25.

80. Ibid., 58.

81. *District of Columbia v. Heller*, 554 U.S. 570, 616 (2008).

82. Ibid., 629.

83. Dennis A. Henigan, "Book Review of *Out of Range: Why the Constitution Can't End the Battle Over Guns*, by Mark V. Tushnet," *Journal of Legal Education*, 60 (2) (2010).

84. Siegel, "Dead or Alive," 201.

85. J. Harvie Wilkinson III, "Of Guns, Abortions, and the Unraveling Rule of Law," *Virginia Law Review*, 95 (2)(2009), 274.

86. Siegel, "Dead or Alive," 193.

87. *District of Columbia v. Heller*, 629.

88. Ibid., 570.

89. George P. Fletcher, *A Crime of Self-Defense: Bernhard Goetz and the Law on Trial* (University of Chicago Press 1988), 18.

90. Mary Anne Franks, "Democratic Surveillance," *Harvard Journal of Law and Technology*, 30 (2017), 462.

91. Mary Anne Franks, "Men, Women, and Optimal Violence," *University of Illinois Law Review*, 2016 (2016), 940.

92. Fletcher, *A Crime of Self-Defense*, 18.

93. John Locke, *Second Treatise on Government*, Section 19 (1690), http://libertyonline.hypermall.com/Locke/second/second-frame.html https://static.prisonpolicy.org/scans/bjs/jv003.pdf 94. Katrina Baum, "Juvenile Victimization and Offending, 1993–2003," Bureau of Justice Statistics, Special Crime Report, National Crime Victimization Survey (August 2005), https://static.prisonpolicy.org/scans/bjs/jv003.pdf

95. Erika Harrell, "Crime Against Persons with Disabilities, 2009–2012," Bureau of Justice Statistics, (February 2014), https://www.bjs.gov/content/pub/pdf/capd0912st.pdf

96. According to the Bureau of Justice Statistics,

Persons in poor households at or below the Federal Poverty Level (FPL) (39.8 per 1,000) had more than double the rate of violent victimization as persons in high-income households (16.9 per 1,000) for the period 2008–12. Serious violence (rape or sexual assault, robbery and aggravated assault) accounted for a greater percentage of violence among persons in poor households (38 percent) than in high-income households (27 percent). ("Household Poverty and Nonfatal Violent Victimization, 2008–2012," https://www.bjs.gov/index.cfm?ty=pbdetail&iid=5137)

97. Brad J. Bushman, "The 'Weapons Effect,'" *Psychology Today* (Jan. 18, 2013), https://www.psychologytoday.com/blog/get-psyched/201301/the-weapons-effect

98. Debra Dobray and Arthur J. Waldrop, "Regulating Handgun Advertising Directed at Women," *Whittier Law Review,* 12 (1991), 115.

99. Mayors Against Illegal Guns, "Shoot First: 'Stand Your Ground' Laws and Their Effect on Violent Crime and the Criminal Justice System," *Everytown for Gun Safety* (Sept. 2013), https://everytownresearch.org/reports/shoot-first/

100. Popken, "America's Gun Business, by the Numbers."

101. Children's Safety Network, Injury and Violence Policy Center, https://www.childrenssafetynetwork.org/publications/cost-firearm-violence

102. Kara Fox, "How US Gun Culture Compares with the World," *CNN* (July 19, 2017), http://www.cnn.com/2017/07/19/world/us-gun-crime-police-shooting-statistics/index.html

103. Daniel White, "America's Gun Homicide Rate Is 25 Times Higher Than Other Rich Countries," *Time* (Feb. 3, 2016), http://time.com/4206484/america-violent-death-rate-higher/

104. Ibid.

105. Ibid.

106. Ben Casselman, Matthew Conlen and Reuben Fischer-Baum, "Gun Deaths in America," *Five Thirty Eight*, https://fivethirtyeight.com/features/gun-deaths/

107. Melissa Healy, "Guns Kill Nearly 1,300 Children in the U.S. Each Year and Send Thousands More to Hospitals," *Los Angeles Times* (June 19, 2017), http://www.latimes.com/science/sciencenow/la-sci-sn-gun-deaths-children-20170619-story.html

108. Brady Campaign to Prevent Gun Violence, "Key Gun Violence Statistics," https://www.bradycampaign.org/key-gun-violence-statistics

109. Dave Mosher and Skye Gould, "Americans Are More Likely to Die from Gun Violence Than Many Leading Causes of Death Combined," *Business Insider* (Oct. 2, 2017), http://www.businessinsider.com/gun-death-statistics-assault-mass-shootings-accidents-2017-10

110. Claims that guns are frequently used defensively are drawn principally from the dubious work of two gun rights advocates, John Lott and David Kopel. Lott's research and reputation have been repeatedly discredited, and it has been revealed that Kopel and his research institute have received more than $1.42 million in funding from the NRA over eight years. See Alex Seitz-Wald, "Why Is the Media Rehabilitating John Lott?" *Salon* (Dec. 21, 2012), *http://www.salon.com/2012/12/21/why_is_the_media_rehabilitating_john_lott/*; Evan DeFilippis and Devin Hughes, "The GOP's Favorite Gun '"Academic" Is a Fraud," *Think Progress* (Aug. 12, 2016), https://thinkprogress.org/debunking-john-lott-5456e83cf326/; Frank Smyth, "The Times Has Finally (Quietly) Outed an NRA-Funded

'Independent' Scholar," *Progressive* (April 24, 2014), *http://progressive.org/dispatches
/times-finally-quietly-outed-nra-funded-independent-scholar/*. One of the gun lobby's most
repeated claims is that there are 2.5 million defensive gun uses (DGUs) every year. As Philip J.
Cook and Kristin A. Goss point out, there is very good reason to be skeptical of that number,
as it is more than double the number of total gun crimes reported by the National Crime
Victimization Survey. According to the *New York Times*, the number of actual defensive
gun uses is probably closer to 67,740 per year. Philip J. Cook and Kristin A. Goss, *The Gun
Debate: What Everyone Needs to Know* (Oxford University Press 2014), 20; Juliet Lapidos,
"Defensive Gun Use," *New York Times* (April 15, 2013), https://takingnote.blogs.nytimes
.com/2013/04/15/defensive-gun-use/

111. Julia Glum, "ISIS in America: Militants Can Easily Buy Guns at U.S. Gun Shows,
Islamic State Tells Its Fighters," *Newsweek* (May 5, 2017), http://www.newsweek.com
/isis-magazine-gun-shows-loophole-595295

112. Evan DeFilippis and Devin Hughes, "Gunfight or Flight: New Study Finds No Advantages to Using a Firearm in Self-Defense Situations," *The Trace* (July 14, 2015), https://www
.thetrace.org/2015/07/defensive-gun-use-myth/

113. "In 2012 for every justifiable homicide in the United States involving a gun, guns
were used in 32 criminal homicides." Violence Policy Center, "Self-Defense Gun Use Is Rare,
Study Finds" (June 17, 2015), http://vpc.org/press/self-defense-gun-use-is-rare-study-finds/

114. David Hemenway and S. J. Solnick, "The Epidemiology of Self-Defense Gun Use:
Evidence from the National Crime Victimization Surveys 2007–2011," *Preventive Medicine,*
79 (2015), 22–27.

115. Alex Yablon, "How the Las Vegas Shooting Challenges the NRA's 'Good Guy
with a Gun' Argument," *The Trace* (Oct. 2, 2017), https://www.thetrace.org/rounds/las
-vegas-mass-shooting-nra-good-guy-with-a-gun/

116. Bernard D. Rostker et al., "Evaluation of the New York City Police Department Firearm Training and Firearm-Discharge Review Process," RAND Corporation (2008), http://www
.nyc.gov/html/nypd/downloads/pdf/public_information/RAND_FirearmEvaluation.pdf

117. Joshua Holland, "Tactical Experts Destroy the NRA's Heroic Gunslinger Fantasy,"
The Nation (Oct. 5, 2015), https://www.thenation.com/article/combat-vets-destroy-the-
nras-heroic-gunslinger-fantasy/; Duane Thomas, quoted in "Carrying Concealed Weapons:
A Statement to Senate Judiciary Committee" (2002): "Most cops and civilian gun carriers
are *lousy* handgun shots. The level of ineptitude of many people who carry guns on a daily
basis is nothing short of appalling." http://docs.legis.wisconsin.gov/2001/related/public
_hearing_records/sc_jcacfr_judiciary_consumer_affairs_and_campaign_finance_reform/bills
_resolutions/01hr_sc_jcacfr_sb0357_pt04.pdf

118. Joseph J. Vince Jr., Timothy Wolfe, and Layton Field, "Firearms Training and Self-
Defense," *National Gun Victims Action Council* (2015), https://www.gunvictimsaction.org/
downloads22/FirearmsTrainings%20_StudyDocument_F_062115.pdf

119. Andrew Anglemeyer, Tara Horvath, and George Rutherford, "The Accessibility of Firearms and Risk for Suicide and Homicide Victimization Among Household Members: A Systematic Review and Meta-Analysis," *Annals of Internal Medicine* (Jan. 21, 2014), http://annals.org
/aim/article/1814426/accessibility-firearms-risk-suicide-homicide-victimization-among
-household-members-systematic

120. "Among gun assaults where the victim had at least some chance to resist, this

adjusted odds ratio increased to 5.45." Charles C. Branas et al., "Investigating the Link Between Gun Possession and Gun Assault," *American Journal of Public Health,* 99 (11) (2009), 2034–2040.

121. Matthew Miller, Deborah Azrael, and David Hemenway, "Firearm Availability and Unintentional Firearm Deaths," *Accident Analysis and Prevention,* 33 (2001), 477–484.

122. LaPierre, *Guns, Freedom, and Terrorism.*

123. Winkler, *Gun Fight,* 114–117.

124. "No support to the hypothesis that shall-issue laws have beneficial effects in reducing murder rates" (Patricia Grambsch, "Regression to the Mean, Murder Rates, and Shall-Issue Laws," *American Statistician,* 62 (4)(2012)); "No statistically significant association exists between changes in concealed weapon laws and state homicide rates" (L. Hepburn et al., "The Effect of Nondiscretionary Concealed Weapon Carrying Laws on Homicide," *Journal of Trauma,* 56 (3) (2004)); "No evidence that [right-to-carry] laws reduce or increase rates of violent crime" (Tomislav Kovandzic, Thomas Marvell, and Lynne Vieraitis, "The Impact of 'Shall-Issue' Concealed Handgun Laws on Violent Crime Rates," *Homicide Studies* (2005), *https://doi.org/10.1177%2F1088767905279972*); "[T]he rate at which CHLs [concealed handgun licenses] are issued and crime rates are independent of one another—crime does not drive CHLs; CHLs do not drive crime" (Charles D. Phillips et al., "Concealed Handgun Licensing and Crime in Four States," *Journal of Criminology* (2015), https://www.hindawi.com/journals/jcrim/2015/803742/).

125. David Fortunato, "Can Easing Concealed Carry Deter Crime?" *Social Science Quarterly* (2015), http://www.davidfortunato.com/ssq2015.pdf

126. Erik Eckholm, "Rampage Killings Linger in Memory, but Toll of Gun Violence Is Constant," *New York Times* (Oct. 8, 2015), https://www.nytimes.com/2015/10/09/us/rampage-killings-get-attention-but-gun-violence-is-constant.html

127. Everytown for Gun Safety, "Mass Shootings in the United States: 2009–2016" (April 11, 2017), https://everytownresearch.org/reports/mass-shootings-analysis/

128. Mark Follman, "The NRA Myth of Gun-Free Zones," *Mother Jones* (April 1, 2013), http://www.motherjones.com/politics/2013/04/gun-free-zones-mass-shootings/

129. Niraj Chokshi, "Secret Service: We're Not Allowing Firearms at the Republican National Convention," *Washington Post* (March 28, 2016), https://www.washingtonpost.com/news/the-fix/wp/2016/03/28/more-than-42000-people-have-signed-a-petition-to-allow-guns-at-the-republican-national-convention/?utm_term=.cc99a7a1bd48

130. Mark Hensch, "Secret Service: No Guns at Trump NRA Speech," *The Hill* (April 27, 2017), http://thehill.com/homenews/administration/330973-secret-service-no-guns-at-trump-nra-speech

131. "'The totality of the evidence based on educated judgments about the best statistical models suggests that right-to-carry laws are associated with substantially higher rates' of aggravated assault, rape, robbery and murder" (Clifton B. Parker, "Right-to-Carry Gun Laws Linked to Increase in Violent Crime, Stanford Research Shows," *Stanford News* (Nov. 14, 2014), *https://news.stanford.edu/news/2014/november/donohue-guns-study-111414.html*); "A 'shall issue' law that eliminates most restrictions on carrying a concealed weapon may be associated with increased firearm homicide rates" (M. Rosengart et al., "An Evaluation of State Firearm Regulations and Homicide and Suicide Death Rates," *Injury Prevention,* 11 (2) (2005), 77–83); "Changes in gun ownership are significantly positively related to

changes in the homicide rate" (Mark Duggan, "More Guns, More Crime," *Journal of Political Economy*, 109 (5) (2001), https://www.kellogg.northwestern.edu/faculty/dranove /htm/dranove/coursepages/Mgmt%20469/guns.pdf).

132. Parker, "Right-to-Carry Gun Laws Linked to Increase in Violent Crime."

133. Sarah Ferris, "More Homicides Are Reported in States Where You Can 'Stand Your Ground,' Report Finds," *Washington Post* (Aug. 15, 2014), https://www.washingtonpost .com/blogs/govbeat/wp/2014/08/15/more-homicides-are-reported-in-states-where-you-can-stand-your-ground-report-finds/?utm_term=.8335906de724

134. Richard Florida, "The Geography of Gun Deaths," *The Atlantic* (Jan. 13, 2011), https://www.theatlantic.com/national/archive/2011/01/the-geography-of-gun-deaths /69354/

135. Daniel Webster and Jens Ludwig, "Myths About Defensive Gun Use and Permissive Gun Carry Laws," *Berkeley Media Studies Group* (2000), http://www.bmsg.org/pdfs /myths.pdf

136. A Department of Justice study found that 93 percent of violent crimes that victimize college students occur *off* campus. http://www.armedcampuses.org/

137. Sofi Sinozich and Lynn Langton, "Rape and Sexual Assault Victimization Among College-Age Females, 1995–2013," Bureau of Justice Statistics, Special Report (Dec. 2014), https://www.bjs.gov/content/pub/pdf/rsavcaf9513.pdf

138. Department of Justice study, http:www.armedcampuses.org/

139. Campaign to Keep Guns Off Campus, "The Campaign to Keep Guns off Campus' New Study Shows That On-Campus Crime Rates Have Increased in Two States Where Concealed Carry on Campus Is Allowed" (March 17, 2015), http://keepgunsoffcampus.org /blog/2015/03/17/the-campaign-to-keep-guns-off-campus-new-study-shows-that-on-campus -crime-rates-have-increased-in-two-states-where-concealed-carry-on-campus-is-allowed/

140. Peter Overby, "NRA: 'Only Thing That Stops a Bad Guy with a Gun Is a Good Guy with a Gun," *NPR* (Dec. 21, 2012), https://www.npr.org/2012/12/21/167824766/nra-only-thing -that-stops-a-bad-guy-with-a-gun-is-a-good-guy-with-a-gun

141. William Saletan, "Friendly Firearms," *Slate* (Jan. 11, 2011). http://www.slate.com /articles/health_and_science/human_nature/2011/01/friendly_firearms.html

142. Waldman, *The Second Amendment*, 163.

143. Caroline O., "How the NRA Silenced the Science of Gun Violence Prevention," *Medium* (June 9, 2017), https://medium.com/@RVAwonk/how-the-nra-silenced-the-science-of-gun -violence-prevention-25a4e537c29e

144. Andrew Jay McClurg, "The Second Amendment Right to Be Negligent," *Florida Law Review*, 68 (2016), 6–8.

145. Osnos, "Making a Killing: The Business and Politics of Selling Guns."

146. See Caroline E. Light, *Stand Your Ground: A History of America's Love Affair with Lethal Self-Defense* (Beacon Press 2018).

147. Mary Anne Franks, "Real Men Advance, Real Women Retreat: Stand Your Ground, Battered Women's Syndrome, and Violence as Male Privilege," *University of Miami Law Review*, 68 (2014), 1108–1109.

148. Matthew R. Durose et al., "Family Violence Statistics: Including Statistics on Strangers and Acquaintances," Bureau of Justice Statistics (June 2005), https://www.bjs.gov /content/pub/pdf/fvs02.pdf

149. Shannan Catalano, "Intimate Partner Violence in the United States," Bureau of Justice Statistics (2007), https://www.bjs.gov/content/pub/pdf/ipvus.pdf

150. National Center for Injury Prevention and Control, "National Intimate Partner and Sexual Violence Survey: Intimate Partner Violence in the United States," *CDC* (2010) http://www.cdc.gov/violenceprevention/pdf/nisvs_report2010-a.pdf

151. Jennifer Mascia, "Once Every 16 Hours, an American Woman Is Fatally Shot by a Current or Former Romantic Partner," *The Trace* (Feb. 9, 2016), https://www.thetrace .org/2016/02/women-domestic-violence-death-statistics/

152. Susan Sorenson and Rebecca Schut, "Nonfatal Gun Use in Intimate Partner Violence: A Systematic Review of the Literature," *Trauma, Violence, Abuse* (2016), https://www.ncbi .nlm.nih.gov/pubmed/27630138

153. Everytown for Gun Safety, "Guns and Violence Against Women: America's Uniquely Lethal Domestic Violence Problem," https://everytownresearch.org/reports/guns-and -violence-against-women/

154. Caroline Light, "Why the NRA Has Been a Disaster for Black Americans," *Mother Jones* (May 2, 2017), http://www.motherjones.com/politics/2017/05/florida-stand -your-ground-guns-rights-race-donald-trump-national-rifle-association/

155. National Institute of Justice, "Victims and Victimization" (March 15, 207), https://www .nij.gov/topics/victims-victimization/pages/welcome.aspx

156. Malcolm X Grassroots Movement 2013, "Operation Ghetto Storm: 2012 Annual Report on the
Extrajudicial Killings of 313 Black People by Police, Security Guards, and Vigilantes" (April 2013),
https://mxgm.org/wp-content/uploads/2013/04/Operation-Ghetto-Storm.pdf

157. German Lopez, "Open Carry Laws Didn't Stop Cops from Killing Keith Lamont Scott," *Vox* (Sept. 21, 2016), https://www.vox.com/2014/12/13/7384813/black-open-carry

158. B. Keith Payne, "Weapon Bias: Split-Second Decisions and Unintended Stereotyping," *Current Directions in Psychology* (Dec. 1, 2006), http://journals.sagepub.com/doi/abs /10.1111/j.1467-8721.2006.00454.x?journalCode=cdpa

159. Jennifer Carlson, *Citizen-Protectors: The Everyday Politics of Guns in an Age of Decline* (Oxford University Press 2015), 115.

160. David A. Graham, "Do African Americans Have a Right to Bear Arms?" *The Atlantic* (June 21, 2017), https://www.theatlantic.com/politics/archive/2017/06/the-continued -erosion-of-the-african-american-right-to-bear-arms/531093/

161. Kira Lerner, "Black Lives Don't Matter to the NRA," *Think Progress* (July 7, 2016), http://thinkprogress.org/justice/2016/07/07/3796062/nra-black-lives-matter/

162. Wilbert L. Cooper, "This Group of Black Women Is Taking Up Arms to Fight Racism and Misogyny," *Vice* (Feb. 8, 2017), https://www.vice.com/en_us/article/ypqy9w/this -group-of-black-women-is-taking-up-arms-to-fight-racism-and-misogyny

163. John Nichols, "How ALEC Took Florida's 'License to Kill' Law National," *The Nation* (March 22, 2012), https://www.thenation.com/article/how-alec-took-floridas-license -kill-law-national/

164. Adam Weinstein, "How the NRA and Its Allies Helped Spread a Radical Gun Law Nationwide," *Mother Jones* (June 7, 2012), https://www.motherjones.com/politics/2012/06/nra-alec -stand-your-ground/

165. On March 5, 2018, the *New Yorker* published an exposé of Hammer's lobbying work, penned by Mike Spies in connection with *The Trace*, a nonprofit group dedicated to covering firearms in America. As part of his research for the article, Spies pored over thousands of pages of e-mail detailing the nature of the relationship between Hammer and Florida state officials. The documents, obtained through public-records requests, reflect an established hierarchy operating as follows: "[S]he gives orders, and they follow them."

In 2012, a subcommittee of the Florida legislature received a draft piece of legislation that would deny concealed-carry permit holders the right to bring a firearm into a range of government buildings or childcare centers. When Hammer learned of the bill's advancement, she fired off an e-mail to the policy chief of the subcommittee informing her that the NRA was opposed to the legislation and that Hammer hoped "that it will not ever be heard."

The "legislation was left off the voting calendar, and died two months later." Mike Spies, "The N.R.A. Lobbyist Behind Florida's Pro-Gun Policies," *New Yorker* (March 5, 2018), https://www.newyorker.com/magazine/2018/03/05/the-nra-lobbyist-behind-floridas-pro-gun-policies

166. Michael C. Bender, "Pistol-Packing Grandma Helps NRA Push State Pro-Gun Laws," *Bloomberg* (May 11, 2012), https://www.bloomberg.com/news/articles/2012-05-11/pistol-packing-grandma-helps-nra-push-state-pro-gun-laws

167. Paul Solotaroff, "A Most American Way to Die," *Rolling Stone* (April 25, 2013), https://www.rollingstone.com/culture/culture-news/a-most-american-way-to-die-93561/

168. Weinstein, "How the NRA and Its Allies Helped Spread a Radical Gun Law Nationwide."

169. Center for Individual Freedom, "Interview with Marion Hammer" (Nov. 3, 2005).

170. Peter Schorsch, Senator Don Gaetz, and Representative Matt Gaetz, "Op-ed: Standing Up for 'Stand Your Ground,'" *Saint Peters Blog* (May 2, 2012), http://saintpetersblog.com/sen-don-gaetz-rep-matt-gaetz-op-ed-standing-up-for-stand-your-ground/

171. Franks, "Real Men Advance, Real Women Retreat: Stand Your Ground, Battered Women's Syndrome, and Violence as Male Privilege," 1100–1102.

172. Rape, Abuse and Incest National Network (RAINN), "Perpetrators of Sexual Violence: Statistics," https://www.rainn.org/statistics/perpetrators-sexual-violence

173. "Though mass shootings make an outsize psychological impact, they are a tiny fraction of the nation's overall gun violence, which takes more than 30,000 lives annually" (Mark Follman, "America's Mass-Shootings Epidemic," *Los Angeles Times* (Oct. 19, 2014), http://www.latimes.com/opinion/op-ed/la-oe-follman-rise-in-mass-shootings-20141020-story.html).

174. "[N]ot one of 62 mass shootings in the United States over the last 30 years has been stopped [by an armed civilian]. More broadly, attempts by armed civilians to intervene in shooting rampages are rare—and are successful even more rarely" (Mark Follman, "Do Armed Civilians Stop Mass Shooters? Actually, No," *Mother Jones* (Dec. 19, 2012), https://www.motherjones.com/politics/2012/12/armed-civilians-do-not-stop-mass-shootings/).

175. Thomas J. Gardner and Terry M. Anderson, *Criminal Law* (Cengage 2016), 148–149.

176. *Weiand v. State*, 732 So. 2d 1044, Fla. 1999.

177. American Bar Association, "National Task Force on Stand Your Ground Laws" (Sept. 2015), https://www.americanbar.org/content/dam/aba/images/diversity/SYG_Report_Book.pdf

178. Ibid.

179. Elizabeth B. Megale, "Disaster Unaverted: Reconciling the Desire for a Safe and Secure State with the Grim Realities of Stand Your Ground," *American Journal of Trial Advocacy,* 37 (2013), 258, https://scholarship.law.campbell.edu/cgi/viewcontent.cgi?article =1222&context=fac_sw

180. Shankar Vedantam, "'Stand Your Ground' Linked to Increase in Homicides," *NPR* (Jan. 2, 2013), https://www.npr.org/2013/01/02/167984117/-stand-your-ground -linked-to-increase-in-homicide

181. Kameel Stanley and Connie Humburg, "Many Killers Who Go Free with Florida 'Stand Your Ground' Law Have History of Violence," *Tampa Bay Times* (July 20, 2012), https:// www.tampabay.com/news/courts/criminal/many-killers-who-go-free-with-florida-stand -your-ground-law-have-history/1241378

182. Ibid.

183. American Bar Association, "National Task Force on Stand Your Ground Laws," 13.

184. Cheng Cheng and Mark Hoekstra, "Does Strengthening Self-Defense Law Deter Crime or Escalate Violence?: Evidence from Castle Doctrine," *National Bureau of Economic Research* (June 2012), http://www.nber.org/papers/w18134

185. Chandler McClellan and Erdal Tekin, "Stand Your Ground Laws and Homicides," Institute for the Study of Labor, Discussion Paper Series (July 2012), http://ftp.iza.org /dp6705.pdf

186. Jenks cited in American Bar Association, "National Task Force on Stand Your Ground Laws," 22.

187. Texas Penal Code §§ 9.41, 9.42, and 9.43.

188. Adam B. Ellick, "Grand Jury Clears Texan in the Killing of 2 Burglars," *New York Times* (July 1, 2008), https://www.nytimes.com/2008/07/01/us/01texas.html

189. Brian Rogers, Ruth Rendon, and Dale Lezon, "Joe Horn Cleared by Grand Jury in Pasadena Shootings," *Houston Chronicle* (June 30, 2008). https://www.chron .com/neighborhood/pasadena-news/article/Joe-Horn-cleared-by-grand-jury-in-Pasadena -1587004.php

190. Patrik Jonsson, "Martin Killing in Florida Puts 'Stand Your Ground' on Trial," *Christian Science Monitor* (March 16, 2012), https://www.csmonitor.com/USA/Justice/2012/0316 /Trayvon-Martin-killing-in-Florida-puts-Stand-Your-Ground-law-on-trial

191. Patrik Jonsson, "Michael Dunn Loud-Music Life Sentence: A Corrective on Stand Your Ground Laws?" *Christian Science Monitor* (Oct. 18, 2014), https://www.cs-monitor.com/USA/Justice/2014/1018/Michael-Dunn-loud-music-life-sentence-a-corrective-on -stand-your-ground-laws

192. David Kopel, "Stand Your Ground Had Nothing to Do with the Dunn Verdict in Florida," *Washington Post* (Feb. 17, 2014), http://www.washingtonpost.com/news/volokhconspiracy /wp/2014/02/17/stand-your-ground-had-nothing-to-do-with-the-dunn-verdict-inflorida

193. Franks, "Real Men Advance, Real Women Retreat," 1099.

194. Jeannine Amber, "In Her Own Words: Marissa Alexander Tells Her Story," *Essence* (March 4, 2015), http://www.essence.com/2015/03/04/marissa-alexander-exclusive

195. Jim Piggott, "Judge: Marissa Alexander Released to House Arrest," *News 4 Jax* (Jan. 27, 2015), http://www.news4jax.com/news/marissa-alexander-expected-to-be-released/30947974

196. The stand-your-ground laws of other states, such as South Carolina, are closely modeled on Florida's and include the same deliberate exclusions of domestic violence victims.

In November 2012, Whitlee Jones was attempting to leave her partner, Eric Lee, after he punched her and dragged her down the street by her hair. As she gathered up her belongings and tried to exit the house, Lee blocked her way. Jones stabbed him, and Lee died. The case's lead prosecutor, Assistant Solicitor Culver Kidd, stated:

> "[The Legislature's] intent . . . was to provide law-abiding citizens greater protections from external threats in the form of intruders and attackers. . . . We believe that applying the statute so that its reach into our homes and personal relationships is inconsistent with [its] wording and intent."

Quoted in Andrew Knapp, "Charleston Prosecutors Challenge Use of 'Stand Your Ground' Law in Domestic Disputes at Home," *The Post and Courier* (Oct. 11, 2014), https://www.postandcourier.com/archives/charleston-prosecutors-challenge-use-of-stand-your-ground-law-in/article_a065edea-3fab-519e-a144-38f39f96d500.html

197. NRA-ILA, "NRA's Chris Cox Calls on Americans to Support Trump" (July 19, 2016), https://www.nraila.org/articles/20160719/nras-chris-cox-calls-on-americans-to-support-trump

198. Jeremy Diamond, "Trump: I Could 'Shoot Somebody and I Wouldn't Lose Voters,'" *CNN* (Jan. 24, 2016), https://edition.cnn.com/2016/01/23/politics/donald-trump-shoot-somebody-support/

199. Paulina Firozi, "Trump Calls for Police to Take Guns During Stop-and-Frisks," *The Hill* (Sept. 22, 2016), http://thehill.com/blogs/ballot-box/presidential-races/297264-trump-calls-for-police-to-take-guns-away-during-stop-and

200. Tyler Yzaguirre, "Why Gun Owners Should Use the First Amendment to Protect Open Carry," *The Hill* (Aug. 8, 2017), https://thehill.com/blogs/pundits-blog/civil-rights/345675-why-gun-owners-should-use-the-first-amendment-to-protect-open

CHAPTER THREE

1. Phil Helsel and Miguel Almaguer, "Portland Stabbing Suspect Yells 'Free Speech or Die' in Court Appearance," *NBC News* (May 30, 2017), https://www.nbcnews.com/news/us-news/portland-stabbing-suspect-yells-free-speech-or-die-first-court-n766416

2. Doug Brown, "Suspect in Portland Hate Crime Murders Is a Known White Supremacist," *Portland Mercury* (May 27, 2017), https://www.portlandmercury.com/blogtown/2017/05/27/19041594/suspect-in-portland-hate-crime-murders-is-a-known-white-supremacist

3. Helsel and Almaguer, "Portland Stabbing Suspect Yells 'Free Speech or Die' in Court Appearance."

4. Tyler Yzaguirre, "Why Gun Owners Should Use the First Amendment to Protect Open Carry," *The Hill* (Aug. 8, 2017), https://thehill.com/blogs/pundits-blog/civil-rights/345675-why-gun-owners-should-use-the-first-amendment-to-protect-open

5. ACLU, "David Cole: ACLU Legal Director," https://www.aclu.org/bio/david-cole; NRA-ILA, "NRA's Chris Cox Calls on Americans to Support Trump" (July 19, 2016), https://www.nraila.org/articles/20160719/nras-chris-cox-calls-on-americans-to-support-trump

6. NRA-ILA, "NRA's Chris Cox Calls on Americans to Support Trump."

7. ACLU, "Guardians of Freedom," https://www.aclu.org/guardians-freedom

8. Both the ACLU and the NRA claim to be nonpartisan organizations, but they are both widely perceived as having distinct political commitments.

9. It can be argued that yet another organization, the National Association for the Advancement of Colored People (NAACP), which was founded in 1909 in the wake of widespread violence against black people, may have the strongest claim to being "oldest, largest and most widely recognized civil rights organization."

10. Laura Weinrib, *The Taming of Free Speech: America's Civil Liberties Compromise* (Harvard University Press 2016).

11. ACLU, "ACLU Lawsuit Seeks Access to Lawful Information on Internet for Library Patrons in Eastern Washington" (Nov. 16, 2006), https://www.aclu.org/news /aclu-lawsuit-seeks-access-lawful-information-internet-library-patrons-eastern-washington

12. Kat Miller, "ACLU 'Rethinking' the Second Amendment?" *Washington Times* (July 22, 2010), https://www.washingtontimes.com/blog/watercooler/2010/jul/22/aclu-rethinking -second-amendment/

13. David McGrath Schwartz, "Nevada ACLU Supports an Individual's Right to Bear Arms," *Las Vegas Sun* (July 11, 2008), https://lasvegassun.com/news/2008/jul/11/ only-nevada-aclu-opposes-gun-control/

14. Richard Delgado and David H. Yun, "'The Speech We Hate': First Amendment Totalism, the ACLU, and the Principle of Dialogic Politics," *Arizona State Law Journal*, 27 (1995), 1300.

15. Evelyn Beatrice Hall, *The Friends of Voltaire* (G. P. Putnam's Sons 1906), 199.

16. Ron Grossman, "Flashback: 'Swastika War': When the Neo-Nazis Fought in Court to March in Skokie," *Chicago Tribune* (March 10, 2017), http://www.chicagotribune.com/news /opinion/commentary/ct-neo-nazi-skokie-march-flashback-perspec-0312-20170310-story.html

17. Aryeh Neier, "Lessons in Free Speech 40 Years After Nazis Planned Skokie March," *Chicago Sun Times* (April 25, 2017), http://chicago.suntimes.com/columnists/lessons-in-free -speech-40-years-after-nazis-planned-skokie-march/

18. ACLU, "About the ACLU," https://www.aclu.org/about-aclu

19. Delgado and Yun write,

[H]ate speech today lies not at the periphery, but at the center, and that political speech lies at the periphery of First Amendment ideology. The center and the periphery have traded places in a second sense as well: In a striking reversal of Harry Kalven's thesis, injuries to whites are now placed at the fore of constitutional jurisprudence, with redress to blacks' historical injustices allowed only when it coincides with benefits to whites. ("'The Speech We Hate,'" 1286)

20. UVA Center for Politics, "New Poll: Some Americans Express Troubling Racial Attitudes Even as Majority Oppose White Supremacists," *Sabato's Crystal Ball* (Sept. 14, 2017), http:// www.centerforpolitics.org/crystalball/articles/new-poll-some-americans-express-troubling -racial-attitudes-even-as-majority-oppose-white-supremacists/

21. Leslie Kendrick, "Speech, Intent, and the Chilling Effect," *William and Mary Law Review*, 54 (2013), 1655.

22. Jillian C. York, "Onlinecensorship.org Launches Inaugural Report," *Electronic Frontier Foundation* (March 31, 2016), https://www.eff.org/deeplinks/2016/03/onlinecensorshiporg -launches-inaugural-report

23. Kendrick, "Speech, Intent, and the Chilling Effect," 1684.

24. "From the perspective of the First Amendment, we must attend to the silencing effect of hate speech and pornography on disadvantaged groups—how certain forms of speech violate the equal right to free speech of those groups, that is, to the Fourteenth Amendment ramifications of those two forms of speech" (Owen M. Fiss, *The Irony of Free Speech* (Harvard University Press 1996), 26).

25. Cynthia Bowman, "Street Harassment and the Informal Ghettoization of Women," *Harvard Law Review,* 106 (3) (1993), 52; see also Olatokunbo Olukemi Laniya, "Street Smut: Gender, Media, and the Legal Power Dynamics of Street Harassment, or 'Hey Sexy' and Other Verbal Ejaculations," *Columbia Journal of Gender and Law,* 14 (2005), 91.

26. Stop Street Harassment, "Unsafe and Harassed in Public Spaces: A National Street Harassment Report" (Sept. 2014), 20–21, https://www.stopstreetharassment.org/wp-content/uploads /2012/08/2014-National-SSH-Street-Harassment-Report.pdf

27. Mari J. Matsuda, "Public Response to Racist Speech: Considering the Victim's Story," *Michigan Law Review,* 87 (1989), 2337; see also Michel Martin, "Racism Is Literally Bad for Your Health," *NPR* (Oct. 28, 2017), https://www.npr.org/2017/10/28/560444290/racism -is-literally-bad-for-your-health

28. "[T]he conventional understanding of the most familiar metaphor in the First Amendment lexicon, the 'marketplace of ideas,' has had the undesirable effect of focusing attention too much on the truth seeking and self-government values and on the function of free speech as a social mechanism" (Vincent Blasi, "Holmes and the Marketplace of Ideas," *Supreme Court Review* (2004), 1).

29. *Abrams v. United States,* 250 U.S. 616, 630 (1919).

30. Thomas W. Joo, "The Worst Test of Truth: The 'Marketplace of Ideas' as Faulty Metaphor,' *Tulane Law Review,* 89 (2014), 385–386.

31. Wayne Batchis, *The Right's First Amendment: The Politics of Free Speech and the Return of Conservative Libertarianism* (Stanford University Press 2016), x.

32. *Whitney v. California,* 274 U.S. 357 (1927) (J. Brandeis, concurring).

33. Joo, "The Worst Test of Truth," 415.

34. Frederick Schauer, "The Boundaries of the First Amendment: A Preliminary Exploration of Constitutional Salience," *Harvard Law Review,* 117 (2004), 1783–1784.

35. *Whitney v. California* (emphasis added).

36. Joo, "The Worst Test of Truth," 414 ("even where the marketplace eventually exposes misleading speech, it 'may not reveal it sufficiently soon to avoid harm to numerous people'").

37. Ibid.

38. Brian Resnick, "The Science Behind Why Fake News Is So Hard to Wipe Out," *Vox* (Oct. 31, 2017), https://www.vox.com/science-and-health/2017/10/5/16410912/illusory-truth-fake -news-las-vegas-google-facebook

39. Samuel D. Warren and Louis D. Brandeis, "The Right to Privacy," *Harvard Law Review,* 4 (5) (1890), 218.

40. Morrison Torrey, "Thoughts About Why the First Amendment Operates to Stifle the Freedom and Equality of a Subordinated Majority," *Women's Rights Law Reporter,* 21 (1999), 35.

41. Lincoln Caplan, "The Embattled First Amendment," *The American Scholar* (March 4, 2015), https://theamericanscholar.org/the-embattled-first-amendment/#.V7toqI5eyVp

42. John C. Coates IV, "Corporate Speech and the First Amendment: History, Data, and Implications," *Constitutional Commentary*, 30 (2015), 223–224.

43. Batchis, *The Right's First Amendment*, 219.

44. David Niose, *Fighting Back the Right: Reclaiming America from the Attack on Reason* (St. Martin's Press 2014), 45.

45. Joel Bakan, *The Corporation: The Pathological Pursuit of Profit and Power* (Free Press, 2004), 1–2.

46. Adam Winkler, *We the Corporations: How American Businesses Won Their Civil Rights* (Liveright 2018).

47. Jane Mayer, "Covert Operations," *New Yorker* (Aug. 30, 2010), https://www.newyorker.com/magazine/2010/08/30/covert-operations

48. Lee Fang, "Exclusive: David Koch Refuses to Answer Questions About Citizens United, Secret Right-Wing Meetings," *Think Progress* (Jan. 10, 2011), https://thinkprogress.org/exclusive-david-koch-refuses-to-answer-questions-about-citizens-united-secret-right-wing-meetings-e5d111bdod55/

49. Tamara R. Piety, *Brandishing the First Amendment: Commercial Expression in America* (University of Michigan Press 2013), 4.

50. M. Todd Henderson, University of Chicago Law School Faculty Blog (March 12, 2010), http://uchicagolaw.typepad.com/faculty/2010/03/citizens-united-a-defense.html

51. Ronald Dworkin, "The Decision That Threatens Democracy," *New York Review of Books* (May 13, 2010), *http://www.nybooks.com/articles/2010/05/13/decision-threatens-democracy/*; see also Robert C. Post, *Citizens Divided: Campaign Finance Reform and the Constitution* (Harvard University Press 2014).

52. Former Leaders of the American Civil Liberties Union Letter to Chairman Patrick Leahy, U.S. Senate Committee on the Judiciary (Sept. 4, 2014), https://www.brennancenter.org/sites/default/files/analysis/Former_ACLU_Leader_Letter_2014.pdf

53. Leigh Ann Wheeler, *How Sex Became a Civil Liberty* (Oxford University Press 2012), 6.

54. Ibid., 135.

55. Ibid.

56. Ibid., 135–136.

57. The book received very little attention, perhaps due in part to ACLU spokesperson Emily Whitfield's characterization of Fahs as "a disgruntled employee who had been fired for incompetence" (Fahs had in fact resigned).

58. Melvin Wulf cited in Mark Ames, "The Left's Big Sellout—How the ACLU and Human Rights Groups Quietly Exterminated Labor Rights," *Naked Capitalism* (June 24, 2012), https://www.nakedcapitalism.com/2012/06/mark-ames-the-lefts-big-sellout-how-the-aclu-and-human-rights-groups-quietly-exterminated-labor-rights.html

59. Matt Drange, "After $24 Million Anti-Trump Windfall, ACLU Heads to Silicon Valley for Startup Lessons," *Forbes* (Jan. 31, 2017), https://www.forbes.com/sites/mattdrange/2017/01/31/aclu-flush-with-24m-in-wake-of-trump-immigration-orders-partners-with-tech-incubator-y-combinator/#43fa78297ba6

60. Sam Sanders, "'The Resistance' Faces a New Question: What to Do with All That

Money," *NPR* (March 26, 2017), http://www.npr.org/2017/03/26/520854771/the-resistance-faces-a-new-question-what-to-do-with-all-that-money

61. Drange, "After $24 Million Anti-Trump Windfall, ACLU Heads to Silicon Valley for Startup Lessons."

62. Maya Kosoff, "The A.C.L.U. Has Raised So Much Money That Silicon Valley Is Rushing into Help," *Vanity Fair* (Jan 31. 2017), https://www.vanityfair.com/news/2017/01/the-aclu-has-raised-so-much-money-its-enlisted-silicon-valley-to-help-spend-it

63. Sean Higgins, "Did the Kochs Ever Give the ACLU $20 Million? Probably Not," *Washington Examiner* (July 18, 2014), http://www.washingtonexaminer.com/did-the-kochs-ever-give-the-aclu-20-million-probably-not/article/2551030

64. Carl Hulse, "Unlikely Cause Unites the Left and the Right: Justice Reform," *New York Times* (Feb. 18, 2015), https://www.nytimes.com/2015/02/19/us/politics/unlikely-cause-unites-the-left-and-the-right-justice-reform.html?smid=tw-share&_r=0

65. Molly Ball, "Do the Koch Brothers Really Care About Criminal-Justice Reform?" *The Atlantic* (March 3, 2015), https://www.theatlantic.com/politics/archive/2015/03/do-the-koch-brothers-really-care-about-criminal-justice-reform/386615/

66. Zach Carter, "Kochs Embedded in Major Rift on Bipartisan Criminal Justice Reform," *Huffington Post* (Nov. 26, 2015), https://www.huffingtonpost.com/entry/criminal-justice-reform-koch_us_56560fb0e4b079b2818a13fe

67. Alex Kotch, "How Charles Koch Is Helping Neo-Confederates Teach College Students," *The Nation* (March 21, 2018), https://www.thenation.com/article/how-charles-koch-is-helping-neo-confederates-teach-college-students/

68. ACLU, "ACLU Announces New Trone Center for Criminal Justice Reform and Advisory Board of Private Sector and Education Leaders to Promote Reintegration" (Dec. 21, 2015), https://www.aclu.org/news/aclu-announces-new-trone-center-criminal-justice-reform-and-advisory-board-private-sector-and

69. Mary Anne Franks, "'Revenge Porn' Reform: A View from the Front Lines," *Florida Law Review,* 69 (2017), 1253.

70. Annmarie Chiarini, "I Was a Victim of Revenge Porn. I Don't Want Anyone Else to Face This," *The Guardian* (Nov. 19, 2013), https://www.theguardian.com/commentisfree/2013/nov/19/revenge-porn-victim-maryland-law-change; Jack Simpson, "Revenge Porn: What Is It and How Widespread Is the Problem?" *Independent* (July 2, 2014), http://www.independent.co.uk/news/uk/home-news/what-is-revenge-porn-9580251.html

71. Ann Bartow, "Pornography, Coercion, and Copyright Law 2.0," *Vanderbilt Journal of Entertainment and Technology Law,* 10 (2008), 817–818; Marion Brooks, "The World of Human Trafficking: One Woman's Story," *NBC Chicago* (Feb. 22, 2013), http://www.nbcchicago.com/investigations/human-trafficking-alex-campbell-192415731.html

72. Tara Culp-Ressler, "16-Year-Old's Rape Goes Viral on Social Media: 'No Human Being Deserved This,'" *Think Progress* (July 10, 2014), http://thinkprogress.org/health/2014/07/10/3458564/rape-viral-social-media-jada/

73. Charles Ornstein, "Nursing Home Workers Share Explicit Photos of Residents on Snapchat," *ProPublica* (Dec. 21, 2015), https://www.propublica.org/article/nursing-home-workers-share-explicit-photos-of-residents-on-snapchat

74. Chiarini, "I Was a Victim of Revenge Porn."

75. Danielle Keats Citron and Mary Anne Franks, "Criminalizing Revenge Porn," *Wake Forest Law Review,* 49 (2014), 350, 353.

76. Ariel Ronneburger, "Sex, Privacy, and Webpages: Creating a Legal Remedy for Victims of Porn 2.0," *Syracuse Science and Technology Law Reporter,* 21 (2009), 9.

77. Citron and Franks, "Criminalizing Revenge Porn," 352.

78. Emily Bazelon, "Another Sexting Tragedy," *Slate* (April 12, 2013), http://www.slate .com/articles/double_x/doublex/2013/04/audrie_pott_and_rehtaeh_parsons_how_should_the _legal_system_treat_nonconsensual.html

79. Citron and Franks, "Criminalizing Revenge Porn," 353–354; Jill Filipovic, "'Revenge Porn' Is About Degrading Women Sexually and Professionally," *The Guardian* (Jan. 28, 2013), https://www.theguardian.com/commentisfree/2013/jan/28/revenge-porn-degrades-women; Danielle Citron, "Cyber Stalking and Cyber Harassment, a Devastating and Endemic Problem," *Concurring Opinions* (March 16, 2012), http://www.concurringopinions.com/archives/2012/03 /cyber-stalking-and-cyber-harassment-a-devastating-and-endemic-problem.html

80. Megan C. Hills, "How Hugh Hefner Built an Entire Empire Without Marilyn Monroe's Consent," *Marie Claire* (Oct. 2, 2017), http://www.marieclaire.co.uk/news/celebrity -news/hugh-hefner-marilyn-monroe-541688

81. Emily Poole, "Fighting Back Against Non-Consensual Pornography," *University of San Francisco Law Review,* 49 (2015), 186.

82. Ibid.

83. Many of the lawsuits were resolved in favor of the plaintiffs. See *Wood v. Hustler Magazine, Inc.,* 736 F.2d 1084, 1085 (5th Cir. 1984); *Gallon v. Hustler Magazine, Inc.,* 732 F. Supp. 322, 326 (N.D.N.Y 1990).

84. Taylor Linkous, "It's Time for Revenge Porn to Get a Taste of Its Own Medicine: An Argument for the Federal Criminalization of Revenge Porn," *Richmond Journal of Law and Technology,* 20 (2014), 10.

85. In other cases, what is labeled "amateur" or "homemade" porn is in fact professionally produced material made with consenting and compensated individuals.

86. Mary Anne Franks, "Who's Afraid of Hot Girls?" *Huffington Post* (June 26, 2015), http://www.huffingtonpost.com/mary-anne-franks/whos-afraid-of-hot-girls_b_7670514.html

87. New Jersey was the first state to enact such a law in 2003. N.J. Statute § 2C:14–19.

88. Connor Simpson, "Revenge Porn King Hunter Moore Arrested for Hacking Email Accounts," *The Atlantic* (Jan. 23, 2014), https://www.theatlantic.com/national/archive/2014/01 /revenge-porn-king-hunter-moore-arrested-conspiracy-hack-email-accounts/357321/

89. Ibid. In 2015, Moore pled guilty to one count of unauthorized computer access and one count of aggravated identity theft. He was sentenced to two and a half years in federal prison, followed by three years of supervised release. Abby Ohlheiser, "Revenge Porn Purveyor Hunter Moore Is Sentenced to Prison," *Washington Post* (Dec. 3, 2015), https://www.washingtonpost.com/news/the-intersect/wp/2015/12/03/revenge-porn-purveyor -hunter-moore-is-sentenced-to-prison/?utm_term=.22dfee39b06a

90. Crimesider Staff, "Christopher Chaney, So-Called Hollywood Hacker, Gets 10 Years for Posting Celebrities' Personal Photos Online," *CBS News* (Dec. 18, 2012), http:// www.cbsnews.com/news/christopher-chaney-so-called-hollywood-hacker-gets-10-years-for -posting-celebrities-personal-photos-online/

91. See, for example, Chiarini, "I Was a Victim of Revenge Porn."

92. I currently serve as the CCRI's legislative and tech policy director and President.

93. Jessica Roy, "How Tech Companies Are Fighting Revenge Porn—and Winning," *New York Magazine* (June 24, 2015), http://nymag.com/thecut/2015/06/how-tech-companies -are-fighting-revenge-porn.html

94. H.R. 5896, 114th Cong. (2016).

95. Uniform Law Commission, "National Law Group Wraps Up 127th Annual Meeting: Seven New Acts Approved" (July 25, 2018), *http://www.uniformlaws.org/NewsDetail .aspx?title=Uniform%20Law%20Commission%20Wraps%20Up%20127th%20Annual %20Meeting*. I served as the reporter for this act.

96. Eric Schulzke, "California Lawmakers Target 'Revenge Porn' but Miss, Critics Say," *Deseret News* (Sept. 8, 2013), http://www.deseretnews.com/article/865586019 /California-lawmakers-target-revenge-porn-but-miss-critics-say.html (noting that the northern California ACLU had written a confused letter opposing the state's new "revenge porn" bill without making any coherent First Amendment arguments or citing to any relevant cases); see also Liz Halloran, "Race to Stop 'Revenge Porn' Raises Free Speech Worries," *NPR* (March 6, 2014), http://www.npr.org/blogs/itsallpolitics/2014/03/06/286388840 /race-to-stop-revenge-porn-raises-free-speech-worries

97. The reason for the ACLU's change in approach is not clear. "Will Matthews, a spokesman for the ACLU of Northern California, said that the ACLU had no objections to the bill, but he could not offer any explanation for why the initial objection letter was sent, nor what changes in the bill altered their viewpoint" (Schulzke, "California Lawmakers Target 'Revenge Porn' but Miss, Critics Say").

98. Michelle Dean, "Arizona Adds Revenge Porn Law to Its Books," *Gawker* (May 2, 2014), http://gawker.com/arizona-adds-revenge-porn-law-to-its-books-1570757305

99. *Antigone Books L.L.C. v. Brnovich*, Case No. 2:14-cv-02100-PHX-SRB (D. Ariz. 2014).

100. E-mail from American Civil Liberties Union, to Arizona Lawmakers and Arizona House of Representatives Standing Committee on the Judiciary (Feb. 10, 2015), https://drive .google.com/file/d/0B2LoKN1jK5BNX0NsZUdOUng5ZlE/view?usp=sharing

101. See "Criminal Law—Harassment—Revenge Porn: Hearing on H.B. 43 Before H. Judiciary Comm.," 2014 Leg., 434th Sess. 1–2 (Md. 2014) (statement of American Civil Liberties Union of Maryland).

102. ACLU Press Release, "First Amendment Lawsuit Challenges Arizona Criminal Law Banning Nude Images" (Sept. 23, 2014), https://www.aclu.org/news/first-amendment-lawsuit -challenges-arizona-criminal-law-banning-nude-images. I do not share the ACLU's certainty that circulating unedited photos of Abu Ghraib prisoners being sexually humiliated, with their genitalia and identifying features completely exposed (photos that did expose them in this way would not be subject to nonconsensual pornography statutes), should be absolutely protected by the First Amendment. Indeed, given the sensitivity of the imagery, mainstream news outlets blurred or otherwise edited the faces or the genitalia of the men depicted. Every disclosure that reveals the victims' identity potentially not only magnifies their humiliation but also creates the risk of further harm when they return to their communities.

103. *Broadrick v. Oklahoma*, 413 U.S. 601, 615 (1973).

104. As the Supreme Court noted in 1973, "there are limitations in the English language with respect to being both specific and manageably brief." Ibid., 608 (quoting *United*

States Civil Service Comm. v. Letter Carriers, 413 U.S. 548, 578–579 (1973)). No statute will "satisfy those intent on finding fault at any cost," but the Constitution does not require the satisfaction of impossible standards. Ibid. What is required, rather, is that laws be "set out in terms that the ordinary person exercising ordinary common sense can sufficiently understand and comply with, without sacrifice to the public interest." Ibid. To strike down a law on the grounds of constitutional overbreadth is "strong medicine . . . employed by the Court sparingly, and only as a last resort." Ibid., 601.

105. N.J. Statute § 2C:14–19.

106. Alaska Statute § 11.61.120 (2017).

107. Lee Rowland, "VICTORY! Federal Judge Deep-Sixes Arizona's Ridiculously Over-broad 'Nude Photo' Law," *ACLU* (July 10, 2015), https://www.aclu.org/blog/speak-freely /victory-federal-judge-deep-sixes-arizonas-ridiculously-overbroad-nude-photo-law #comments-top

108. Arizona Revised Statute § 13–1425 (2017).

109. Asia A. Eaton, Holly Jacobs, and Yanet Ruvalcaga, "2017 Nationwide Online Study of Nonconsensual Porn Victimization and Perpetration: A Summary Report," *Cyber Civil Rights Initiative* (June 12, 2017), https://www.cybercivilrights.org/wp-content/uploads/2017 /06/CCRI-2017-Research-Report.pdf

110. *Snyder v. Phelps*, 562 U.S. 443, 458 (2011).

111. For example, a Texas court recently held that the state's improper photography statute could not be rescued from constitutional overbreadth because it only criminalized photographs taken with the intent to arouse or gratify a person's sexual desires. In fact, the court found that such an intent requirement was "the regulation of protected thought." *Ex parte* Thompson, 442 S.W.3d 325, 339, 350–351 (Tex. Crim. App. 2014). See also *Snyder v. Phelps*, 562 U.S. at 458.

112. Pub. L. No. 103–322, 108 Stat. 1941 (1994) (codified at 42 U.S.C. § 13981 (2012)), invalidated by *United States v. Morrison*, 529 U.S. 598 (2000).

113. Gabe Rottman, "New Expansion of Stalking Law Poses First Amendment Concerns," *ACLU* (March 12, 2013), https://www.aclu.org/blog/free-speech/new-expansion-stalking -law-poses-first-amendment-concerns

114. Franks, "'Revenge Porn' Reform: A View from the Front Lines," 1331–1332.

115. Ibid., 1288.

116. I repeatedly advised the legislative sponsor against such requirements.

117. Title 18 Pennsylvania Consolidated Statute § 3131.

118. Christian Alexandersen, "Senator Wants to Close 'Revenge Porn' Relationship Ex-emption Amid Penn State Frat Scandal," *Penn Live* (March 19, 2015), http://www.pennlive.com /midstate/index.ssf/2015/03/senator_wants_to_close_revenge.html

119. ACLU, "Privacy and Technology," https://www.aclu.org/issues/privacy-technology

120. Chris Calabrese, "Federal Trade Commission Needs to Move Beyond Reports When It Comes to Data Brokers," *ACLU* (May 28, 2014), https://www.aclu.org/blog/technology -and-liberty/federal-trade-commission-needs-move-beyond-reports-when-it-comes-data

121. ACLU, "Coalition Letter to the Senate in Support of the Genetic Information Nondis-crimination Act (GINA)," https://www.aclu.org/letter/coalition-letter-senate-urging-protection-genetic-information-nondiscrimination-act-gina?redirect=technology-and-liberty/coalition -letter-senate-urging-protection-genetic-information-nondiscriminati

122. ACLU, "ACLU Urges Congress to Define Medical Privacy as Patient Control of Electronic Health Records" (July 23, 2008), https://www.aclu.org/news/aclu-urges-congress-define-medical-privacy-patient-control-electronic-health-records

123. Warren and Brandeis, "The Right to Privacy," 217.

124. ACLU, "ACLU and Bipartisan Supporters Urge Passage of Bill to Check GPS Tracking by Police: It's Time to Bring Privacy Laws Up to Speed with New Technology" (March 20, 2013), https://www.aclu.org/news/aclu-and-bipartisan-supporters-urge-passage-bill-check-gps-tracking-police

125. Robert Ellis Smith, "Statement on Social Security Number Privacy Act Bill H-5202," *Privacy Journal* (Feb. 7, 2011), http://riaclu.org/images/uploads/2011_SSN_Privacy_Act_bill_RES_testimony.pdf

126. Amy Binder, "There's a Well-Funded Campus Industry Behind the Ann Coulter Incident," *Washington Post* (May 1, 2017), https://www.washingtonpost.com/news/monkey-cage/wp/2017/05/01/theres-a-well-funded-campus-outrage-industry-behind-the-ann-coulter-incident/?utm_term=.112bf3354229

127. Moira Weigel, "Political Correctness: How the Right Invented a Phantom Enemy," *The Guardian* (Nov. 30, 2016), https://www.theguardian.com/us-news/2016/nov/30/political-correctness-how-the-right-invented-phantom-enemy-donald-trump

128. Jonathan Chait, "Not a Very P.C. Thing to Say: How the Language Police Are Perverting Liberalism," *New York Magazine* (Jan. 27, 2015), http://nymag.com/daily/intelligencer/2015/01/not-a-very-pc-thing-to-say.html

129. Scott Jaschik, "U Chicago to Freshmen: Don't Expect Safe Spaces," *Inside Higher Ed* (Aug. 25, 2016), https://www.insidehighered.com/news/2016/08/25/u-chicago-warns-incoming-students-not-expect-safe-spaces-or-trigger-warnings

130. Floyd Abrams cited in Jeff Robbins, "Floyd Abrams Speaks Freely to Political Correctness on America's Campuses," *Observer* (May 9, 2016), http://observer.com/2016/05/floyd-abrams-speaks-freely-to-political-correctness-on-americas-campuses/

131. Jeremy W. Peters and Thomas Fuller, "Ann Coulter Says She Will Pull Out of Speech at Berkeley," *New York Times* (April 26, 2017), https://www.nytimes.com/2017/04/26/us/ann-coulter-berkeley-speech.html

132. Daniel Marans, "Bernie Sanders Condemns Threats Against Ann Coulter Speech at Berkeley," *Huffington Post* (April 22, 2017), https://www.huffingtonpost.com/entry/bernie-sanders-ann-coulter-berkeley_us_58fb7006e4b00fa7de14bc3d

133. Meghana Kurup, "Elizabeth Warren on Coulter–Berkeley Controversy: 'Let Her Speak and Don't Show Up,'" *Washington Examiner* (April 25, 2017), https://www.washingtonexaminer.com/elizabeth-warren-on-coulter-berkeley-controversy-let-her-speak-and-dont-show-up

134. David Cole cited in "ACLU Statement on Ann Coulter Speech," *ACLU* (April 26, 2017), https://www.aclu.org/news/aclu-statement-ann-coulter-speech

135. Ibid.

136. Ibid.

137. Binder, "There's a Well-Funded Campus Industry Behind the Ann Coulter Incident."

138. Center for Media and Democracy, "EXPOSED: The State Policy Network—The Powerful Right-Wing Network Helping to Hijack State Politics and Government" (Nov. 2013), 2, https://www.alecexposed.org/w/images/2/25/SPN_National_Report_FINAL.pdf

139. Jim Sleeper, "The Conservatives Behind the Campus 'Free Speech' Crusade,"

American Prospect (Oct. 19, 2016), http://prospect.org/article/conservatives-behind-campus-%E2%80%98free-speech%E2%80%99-crusade

140. Jim Sleeper, "What the Campus 'Free Speech' Crusade Won't Say," *AlterNet* (Sept. 4, 2016),

https://www.alternet.org/education/what-campus-free-speech-crusade-wont-say-0

141. National Center for Educational Statistics, "Fast Facts: Educational Institutions," https://nces.ed.gov/fastfacts/display.asp?id=84

142. Mike Carter and Steve Miletich, "Couple Charged with Assault in Shooting During UW Speech by Milo Yiannopoulos," *Seattle Times* (May 1, 2017), http://www.seattletimes.com/seattle-news/crime/couple-charged-with-assault-in-shooting-melee-during-uw-speech-by-milo-yiannopoulos/

143. Thomas Healy, "Who's Afraid of Free Speech? What Critics of Campus Protest Get Wrong About the State of Public Discourse," *The Atlantic* (June 18, 2017), https://www.theatlantic.com/politics/archive/2017/06/whos-afraid-of-free-speech/530094/

144. Kyla Morgan Young, "'Even Princeton': Vietnam and a Culture of Student Activism, 1967–1972," *Mudd Manuscript Library Blog* (Feb. 24, 2016), https://blogs.princeton.edu/mudd/2016/02/even-princeton-vietnam-and-a-culture-of-student-activism-1967–1972/; Alison Pohle, "Today's College Freshmen Are More Likely to Protest Than Students in the '60s and '70s," *Boston Globe* (Feb. 11, 2016), https://www.boston.com/news/education/2016/02/11/todays-college-freshmen-are-more-likely-to-protest-than-students-in-the-60s-and-70s

145. See Aaron Hanlon, "What Stunts Like Milo Yiannopoulos's 'Free Speech Week' Cost," *New York Times* (Sept. 24, 2017), https://www.nytimes.com/2017/09/24/opinion/milo-yiannopoulos-free-speech-week-berkeley.html

146. Stanley Kurtz, James Manley, and Jonathan Buther, "Campus Free Speech: A Legislative Proposal," *Goldwater Institute* (Jan. 30, 2017), https://goldwaterinstitute.org/wp-content/uploads/cms_page_media/2017/2/2/X_Campus%20Free%20Speech%20Paper.pdf

147. Ralph Wilson, "Koch Network's Student Protest Ban Disguised as 'Campus Free Speech,'" *UnKoch My Campus* (March 1, 2017), http://www.unkochmycampus.org/mar-1-2017-protest-ban-sold-as-free-speech/

148. Todd Richmond, "University of Wisconsin Approves Free Speech Policy That Punishes Student Protesters," *Chicago Tribune* (Oct. 6, 2017), http://www.chicagotribune.com/news/nationworld/midwest/ct-university-of-wisconsin-protest-punishment-20171006-story.html

149. Ralph Wilson, "Koch Network's Student Protest Ban Disguised as 'Campus Free Speech.'"

150. John K. Wilson, "The Tennessee Legislature's Attack on Free Speech," *Academe Blog* (Feb. 12, 2017), https://academeblog.org/2017/02/12/the-tennessee-legislatures-attack-on-free-speech/

151. Ibid.

152. Ibid. John Wilson wrote a much more positive follow-up post in May 2017 after the bill was rewritten in consultation with FIRE to remove its most censorious aspects.

153. Krissy Eliot, "Ann Coulter at Berkeley: Untangling the Truth," *California Magazine* (May 8, 2017), https://alumni.berkeley.edu/california-magazine/just-in/2017-05-08/ann-coulter-berkeley-untangling-truth

154. Ibid.

155. Peters and Fuller, "Ann Coulter Says She Will Pull Out of Speech at Berkeley."

156. Nicholas Dirks, "New Message from the Chancellor About Possible Coulter Visit," *Berkeley News* (April 26, 2017), http://news.berkeley.edu/2017/04/26/new-message-from -the-chancellor-about-possible-coulter-visit/

157. Hanlon, "What Stunts Like Milo Yiannopoulos's 'Free Speech Week' Cost."

158. Anonymous e-mail cited in Erin Alberty, "Anita Sarkeesian Explains Why She Canceled USU Lecture," *Salt Lake Tribune* (Oct. 16, 2014), http://archive.sltrib.com/article.php?id =58528113&itype=CMSID

159. Annie Knox, "Campus Gun Laws Are Not Carved in Stone," *Salt Lake Tribune* (Jan. 20, 2015), http://archive.sltrib.com/article.php?id=2063657&itype=CMSID

160. Alberty, "Anita Sarkeesian Explains Why She Canceled USU Lecture."

161. Ibid.

162. Ibid.

163. Krystal Knapp, "Princeton Professor Who Criticized Donald Trump Cancels Talks After Receiving Death Threats," *Planet Princeton* (May 31, 2017), https://planetprinceton .com/2017/05/31/princeton-professor-who-criticized-donald-trump-cancels-talks-after -receiving-death-threats/

164. Sarah Larimer, "What It Feels Like When a Professor's Comments Ignite a Fury," *Washington Post* (Sept. 10, 2017), https://www.washingtonpost.com/local/education/what-it-feels-like -when-a-professors-comments-ignite-a-fury/2017/09/10/f5702dac-80f6-11e7-b359-15a361 7c767b_story.html?utm_term=.c2379293f49e

165. Steve Kolowich, "What Is a Black Professor in America Allowed to Say?" *The Guardian* (Aug. 3, 2017), https://www.theguardian.com/world/2017/aug/03/what-is-a-black-professor-in -america-allowed-to-say-tommy-j-curry

166. Tommy Curry cited in ibid.

167. Ibid.

168. Sarita Farnelli, "Attack on Academia, Part 5: Interview with Tommy Curry," *Weave News* (Sept. 21, 2017), http://www.weavenews.org/stories/2017/9/21/attack-on-academia-part-5 -interview-with-tommy-curry

169. " "No Action Against Tennessee Professor over Protest Tweet," *USA Today* (Sept. 27, 2016), https://www.tennessean.com/story/news/2016/09/27/no-action-against-tennessee -professor-over-protest-tweet/91167524/

170. American Association of University Professors, "Targeted Online Harassment of Faculty" (Jan. 31, 2017), https://www.aaup.org/news/targeted-online-harassment-faculty

171. *Cohen v. California*, 403 U.S. 15, 20, 91 S. Ct. 1780, 1785–1786, 29 L. Ed. 2d 284 (1971).

172. "It is firmly settled that under our Constitution the public expression of ideas may not be prohibited merely because the ideas are themselves offensive to some of their hearers" (*Street v. New York*, 394 U.S. 576, 592, 89 S. Ct. 1354, 1366, 22 L. Ed. 2d 572 (1969)).

173. *Village of Skokie v. National Socialist Party of America*, 69 Ill. 2d 605, 614–615, 373 N.E.2d 21, 24 (1978).

174. Jewish Telegraphic Agency, "JDL to Deal with Nazi Rally" (June 29, 1977), https://www .jta.org/1977/06/29/archive/jdl-to-deal-with-nazi-rally

175. *Chaplinsky v. New Hampshire* (1942), 572 (emphasis added).

176. David Guttman cited in Mark A. Rabinowitz, "Nazis in Skokie: Fighting Words or Heckler's Veto?" *Depaul Law Review,* 28 (1979), footnote 143, 280–281.

177. Ibid., 283.

178. Joseph Goldstein, "Alt-Right Gathering Exults in Trump Election with Nazi-Era Salute," *New York Times* (Nov. 20, 2017), https://www.nytimes.com/2016/11/21/us/alt-right-salutes -donald-trump.html?_r=0

CHAPTER FOUR

1. *Doe ex rel. Roe v. Backpage.com, LLC,* 104 F. Supp. 3d 149, 153 (D. Mass. 2015), aff'd sub nom. *Jane Doe No. 1 v. Backpage.com, LLC,* 817 F.3d 12 (1st Cir. 2016).

2. Communications Decency Act, 47 U.S.C. 230(c)(1) (1996).

3. *Doe ex rel. Roe v. Backpage.com, LLC,* 104 F. Supp. 3d 149, 165 (D. Mass. 2015), aff'd sub nom. *Jane Doe No. 1 v. Backpage.com, LLC,* 817 F.3d 12 (1st Cir. 2016).

4. John Perry Barlow, "A Declaration of the Independence of Cyberspace," *Electronic Frontier Foundation* (Feb. 8, 1996), https://www.eff.org/cyberspace-independence

5. 47 U.S.C. § 230.

6. John Locke, *Second Treatise on Government,* Section 4 (1690), http://libertyonline .hypermall.com/Locke/second/second-frame.html

7. See Mary Anne Franks, "Unwilling Avatars: Idealism and Discrimination in Cyberspace," *Columbia Journal of Gender and Law,* 20 (2011).

8. Ethan Katsh and Orna Rabinovich-Einy, *Digital Justice: Technology and the Internet* (Oxford University Press 2017), 30.

9. "Top 75 Reasons Why Women Should Not Have Freedom of Speech," http://www.angelfire .com/hi2/jimb/womenshouldnothavefreedomofspeech.html

10. *United States v. Alkhabaz,* 104 F.3d. 1492,1496 (6th Cir. 1997).

11. Wayne King, "Computer Network Links Rightist Groups and Offers 'Enemy' List," *New York Times* (Feb. 15, 1985), https://www.nytimes.com/1985/02/15/us/computer-network -links-rihtist-groups-and-offers-enemy-list.html

12. Ibid.

13. Robert J. Klotz, *The Politics of Internet Communication* (Rowman & Littlefield 2004), 24.

14. Danielle Keats Citron, "Cyber Civil Rights," *Boston University Law Review,* 89 (2009), 99.

15. Jonathan Taplin, *Move Fast and Break Things: How Facebook, Google, and Amazon Cornered Culture and Undermined Democracy* (Little, Brown and Company 2017), 54.

16. Mary Anne Franks, "Democratic Surveillance," *Harvard Journal of Law and Technology,* 30 (2017), 455.

17. Cass R. Sunstein, *#Republic: Divided Democracy in the Age of Social Media* (Princeton University Press 2017), 179 (emphasis added).

18. Lawrence Lessig, "Code Is Law: On Liberty in Cyberspace," *Harvard Magazine* (Jan. 1, 2000), https://harvardmagazine.com/2000/01/code-is-law-html

19. See Mary Anne Franks, "Sexual Harassment 2.0," *Maryland Law Review,* 71 (2012).

20. *Cubby, Inc. v. CompuServe, Inc.,* 776 F. Supp. 135 (S.D.N.Y. 1991).

21. 1995 WL 323710 (N.Y. Sup. Ct. 1995).

22. Ryan J. P. Dyer, "The Communication Decency Act Gone Wild: A Case for Renewing the Presumption Against Preemption," *Seattle University Law Review,* 37 (2014), 851.

23. Ibid.

24. *Zeran v. AOL,* 129 F.3d 327 (4th Cir. 1997).

25. David Lukmire, "Can the Courts Tame the Communications Decency Act?: The Reverberations of *Zeran v. America Online,*" *NYU Annual Survey of American Law,* 66 (2010), 403.

26. Ibid.

27. David Niose, *Fighting Back the Right: Reclaiming America from the Attack on Reason* (St. Martin's Press 2014), 41, 45.

28. Kalev Leetaru, "Do Social Media Platforms Really Care About Online Abuse?" *Forbes* (Jan. 12, 2017), https://www.forbes.com/sites/kalevleetaru/2017/01/12/do-social-media-platforms -really-care-about-online-abuse/#a8851ca45f15

29. Astra Taylor, *The People's Platform: Taking Back Power and Culture in the Digital Age* (Metropolitan Books 2014), 221.

30. Taplin, *Move Fast and Break Things,* 9.

31. Aamer Madhani, "Visa Follows MasterCard, Cuts Off Business with Backpage.com," *USA Today* (July 1, 2015), https://www.usatoday.com/story/money/2015/07/01/visa-mastercard -stop-business-with-backpage/29558315/

32. Thomas J. Dart, Cook County Sheriff, "Letter to the Members of the Board of Directors, MasterCard Incorporated" (June 29, 2015), http://blogs.chicagotribune.com/files/letter-from -cook-county-sheriff-to-mastercard.pdf

33. *Bantam Books, Inc. v. Sullivan,* 372 U.S. 58, 61 (1963).

34. *Bantam Books, Inc. v. Sullivan,* 372 U.S. 58, 61–63, 83 S. Ct. 631, 634–635, 9 L. Ed. 2d 584 (1963) (internal citations omitted).

35. *Bantam Books, Inc. v. Sullivan,* 372 U.S. 66–67, 83 S. Ct. 631, 637, 9 L. Ed. 2d 584 (1963).

36. *Bantam Books, Inc. v. Sullivan,* 372 U.S. 68–69, 83 S. Ct. 631, 638, 9 L. Ed. 2d 584 (1963).

37. *Backpage.com, LLC v. Dart,* 807 F.3d 229, 239 (7th Cir. 2015), *cert. denied,* 137 S. Ct. 46, 196 L. Ed. 2d 28 (2016).

38. Scott Higham and Ellen Nakashima, "Why the Islamic State Leaves Tech Companies Torn Between Free Speech and Security," *Washington Post* (July 16, 2015), https://www.wash-ingtonpost.com/world/national-security/islamic-states-embrace-of-social-media-puts-tech-companies-in-a-bind/2015/07/15/0e5624c4-169c-11e5-89f3-61410da94eb1_story.html?utm _term=.b62354466059

39. Patrick Howell O'Neill, "8chan, the Central Hive of Gamergate, Is Also an Active Pedophile Network," *Daily Dot* (Nov. 17, 2014), https://www.dailydot.com/layer8/8chan -pedophiles-child-porn-gamergate/

40. Ibid.

41. 4chan, "Rules," https://www.4chan.org/rules

42. Julia Angwin, "Facebook's Secret Censorship Rules Protect White Men from Hate Speech But Not Black Children," *ProPublica* (June 28, 2017), https://www.propublica.org /article/facebook-hate-speech-censorship-internal-documents-algorithms

43. Ibid.

44. Ibid.

45. Ibid.

46. Zeynep Tufekci, "The Real Bias Built in at Facebook," *New York Times* (May 19, 2016), https://www.nytimes.com/2016/05/19/opinion/the-real-bias-built-in-at-facebook.html?_r=0

47. Ibid.

48. Ibid.

49. See Frank Pasquale, *The Black Box Society: The Secret Algorithms That Control Money and Information* (Harvard University Press 2016); see also Cathy O'Neil, *Weapons of Math Destruction: How Big Data Increases Inequality and Threatens Democracy* (Crown 2016).

50. Tufekci, "The Real Bias Built in at Facebook."

51. Jon Penney, "Can Cyber Harassment Laws Encourage Online Speech?" *Medium* (Aug. 15, 2017), https://medium.com/berkman-klein-center/can-cyber-harassment-laws-encourage-online-speech-4e1ae884bfba

52. Ibid.

53. Jessica Moreno, "Reddit: We Won't Tolerate Revenge Porn—And You Shouldn't Either," *CNN* (April 27, 2015), http://money.cnn.com/2015/04/26/technology/reddit-revenge-porn/index.html

54. CBS News, "More Than 100 Celebrities Hacked, Nude Photos Leaked" (Sept. 1, 2014), https://www.cbsnews.com/news/jennifer-lawrence-mary-elizabeth-winstead-kate-upton-hacked-dozens-of-nude-photos-leaked/

55. Adario Strange, "Jennifer Lawrence and Other Celebs Hacked as Nude Photos Circulate on the Web," *Mashable* (Aug. 31, 2014), http://mashable.com/2014/08/31/celebrity-nude-photo-hack/

56. Ibid.

57. Ibid. Wong's manifesto prompted one commentator to note, "If Reddit wants to be thought of as a government, we'll call it what it is: a failed state, unable to control what happens within its borders." (T. C. Sottek, "Reddit Is a Failed State: The 'Front Page of the Internet' Is Run by Warlords," *The Verge* (Sept. 8, 2014), http://www.theverge.com/2014/9/8/6121363/reddit-is-a-failed-state).

58. Tom Cheredar, "Reddit CEO Yishan Wong Resigns in Surprise Leadership Change," *Venture Beat* (Nov. 13, 2014), https://venturebeat.com/2014/11/13/reddits-ceo-yishan-wong-resigns-following-50m-raise/

59. Strange, "Jennifer Lawrence and Other Celebs Hacked as Nude Photos Circulate on the Web."

60. "From 1 to 9,000 Communities, Now Taking Steps to Grow Reddit to 90,000 Communities (and Beyond!)," *Reddit* (2015), https://www.reddit.com/r/announcements/comments/2x0g9v/from_1_to_9000_communities_now_taking_steps_to/

61. Hayley Tsukayama, "Twitter Updates Its Rules to Specifically Ban 'Revenge Porn,'" *Washington Post* (March 11, 2015), https://www.washingtonpost.com/news/the-switch/wp/2015/03/11/twitter-updates-its-rules-to-specifically-ban-revenge-porn/?utm_term=.82606f62a083

62. "The Twitter Rules," *Twitter*, https://help.twitter.com/en/rules-and-policies/twitter-rules

63. Kashmir Hill, "Twitter Bans Nonconsensual Intimate Photos, A.K.A. 'Revenge Porn,'" *Fusion* (March 11, 2015), https://splinternews.com/twitter-bans-nonconsensual-intimate-photos-a-k-a-reve-1793846345

64. Rob Price, "Facebook Has Banned Revenge Porn," *Business Insider* (March 16, 2015), https://www.businessinsider.com/facebook-bans-revenge-porn-community-guidelines-2015-3

65. Amit Singhal, "'Revenge Porn' and Search," *Google: Public Policy Blog* (June 19, 2015), https://publicpolicy.googleblog.com/2015/06/revenge-porn-and-search.html

66. Ibid.

67. Deepa Seetharaman, "Facebook Takes Aim at 'Revenge Porn,'" *Wall Street Journal* (April 5, 2017), https://www.wsj.com/articles/facebook-takes-aim-at-revenge-porn-1491428994

68. "New Technology Fights Child Porn by Tracking Its 'PhotoDNA,'" *Microsoft* (Dec. 15, 2009), https://news.microsoft.com/2009/12/15/new-technology-fights-child-porn-by-tracking-its-photodna/#sm.0001mpmupctevct7pjn11vtwrw6xj

69. Ibid.

70. Stephanie Mlot, "'Hash List' to Help Google, Facebook, More Remove Child Porn," *PC Magazine* (Aug. 11, 2015), http://www.pcmag.com/article2/0,2817,2489399,00.asp

71. Kaveh Waddell, "A Tool to Delete Beheading Videos Before They Even Appear Online," *The Atlantic* (June 22, 2016), http://www.theatlantic.com/technology/archive/2016/06/a-tool-to-delete-beheading-videos-before-they-even-appear-online/488105/

72. Amanda Hess, "Reddit Has Banned Revenge Porn. Sort Of," *Slate* (Feb. 25, 2015), http://www.slate.com/blogs/the_slatest/2015/02/25/reddit_bans_revenge_porn_victims_advocates_and_the_aclu_react_to_the_new.html

73. Eshwar Chandrasekharan et al., "You Can't Stay Here: The Efficacy of Reddit's 2015 Ban Examined Through Hate Speech," *Proceedings of the ACM on Human–Computer Interaction*, 1 (2017), http://comp.social.gatech.edu/papers/cscw18-chand-hate.pdf

74. Adi Robertson, "Welcome to Voat: Reddit Killer, Troll Haven, and the Strange Face of Internet Free Speech," *The Verge* (July 10, 2015), https://www.theverge.com/2015/7/10/8924415/voat-reddit-competitor-free-speech

75. Noa Yachot, "The 'Magna Carta' of Cyberspace Turns 20: An Interview with the ACLU Lawyer Who Helped Save the Internet" (June 22, 2017), https://www.aclu.org/blog/free-speech/internet-speech/magna-carta-cyberspace-turns-20-interview-aclu-lawyer-who-helped

76. Matthew Prince, "Cloudflare and Free Speech," *Cloudflare* (Aug. 9, 2013), https://blog.cloudflare.com/cloudflare-and-free-speech/

77. Ken Schwencke, "How One Major Internet Company Helps Serve Up Hate on the Web," *ProPublica* (May 4, 2017), https://www.propublica.org/article/how-cloudflare-helps-serve-up-hate-on-the-web

78. Prince, "Cloudflare and Free Speech."

79. Matthew Prince, "Why We Terminated Daily Stormer," *Cloudflare* (Aug. 16, 2017), https://blog.cloudflare.com/why-we-terminated-daily-stormer/

80. Ibid.

81. Kate Conger, "Cloudflare CEO on Terminating Service to Neo-Nazi Site: 'The Daily Stormer Are Assholes,'" *Gizmodo* (Aug. 16, 2017), https://gizmodo.com/cloudflare-ceo-on-terminating-service-to-neo-nazi-site-1797915295

82. Prince, "Why We Terminated Daily Stormer."

83. Jeremy Malcolm, Cindy Cohn, and Danny O'Brien, "Fighting Neo-Nazis and the Future of Free Expression," *Electronic Frontier Foundation* (Aug. 17, 2017), https://www.eff .org/deeplinks/2017/08/fighting-neo-nazis-future-free-expression

84. Ibid.

85. Barlow, "A Declaration of the Independence of Cyberspace."

86. Malcolm, Cohn, and O'Brien, "Fighting Neo-Nazis and the Future of Free Expression."

87. See Danielle Keats Citron, *Hate Crimes In Cyberspace* (Harvard University Press 2014).

88. Barlow, "A Declaration of the Independence of Cyberspace."

89. See Mary Anne Franks, "Sexual Harassment 2.0," *Maryland Law Review,* 71 (2012).

90. See Cindy Southworth and Sarah Tucker, "Technology, Stalking, and Domestic Violence Victims," *Mississippi Law Journal,* 76 (2007).

91. Danielle Keats Citron and Mary Anne Franks, "Criminalizing Revenge Porn," *Wake Forest Law Review,* 49 (2014).

CONCLUSION

1. Robert Jay Lifton, *Thought Reform and the Psychology of Totalism: A Study of "Brainwashing" in China* (Norton 1963), 436.

2. Ibid.

3. Dana Branham, "Who's the Texas Man at the Center of the Debate over 3-D Printable Guns?," *Dallas News* (Aug. 1, 2018), https://www.dallasnews.com/news/guns/2018/07/14 /texans-blueprints-homemade-guns-get-government-ok-says-spells-doom-gun-control

4. Deanna Paul, Meagan Flynn, and Katie Zezima, "Federal Judge Blocks Posting of Blueprints for 3-D-Printed Guns Hours Before They Were to Be Published," *Washington Post* (July 31, 2018), https://www.washingtonpost.com/news/morning-mix/wp/2018/07/31 /in-last-minute-lawsuit-states-say-3-d-printable-guns-pose-national-security-threat/?utm _term=.e1a60cab06af

5. Ibid.

6. Henry Mayer, *All on Fire: William Lloyd Garrison and the Abolition of Slavery* (Norton 2008), 445.

7. William Lloyd Garrison, "On the Constitution and the Union" (Dec. 29, 1832), http://fair-use.org/the-liberator/1832/12/29/on-the-constitution-and-the-union

8. See Louis Michael Seidman, *On Constitutional Disobedience* (Oxford University Press 2012); Sanford Levinson, *Our Undemocratic Constitution: Where the Constitution Goes Wrong (And How We the People Can Correct It)* (Oxford University Press 2008).

9. George Washington, Letter to Bushrod Washington (Nov. 10, 1787), https://founders .archives.gov/GEWN-04-05-02-0388

10. Immanuel Kant, *Grounding for the Metaphysics of Morals* (1993 [1785]).

11. Edmund Burke, "Letter to John Farr and John Harris, Esqrs., Sheriffs of the City of Bristol, on the Affairs of America" (1777).

12. Kimberlé Crenshaw, "Demarginalizing the Intersection of Race and Sex: A Black Feminist Critique of Antidiscrimination Doctrine, Feminist Theory, and Antiracist Politics," *University of Chicago Legal Forum,* 1989 (1) (1989), 167.

13. Ibid.

INDEX